RESEARCH METHODS IN INTERNATIONAL RELATIONS

SAGE | 50 YEARS

SAGE was founded in 1965 by Sara Miller McCune to support the dissemination of usable knowledge by publishing innovative and high-quality research and teaching content. Today, we publish more than 750 journals, including those of more than 300 learned societies, more than 800 new books per year, and a growing range of library products including archives, data, case studies, reports, conference highlights, and video. SAGE remains majority-owned by our founder, and after Sara's lifetime will become owned by a charitable trust that secures our continued independence.

Los Angeles | London | Washington DC | New Delhi | Singapore

RESEARCH METHODS IN INTERNATIONAL RELATIONS
CHRISTOPHER LAMONT

Los Angeles | London | New Delhi
Singapore | Washington DC

Los Angeles | London | New Delhi
Singapore | Washington DC

SAGE Publications Ltd
1 Oliver's Yard
55 City Road
London EC1Y 1SP

SAGE Publications Inc.
2455 Teller Road
Thousand Oaks, California 91320

SAGE Publications India Pvt Ltd
B 1/I 1 Mohan Cooperative Industrial Area
Mathura Road
New Delhi 110 044

SAGE Publications Asia-Pacific Pte Ltd
3 Church Street
#10-04 Samsung Hub
Singapore 049483

Editor: Natalie Aguilera
Assistant editor: James Piper
Production editor: Katie Forsythe
Copyeditor: Clare Weaver
Proofreader: David Hemsley
Indexer: Anne Solamito
Marketing manager: Sally Ransom
Cover design: Jen Crisp
Typeset by: C&M Digitals (P) Ltd, Chennai, India
Printed in Great Britain by Ashford Colour Press
Ltd

Library of Congress Control Number: 2014948711

British Library Cataloguing in Publication data

A catalogue record for this book is available from
the British Library

MIX
Paper from
responsible sources
FSC
www.fsc.org
FSC® C011748

ISBN 978-1-4462-8604-3
ISBN 978-1-4462-8605-0 (pbk)

For Hannah

CONTENTS

ABOUT THE AUTHOR

Dr. Christopher Lamont is Assistant Professor of International Relations in the Department of International Relations and International Organization at the University of Groningen in the Netherlands. He is also co-Chair of Research in Ethics and Globalisation within the Globalisation Studies Groningen institute. He has taught a number of research methods classes in International Relations, including Methodologies in International Relations, Methodologies and Research Practice, Research Methods in History and International Relations and Research Methods for Area Studies. Previously, Dr. Lamont was a RCUK postdoctoral research fellow in the Transitional Justice Institute at the University of Ulster in Northern Ireland and a Fulbright fellow at the University of Zagreb in Croatia. He holds a PhD in Politics from the University of Glasgow, an MSc in International and European Politics from the University of Edinburgh and a BA in International Studies from the University of Mississippi. His research interests include human rights and transitional justice, and his current research focuses on transitional justice in the Middle East and North Africa with a particular focus on Libya and Tunisia. He has published widely on the subject, including his monograph, *International Criminal Justice and the Politics of Compliance* (Ashgate, 2010), numerous peer reviewed journal articles and contributions to edited volumes.

ACKNOWLEDGEMENTS

Research Methods in International Relations is a textbook that owes its existence, in large part, to a number of undergraduate and postgraduate research methods classes I have taught over the past several years at the University of Groningen. Students of International Relations (IR), perhaps more so than other fields of study within the social sciences, are expected to engage with a broad range of scholarly subjects that span a number of related fields such as political science, international law, economics, sociology, and philosophy. Indeed, the core curriculum of many IR programs at both the undergraduate and postgraduate levels now contain courses from these related fields. As such, it should come as no surprise that there is no unified approach to research methods that underpins the discipline. Instead, students of IR are often confronted with the task of learning how to write academic papers without discipline specific academic training, and instead look to fields such as political science for research methods guidance. Nevertheless, given IR's engagement with a number of related fields in the social sciences, an understanding of a broad range of methods and methodological traditions is certainly a prerequisite for research and writing in IR. To be sure, for students of IR to critically engage with, and contribute to, scholarly and policy debates within the discipline, or in the IR policy community, they must first familiarize themselves with a broad range of research traditions, methods, and techniques.

Paradoxically, despite the broad range of methods utilized by students and scholars of IR, research methods texts in the field remain inwardly focused on presenting one particular method or research tradition, or do not substantively engage with the question of methods. In short, they either engage with or advocate one particular methodological approach, without providing students with a holistic overview of the field. The result is that students embarking on research and writing in IR often start with a confused perspective on methods and methodology in which methodological debates are seen as constituting just another front in the theoretical battles that have become an almost defining feature of contemporary IR scholarship.

It was student feedback that highlighted the need for a more practical approach to research methods that took a step back from the aforementioned theoretical battles, and instead focused on providing students with a comprehensive guide to research methods in IR, which led me to undertake the task of writing this book. In short, *Research Methods in International Relations* aims to provide just that.

I would like to express my thanks to my colleagues and students for providing feedback on the methods discussed in this textbook. In particular, I would like to express my gratitude to colleagues with whom I have had the pleasure to teach research methods at Groningen. I would like to thank Dr. Barbara Henkes, Mr. Benjamin Herborth, Dr. Menno Kamminga, and Dr. Richard Papping. I would also like to thanks Hannah Pannwitz and Arnaud Kurze who provided feedback on draft chapters. And of course, I would like to express my thanks to students who I taught in my *Methodologies in International Relations*, *Methodology and Research Practice*, and *Research Methods in History and International Relations* classes at Groningen for providing inspiration for this textbook.

At Sage I would like to thank Natalie Aguilera and James Piper. Both tirelessly supported me during the writing process, and without their encouragement, this textbook would not have been possible. Furthermore, I would also like to thank the anonymous reviewers who provided valuable feedback on draft chapters and did much to improve this work.

Finally, I would like to thank my family, friends, colleagues, and of course my students for their patience and understanding while I worked on this manuscript.

Christopher K. Lamont
Tunis, Tunisia
August 2014

INTRODUCTION

Research Methods in International Relations is a resource for students and researchers of International Relations (IR) to consult in order to make sense of the wide range of research methods and methodologies that we routinely encounter in the discipline.[1] A firm grasp of the diverse set of methods, and methodologies, used by scholars of IR is both a necessary prerequisite to understanding and evaluating existing scholarly work and to designing your own research. As such, research methods and methodologies are the building blocks that allow us to understand and interpret the world around us.

But, despite the unquestioned importance of research methods, students often cautiously, or even skeptically, engage with texts devoted to the subject. Students of IR, whose interest is in international politics, and who have little time for the dense technical language of methods, can be forgiven for not enthusiastically greeting their initiation to research methods. To be sure, methodologists often bury their observations deep in jargon. The result is a perception of inaccessibility surrounding texts devoted to methods, and a sense that serious reflections on methods in IR are only accessible to those who have received advanced research methods training.

The forthcoming chapters will illustrate that rather than seeing research methods as inaccessible, methods form the basic foundations upon which we design our research projects. Understanding methods is about understanding the underlying logic of our research project. In fact, the best way to approach the question of methods is through an interrogation of the aims of your own particular research project. Discussing research methods in the abstract, while useful in illustrating the strengths and limitations of a particular data collection or data analysis technique, cannot in itself tell you whether or not the use of these techniques are appropriate for your own research project. In order to build the bridge between research and methods you will need to integrate methods into a set of choices that you will make during the course of your essay, dissertation, or thesis writing process.

Research Methods in International Relations provides a comprehensive guide to methods and methodologies that is integrated into a guide to research and writing in International Relations. In addition to helping you contextualize your methods choices in the context of broader topics such as research question selection and **research design**, this textbook also provides you with a practical guide to writing. Indeed, no matter how skillfully we have collected our data and conducted our data analysis, if we are unable to communicate it, our contribution to the field will remain either unintelligible to our audience, or will be simply ignored. In a fast-paced world characterized by instant access to an ever-growing body of information, the need to be able to concisely and effectively communicate our research has never been greater. As students and researchers in IR, we should endeavor to develop the writing skills necessary to effectively communicate our research findings.

After all, if our aim is to understand or explain events in international politics, we must keep in mind that every contribution to IR scholarship is potentially a contribution to policymaking. For example, our studies of the role of civil society during political transitions can inform development or democracy assistance programs that target civil society organizations in countries experiencing dramatic political changes. The more effectively we communicate our findings, the more likely those findings will be used to address policy shortcomings. In short, a well-designed and methodologically sound research project can make a contribution to the field that goes far beyond the academe. From this perspective, research methods can help us evaluate the effectiveness of impact of real-world policies. While some scholars strike a more ambivalent note on the question of IR scholarship informing the practice of international relations, we should always remember that one of our central tasks, as students and scholars of IR, is to also be able to communicate our findings to a wider community of students and real-world practitioners. Using robust methods and being explicit about our methodological choices aids us in our task to communicate our findings because they point to two things real-world practitioners value, a clear presentation of an argument and conclusions that are evidence-based.

In the past, however, far from being seen as a communicative tool, IR research methods have been perceived as forming a barrier between IR scholarship and the wider policy community. Indeed, research methods were accused of constituting a growing obstacle to communicating disciplinary knowledge to a wider audience on the one hand, and narrowing the focus of IR inquiry to trivial questions that were unlikely to be of interest to the policy community on the other.[2] Indeed, Nicholson (2002: 31) noted that certain methods within the discipline have even been alleged to do nothing more than 'restating the obvious in complicated language.' The purpose of research methods is not to shroud our research findings in impenetrable language, put rather it is to clearly communicate our research choices. Research methods allow us to answer the most basic questions that are asked of research: why did we take into consideration certain evidence? How did we evaluate that evidence? How did we arrive at our conclusions? The following chapters of this textbook will help you provide responses to these questions within your own writing.

Research and Writing in International Relations

Research Methods in International Relations is not a textbook that aims to engage with methods for the sake of solely highlighting the latest methodological innovations in the field, but rather it aims to provide you with the tools and guidance necessary to navigate the multitude of research choices you will confront during the research process. It also contains a practical guide for writing research papers, theses, or dissertations. At the outset, however, it is important to make clear that there is not necessarily a trade-off between methodological sophistication and accessible writing. Indeed, as the forthcoming chapters will illustrate, the two often go together. Thus, this textbook is able to integrate a discussion of research methods into a roadmap of the broader research process, from research question formulation and research design, to data collection and analysis, to writing up your research.

Effective and concise writing forms a bridge between our research and our audience. Writing up is thus a crucial component of the research process as our contribution to the field aspires to help make sense of the myriad of urgent and complex questions confronting decision-makers working for governments, NGOs, or businesses. IR scholarship has long aspired to transform international politics through the provision of policy subscriptions to address contemporary challenges, such as environmental degradation, armed conflict, climate change, territorial disputes, human rights abuses, and economic injustice. These aims require us to observe empirical phenomena and draw our own lessons to inform often heated scholarly and policy debates. Indeed, given the strong passions and beliefs that characterize these debates, analytical skills that force us to question our pre-existing beliefs and assumptions are essential to distinguishing informed research from the dull drone of opinions and beliefs that are expressed through blogs, online and print media or on television programs.

Research Methods in International Relations therefore equips us with a set of tools for collecting, interpreting, and analyzing a wide body of information that we will gather from Internet media sources, television, newspapers, expert **interviews**, or large **datasets**. These tools will, in the short term, help us hone our ability to make an impactful contribution to these debates through research essays, theses or dissertations. However, and perhaps more importantly, these tools will make us more effective decision-makers and communicators in the policy, business or academic communities upon leaving higher education. Scholarly research in International Relations should therefore not be viewed as a rarified form of writing but rather a skill that will help students search through vast bodies of data available to decision-makers in international relations and inform critical thinking.

Research essays and dissertations are therefore exercises that go far beyond the narrow classroom assessment function, which primarily serves as an indicator of student performance or understanding of a particular subject matter. Rather, these academic research outputs assist us in making informed choices about why we pose the questions we ask. What kind of knowledge do we seek to gain from our research interests? These questions, as we will learn in Chapter 1, already bring us into the realm of thinking about **methodology**, or ways we go about acquiring knowledge. However, this textbook does not present you with

methods and methodology for the sake of learning about methods and methodology alone. Instead, this textbook is a roadmap that will assist you in thinking
critically about research practice in International Relations. Indeed, one of the
core challenges we encounter as students of International Relations is how to
make sense of salient global events, such as war and peace, environmental degradation, or revolutionary change and internal conflicts. It is within this context of
a messy world, that the analytical and critical thinking skills presented here will
provide you with the requisite skills necessary for most career paths of interest
to students of International Relations.

Thus, rather than seeing a research methods course, or this textbook, as
an initiation into a rarified form of writing and research that is of interest,
or even readable, by scholars alone, we should see research and writing in
International Relations as constituting an opportunity to develop skills that
can be put to use in a number of careers far beyond the university. Approached
from this perspective many of the puzzling aspects of methods dilemmas will
take on a new urgency and appeal as you begin see how research skills for the
student of IR are not just an essential foundation for your studies, but also for
your professional career, whether that be in business, government, civil society,
or the academe.

Take, for example, the assumption that democracies do not go to war
with other democracies. During the late 1990s, and later during the early
years of the George W. Bush presidency in the United States, this assumption
informed a wide range of policy debates. But, at the same time, while we
might be able to agree on the importance of political systems that recognize
civil and political rights and allow for citizen participation in free and fair
elections, do we really know whether or not a particular type of government
makes states more or less likely to go to war? We could start by turning our
assumption into a testable **hypothesis**. Democracies do not go to war with
other democracies. Next, we can test this hypothesis against empirical data
that we will gather as part of our research process. Of course, at this point,
you have probably already recognized that this process, even in relation to
a relatively simple statement like the one presented above is fraught with
choices related to research design and methods. Do you gather statistical
data on all wars that have been fought in the last two centuries and try to
find correlations between regime types and conflict or do we look at in-depth
case studies of events where democracies were in conflict with each other but
war did not break out? The chapters that follow will provide guidance on the
choices presented above.

At this point, it should be pointed out that there is not necessarily always a
definitive right or wrong answer to questions of research design, but rather there
are strengths and limitations inherent to each particular research design you may
pursue. An awareness of these strengths and limitations will prevent you from
making many of the common mistakes found in essays and dissertations.

Research Methods as a 'How to' Guide

At the beginning the research process, you may find yourself confronted by a number of questions about *how to conduct research*. These questions that deal with issues such as how to design your research project or how to collect data, are questions that require you to start thinking about research methods and methodology. And in order to start thinking about research methods and methodology, you will need to understand the wide range of methods and methodologies that may assist you in responding to your research question.

Research methods and methodology might not at first appear to be a topic that you would want to spend a significant time reading and thinking about, especially since what led you to study International Relations in the first place were most likely *not* questions about the philosophy of science, but rather it was your interest in tackling complex challenges in international politics. For example, war, terrorism, revolutions, great power rivalry, regional integration, economic crisis, and human rights are among the many salient issues in international politics that students set out to explore in research essays.

Nevertheless, when attempting to address these questions, you will notice that textbooks on research methods, which have become defining features of other fields of study such as political science, are relatively absent within IR.[3] But, it would be a mistake to assume that this gap in literature does not mean that IR has not engaged with questions of methods. While research methods texts in IR are harder to come by, wider debates on methodology are often at the center of theoretical contestations within the discipline.[4] Perhaps no question is more contested within IR than methodological debates on how we can make use of empirical observations to understand and explain international politics (Katzenstein et al., 1998). However, it is important to understand that these theoretical contestations within IR make little sense without an underlying understanding of methodological assumptions that are contained within dueling research agendas.

Indeed, the narrative history of 20th-century IR is often presented through the lens of an evolving theoretical debate that emerged along with the discipline itself in the aftermath of the First World War. While there is no need to revisit this narrative at length here, as you will have most likely encountered it in an introductory International Relations course, it is instructive to recall that in the early 20th century IR was a discipline that coalesced around the fundamental normative aim of securing world peace through novel international organizations, such as the League of Nations, embedded within a new international legal order and its penultimate dispute settlement body, the International Court of Justice. Realists, such as E.H. Carr and Hans Morgenthau accused these early 20th-century liberals of describing a world as it ought to be as opposed to as it is. Realism sought to rectify this through its attempt to uncover objective laws of international politics. Although Morgenthau turned to human nature to explain the seemingly eternal pursuit of power by states, subsequent realists sought to identify more scientifically sound explanations for state behavior grounded in the international system itself.

While you are most likely already familiar with these debates, what you might not be aware of is that a question of methodology underlies this contestation between idealists and realists. How did these two theoretical traditions in IR look at the same world to arrive at such starkly different conclusions on the nature of world politics? In order to respond to this question, an understanding of how we know what we think we know about the world around us is essential.

It is within this context of contested theories and methodologies that, in the past, students of IR were confronted with basic questions of research design, data collection and data analysis, without practical guidance on core research methods that are widely used in the social sciences. This textbook aims to help address this lack of guidance with what can be thought of as a 'How to' guide for research practice in International Relations that will take you through framing research questions, research design, **field research**, and data analysis.

The forthcoming chapters will provide guidance on all of the above in the form of a 'How to' guide for the research process that spans from generating a research question, to selecting appropriate research methods, to data collection and analysis, to finally writing up. As such, this textbook constitutes a valuable resource for researchers and students of IR, whether at the BA, MA, or PhD level of study. Furthermore, given the broad lessons that can be drawn from these pages for research careers outside of the academe, it can serve as a desk reference for future research you may conduct long after you complete your studies.

Given the plurality of methods deployed in IR, you will be provided here with the tools needed to establish a strong understanding of both qualitative and quantitative methods and a balanced assessment of a broad spectrum of methodological debates and research methods within the discipline. Indeed, a practical guide to research methods in IR cannot ignore contested methodologies. Yet despite the plurality of methods with which this book engages, it remains IR specific and includes a wide spectrum of examples that fall within this broad field which encompasses International Political Economy, Foreign Policy Analysis, Comparative Politics, International Organizations, Human Rights, International Political Sociology, and Political Theory, among other fields.

Chapter Outline

Research Methods in International Relations is divided into ten chapters. The textbook begins here in the Introduction, which has thus far provided an introduction to the task of research and writing in International Relations and goes on in this section to provide a chapter overview. After being introduced to how theoretical contestations within IR reflect shifting methodological perspectives on how we can make sense of international politics, we will explore two broad research traditions in IR in Chapter 1. You will be introduced to broad methodological debates that will serve to contextualize the research design and methods choices you will be asked to make in later chapters. IR's contested methodologies will be explored through a reflection on principal methodological disagreements in the field. The empirical–interpretive divide will be used to illustrate distinct approaches to studying the world around us. This debate will be framed against other binaries in IR scholarship, such as **positivism** vs. **post-positivism** and quantitative vs. qualitative research methods.

In Chapter 1, you will also be challenged to interrogate the purpose of your own research in order to better understand the insights and limitations of research methods presented in later chapters. Framed as a debate, this chapter contains a balanced overview of competing research agendas within the discipline and illustrates how these contested approaches are reflected in research topic and question selection, research design and research methods. You will also be presented with tables that provide a mapping of key characteristics of different methodological traditions in IR.

Chapter 2 provides a transition from methodological debates to research methods through a practical guide to selecting a research question and research design in IR. Here you will be further exposed to the plurality of research agendas and traditions within the discipline. You will be introduced to topic selection and research question development in the context of a chapter that also aims to provide a unique resource that brings together different avenues for research in IR and cogently maps how various types of research questions show affinities for distinct methods. Thus, the interaction between methodological presumptions and research design will be illuminated through examples that will guide you through the research process with special attention being paid to how research purpose is closely linked to choices students and scholars make in relation to research methods. Indeed, as research questions within the discipline take on many different forms from exploratory to explanatory and evaluative, Chapter 2 constitutes an important foundational chapter that will transition readers from broader methodological debates to research methods deployed within the discipline. Furthermore, after a discussion of research design, the chapter will also provide you with an overview of how to write a research proposal.

Chapter 3 will explore an increasingly common and challenging research dilemma confronted by researchers in IR, that of ethics. Research ethics in IR is an important part of the research process, from critical reflections on the research questions you ask, to the question of research funding, research involving **human subjects**, or securing ethical approval for research projects from research funding bodies and research institutions, to basic academic honesty within your research papers. As more and more students and scholars of IR go into the field and gather their data from interviews or other forms of interaction with research participants, questions of research ethics, and how they interact with different codes of ethics, from personal ethics to institutional and professional ethics, require greater attention within the discipline. Thus research ethics go far beyond traditional questions of **plagiarism** and academic dishonesty.

In short, IR research cannot be carried out without at least some reflection on the question of research ethics. Thus, Chapter 3 will highlight that rather than seeing ethics as just another part of the research processes, it should be approached holistically and taken into account at every stage of your research project.

In Chapter 4 you will be provided with an overview of how to write a **literature review**. This chapter aims to provide practical guidance on the literature review reading and writing processes. When conducting IR research, it is essential to nest your own research in existing scholarship on the research topic at hand. In order to conduct a systemic study of a given topic, a firm grasp of scholarly engagement with existing literature is a necessary antecedent to formulating a coherent research paper. Therefore, this chapter will guide you through the process of collecting and reading relevant literature and on structuring and writing a literature review. It also highlights the purpose of literature reviews as both a tool to assist you in familiarizing yourself with existing scholarship and providing your readers with a comprehensive overview of existing scholarship, points of disagreement, or gaps in knowledge, on a given research topic.

Chapter 5 will mark a transition in the textbook from broader questions of methodology, design, ethics, and reviewing the literature, to data collection and analysis techniques widely used in IR. The first of these, which we will explore, is **qualitative methods**. Qualitative methods in IR have been deployed within a broad body of scholarship that spans from empiricist explanatory studies of norm evolution that came to occupy a central position within IR scholarship in the 1990s (Risse et al, 1999) to more recent interpretive studies that reflect on changed understanding of specific vocabularies, phenomena, or events (see for example, Jackson, 2007: 394–42). Chapter 5 will first introduce you to this diverse body of both positivist and interpretive qualitative research in IR through an in-depth overview of constructivist deployment of qualitative research methods in IR scholarship. Next you will be provided with both an assessment of the utility and insight of qualitative research, which will be followed by a practical guide on operationalizing qualitative methods for your own research.

Chapter 5 then goes on to introduce you to commonly used qualitative research techniques in IR. In particular you will be introduced to the process of conducting interview research, from identifying relevant interview subjects to conducting interviews along with other commonly used methods including **content analysis** and **discourse analysis** in IR. In relation to data collection, Chapter 5 will also highlight how the data collection process has been affected by the rapid growth in social media and Internet communications technologies. Indeed, despite the multitude of data collection techniques at our disposal, often students embark on collecting research data without first having reflected on the advantages and disadvantages of various qualitative research methods.

For example, students often seek guidance on the selection of an interview format and problems encountered when generating interview questions. In relation to quantitative data analysis, this chapter will explore content and discourse analysis. Here you will be provided with techniques for collecting relevant data and then organizing your data. Next, an introduction to discourse analysis will provide you with an overview of how to use this particular data collection and analysis tool in IR. It will also examine the focus of discourse analysis, which is on reflecting upon the meaning of official or unofficial pronouncements through the textual analyses of documents.

Chapter 6 then provides an introduction to **quantitative methods**. Quantitative methods, deeply rooted in North American political science, have been deployed with frequency in IR, yet remain inaccessible to many students and scholars who lack advanced mathematical or statistical training. This chapter will provide an introduction to the contributions and utility of quantitative research. It will then go on to provide an overview of the behavioralist-quantitative tradition in IR through an introduction to the mathematical modeling of strategic interactions. Following this introduction to mathematical modeling, some widely used methods to collect quantitative data, such as questionnaires, surveys, and datasets, will be explored. After an overview of quantitative data collection in IR, readers will be provided with strategies for operationalizing quantitative methods in their own research. This will transition readers to the next section of this chapter, which will deliver practical guidance on more common IR quantitative methods. Statistics and formal methods remain widely used in IR and appear frequently in the discipline's leading journals (Zinnes, 2002: 99). Indeed, scholars have attempted to model a wide range of issue areas in the study of international relations from cooperation to conflict. Thus, literacy in formal methods, in particular an ability to draw and understand relationships between variables, is increasingly necessary for both students and scholars to access a growing body of IR scholarship. In sum, this chapter will provide you with an introduction to statistics and formal methods in IR, an overview of formal methods and modeling within the discipline, and a practical guide to operationalizing formal methods in research.

Chapter 7 will turn to mixed methods research. Research methods curricula are often divided along the lines of quantitative and qualitative research methods; however, increasingly students and scholars are turning to mixed methods, which include elements of both in their research. Therefore, this chapter will serve to provide a guide to mixed methods, or methods that seek to combine quantitative and qualitative methods, in IR. To be sure, **triangulation** among methods, and more broadly research traditions, allows students and scholars to draw new and relevant findings from their data. Furthermore, complementarity and gathering a more holistic body of data also constitute two important contributions provided by mixed methods research. Chapter 7 will include examples drawn from the field to illustrate mixed methods research design and operationalization. For example, discursive approaches to both explaining and understanding treaty compliance bring together both quantitative and qualitative methods along with elements of **interpretivism** (Lamont, 2010) and **agent-based modeling** will serve as an example of where mathematical models have been used to shed light on complex social processes (Axelrod, 1997).

After surveying mixed methods research we return to case study design in order to explore in greater detail one of the most common research designs deployed in IR research. Because case studies often include elements of quantitative, qualitative or mixed methods, case study research design is explored in Chapter 8 in order to provide a more complete picture of some of the research choices you will face in designing your case study. Qualitative methods that commonly feature in case studies, such as **process-tracing**, will also be introduced within this chapter. Indeed, although widely associated with qualitative research (Levy, 2002), case studies are increasingly featured within mixed-methods research design and case studies remain a common feature across a broad range of IR scholarship. It has even been argued that case studies constitute the most commonly employed method for IR research (Maoz, 2002). Of course, case studies come in many different forms, for example, exploratory, evaluative, and explanatory. This chapter will provide an overview of different types of case studies while also providing the methodological insights and limitations of case study research. Therefore, Chapter 8 will provide you with both an overview of types of case studies in IR and an assessment of the utility and limits of case study research. The chapter also contains a practical guide for case study research in IR. Building on an overview of different forms of case studies and their insights and limitations, this chapter takes readers through the process of case study design and addresses questions of case selection to assist students in matching an appropriate case study design to prospective research questions. Illustrative examples of case study research in IR will be provided to illuminate this process.

Chapter 9 takes into account an increasing focus on research agendas in IR that require some form of field research, such as those that characterize sub-fields such as area studies, human rights, conflict, and conflict resolution research. Furthermore, sometimes research in these sub-fields requires researchers to conduct field research in fragile political environments and conflict or post-conflict zones. Nevertheless, despite the growth of fieldwork in IR, there is only one text that specifically addresses dilemmas of access, consent, and safety that students of IR are confronted with during field research (Sriram et al., 2009). Chapter 9 will outline the process of field research and introduce students to challenges that they will encounter in the field. They will gain an insight into conducting research in a wide range of fieldwork settings with examples drawn from field research that will also include conflict and post-conflict zones.

Chapter 10 then concludes this textbook with a practical guide to writing up research projects. Writing up often proves the most challenging part of the research process as students are confronted with the task of distilling a wide body of information collected during the research process into a cogent research paper. Chapter 10 will provide an overview of the core components and structure of research papers that will be relevant for undergraduate essays, postgraduate theses, and scholarly journal articles alike. It will also impart important lessons on the writing-up process that integrates lessons learned from research design and operationalization.

Conclusions

Without a firm grasp of methodological debates and research methods deployed within IR, the ability of students and scholars to engage with theoretical debates within the discipline or derive policy relevant lessons from IR scholarship will remain limited. At best, methodologically uniformed research will be drowned out by the vast body of written work that is being produced on a daily basis on international politics, while at worst these flawed assumptions may find themselves widely read and serve to inform policy choices that result in catastrophic consequences. History provides no shortage of examples of the latter.[5] The following pages of this textbook seek to provide you with a practical guide to avoiding these pitfalls.

Most immediately, the introductory section, taken in conjunction with Chapter 1 of this textbook, aims to impart that fundamental choices related to research topic and question selection and research design are all informed by methodological presumptions held by students and scholars. What kind of contribution do we wish to make to existing knowledge about IR? What kinds of research questions are most urgent for us to answer? How do we go about responding to these questions? How do we know we are right? Might we be wrong? These are the questions that you should be able to answer in the context of your own research papers, theses, or dissertations.

Notes

1   This book makes a distinction between research methods and methodologies. While this distinction will be elaborated upon in Chapter 1, here it should be noted that methods refer to the tools and techniques for data collection and analysis, while methodologies refer to the ways through which we acquire knowledge.
2   For example, Stephen M. Walt warns that the professional field of IR has encouraged '... scholars to employ specialized jargon and arcane methodological techniques, because these devices reinforce the idea that members of the discipline are privy to specialized knowledge that non-members lack.' Stephen M. Walt, 'International Affairs and the Public Sphere', *Essay Series: Transformations of the Public Sphere*, Social Science Research Council (SSRC), July 21, 2011, available at: http://publicsphere.ssrc.org/walt-international-affairs-and-the-public-sphere/#foot_2

3   While research methods texts in political science constitute too broad a field of litera-
    ture to review here, one positivist text that is at times also used in the context of IR
    is Stephen Van Evera, *Guide to Methods for Students of Political Science*. Ithaca, NY:
    Cornell University Press, 1997. One of the few examples of texts that engage with both
    qualitative and quantitative research in IR is Frank P. Harvey and Michael Brecher's
    Evaluating Methodology in International Studies. Ann Arbor, MI: University of Michigan
    Press, 2002. Another, yet narrower text, Detleft F. Sprinz and Yael Wolinsky-Nahmias'
    Cases, Numbers, Models: International Relations Research Methods. Ann Arbor, MI:
    University of Michigan Press, 2004.
4   While the terms methods and methodologies are sometimes used interchangeably, here the
    distinction between the two drawn by Moses and Knutsen is used, which sees methodolo-
    gies as posing wider questions about how we know something, whereas methods are refers
    to specific research techniques or tools. See Jonathon W. Moses and Torbjorn L. Knutsen,
    Ways of Knowing: Competing Methodologies in Social and Political Research, 2nd edi-
    tion. New York: Palgrave, 2012, pp. 1–9.
5   For some examples of how IR theory helped bring about foreign policy disasters see
    Stephen M. Walt, 'The Relationship between Theory and Policy in International Relations',
    Annual Review of Political Science, vol. 8, 2005, pp. 28–29. Note that on p. 29 Walt also
    points to examples of the opposite.

1
RESEARCH METHODS IN INTERNATIONAL RELATIONS

International Relations (IR) is a field of study with a rich genealogy of methodological contestation that draws upon diverse traditions of research in the social sciences. From IR's emergence as an academic field of inquiry in the early 20th century, it has drawn inspiration from a number of diverse disciplines: law, economics, political science, history, and sociology, to name a few examples.[1] Importantly, IR also incorporated methodological traditions, and research methods, from these disciplines. At times the traditions of some of these disciplines, such as economics, made a deep imprint upon IR scholarship. Yet, this cross-disciplinary engagement, which gave us the diverse toolbox of research methods presented within this book, should not be interpreted as suggesting that IR is a discipline where 'anything goes' in terms of research practice. Indeed, although Stephen Walt (2011b) points out that we should avoid attempts to impose a single method or theoretical perspective on the field as this would limit research agendas to a narrow scope of questions that could be addressed by the popular method of the day, we should also strive to produce methodologically rigorous research that meets the standards of inquiry within the methods and methodological traditions with which we engage. To be sure, far from IR scholarship lacking methodological rigor, we, as students or scholars of IR, are confronted with the task of reconciling a field of study that welcomes methodological plurality while also adhering to rigorous standards in methods.

This textbook on research methods recognizes this plurality of methods and does not aim to promote a single approach or method for the field. Nevertheless, IR research methods should be held to the same standard demanded across the social sciences. This allows for a unified approach to methods that vigorously interrogates research methods and methodologies even in the context of the diverse research agendas that fluctuate in response to rapid transformations and heated policy debates that characterize our rapidly evolving field of study and practice.

IR's diverse methodological traditions have resulted in researchers, in both scholarship and practice, making use of a diverse array of research methods. Unlike fields of study such as anthropology, which make use of core methods built around ethnography and group observation, IR has brought with it research methods from a number of fields: anthropology, economics, law, political science, and sociology. Thus, an understanding of a broad spectrum of social science methods is a necessary prerequisite for academic or policy literacy. A strong grasp of research methods not only unlocks the tools necessary for you to contribute to IR scholarship, but also reinforces critical thinking skills that constitute prerequisites for a number of research-focused careers that range from policy roles within foreign ministries, to decision-making roles within business or financial forecasting, or research intensive positions within inter-governmental or non-governmental organizations. As such the forthcoming chapters can be seen as a roadmap for academic writing, but they also contain a wider relevance for anyone pursuing research on topics or themes related to international politics.

The relative absence of research methods textbooks in the field has created an unnecessary barrier to research for students of IR, which might leave you questioning what **methodology** and methods mean in a field as broad and diverse as IR.[2] Unlike North American political science, where research methods training is a core part of the curriculum across political science programs (Van Evera, 1997), students of IR are often introduced to, and asked to, contribute to theoretical debates within the field without a firm grasp of underlying methodological debates. Indeed, theoretical and methodological contestations have long frustrated those who attempt to engage with salient topics in international politics.

Most research essays in IR are empirically grounded in some event in international politics and aspire to be policy relevant. For example, you probably approach the field from the perspective of an interested observer of international politics rather than as a partisan to hotly contested theoretical warfare, and thus you would like to explain what you observe rather than use theory as your initial point of departure. This discrepancy alone creates a certain amount of discomfort for those who attempt to link their interests to theories of IR that are of a more general and abstract hue. In sum, research topics that are often of interest include a wide range of issues often plucked from the day's headlines: the causes of conflict in a particular country, or the outbreak of revolutions, the negotiation and durability of peace agreements, political violence and terrorism, corporate accountability for human rights abuses, to international responses to climate change, to name a few.

Meanwhile, although the general focus of theoretical contestation within IR migrates over time: from liberalism to realism, to neo-realism and neo-liberal institutionalism, to **constructivism** and beyond, the underlying methodological contestations between those who embed their research within an empiricist natural science tradition and those who embed their research within a more reflexive interpretive tradition endure. This enduring rivalry between these two broad traditions, which will be elucidated in greater detail shortly, is reflected across the diverse array of subfields in IR with which students of IR are likely to engage with during the course of their undergraduate or postgraduate studies. These subfields include, for example, international security, international political economy, foreign policy analysis, international organizations, and comparative politics.

In part because of the theory-focused nature of major debates within IR, starting a research project, for either an undergraduate essay or postgraduate dissertation, can appear a daunting task as students are faced with the initial problem of reconciling their interest in international politics with scholarly debates in the field. Students of IR have long sought to respond to questions that attempt to either explain or understand the world around us. In fact, the discipline of IR itself emerged from an attempt to understand the causes of war and peace in international politics. Recall that fundamental questions, such as those which sought to elucidate these determinants of war and peace, launched IR as a field of study in the aftermath of the First World War, when the first Chair of International Relations was established in Aberystwyth in 1919 (Burchill, 2001), and it remained a focus of inquiry throughout the Cold War as IR scholars sought to mitigate the risk of a nuclear conflict between the United States and the Soviet Union through deterrence theories grounded in rationalist assumptions regarding superpower behavior.[3]

In the post-Cold War years, intra-state conflicts expanded the focus of IR research as students and scholars sought to understand the proliferation of internal armed conflicts. Furthermore, developments such as the liberalization of international trade and regional political and economic integration saw the deeper integration of the study of domestic politics within states and bargaining models that reflected domestic interests into the field. In addition, the proliferation of human rights activism and human rights commitments entered into by states also led students of IR to attempt to understand what appeared to be a transformation in world politics as state interests, once argued by realists to be narrowly defined in terms of power, now seemed to encompass an expanding range of values and norms of appropriate behavior.

As you embark on research paper writing, you might not be aware that the questions you ask are embedded in underlying assumptions about how to interpret the social world. Every research article read you have read within your IR curriculum, and every research paper you will write, is embedded within a certain methodological framework and can be placed along the enduring divide between **empiricism**, on the one hand, and **interpretivism**, on the other. For example, when reading Cold War literature on international nuclear conflict, you might not be aware of the empiricist assumptions of those scholars who apply scientific methods to explain the conditions under which international nuclear conflict is likely to escalate into a nuclear exchange. In short, academic writing cannot be disentangled from methodology, and methodology cannot be disentangled from academic writing.

While many students, and scholars embark upon selecting research methods without a deeper reflection upon the logic of their use, this chapter will draw linkages between methodologies and research methods through two broad epistemological approaches to IR research, empiricism and interpretivism, which will be explained in greater detail later in this chapter. While empiricism dominated the discipline during the latter half of the 20th century, IR after the turn of the century is now characterized by greater methodological plurality, with leading journals in the field containing a broad range of research that ranges from statistical methods and formal modeling to interpretive research.

From Methodology to Method

It is within this context that we turn to a fundamental question that will shape our research: how do we understand, interpret, or explain the social world around us? In fact, it is helpful to recall here that this question itself defines the very nature of research. Indeed, Pole and Lampard (2002) adopt a process-focused definition of research, which defines research as 'the search for knowledge' (p. 3). With this definition of research in mind, it is not surprising that the preceding question has been at the heart of philosophy of science debates and has produced a wide array of responses that range from claims that the scientific method used to understand the natural sciences can be applied to the social sciences to a complete rejection of the scientific method. Later, this chapter will chart these traditions with a focus on how they relate to student research topics and research methods choices with which students of IR are confronted.

Of course, at the very outset of the research process it is important not to get lost, or misdirected, by questions of methodology. IR's plurality in methodologies and its diversity in research methods often generates a significant amount of confusion, even among scholars in the field, as highlighted by Keohane's early challenge to feminist IR scholars to develop a research agenda that would allow for testable conjecture and **hypothesis** testing, something explicitly rejected on epistemological grounds by many feminist scholars within the field (Tickner, 2005). It is essential to remember that distinct methodological traditions not only deploy different methods, but also emerge from distinct traditions, theories, and principles of reasoning that have shaped research techniques used in the field. Therefore, they often ask fundamentally different questions.

Keohane's challenge is illustrative of a tendency to adopt a narrow view of methods that discounts alternative ways of asking questions and finding answers. In order to capture a broader perspective on IR research methods this chapter presents an empirical–interpretive dichotomy to conceptualize the methodological divide within the field. This is not to make a claim that all research fits nicely along this continuum, nor should this divide be conceptualized as firm, or mutually exclusive. Rather, it is helpful to think of the empirical–interpretive divide as a fluid continuum along which researchers use a wide range of methods.[4] In order to determine where a student's own research falls along this continuum, students must first establish their research topic. Then, they must reflect upon the purpose of their research.

In sum, with IR reading lists containing works positing competing methodological claims and with classroom lecturers whose own research agendas fall within methodologically divergent research traditions, it is evident that IR is a discipline defined by its *inclusiveness* of competing approaches to methodology, although at times the perception that there is a certain methodological intolerance toward research that falls outside a particular tradition is also visible. However, overall, IR's inclusiveness comes at the cost of disciplinary cohesiveness and is therefore also a source of confusion among students seeking methodological guidance because unlike in other fields within the social sciences, where there is greater consensus around dominant methodological traditions, in IR no such consensus exists. Thus rather than conceptualize a hierarchy of research methodologies or methods, the following sections will introduce students to choices they will be confronted with in the research process. And, it will be these choices that will serve as a guide to both the research process and research methods. The next sections will therefore provide students with a roadmap to research practice within the context of these contested methodologies and will act as a basis for choices in **research design** and method that will be presented in forthcoming chapters. However, before moving on to questions of research design and method, it is first important to present the empirical–interpretive divide in greater detail.

Dueling Epistemologies: Empiricism and Interpretivism

When surveying existing literature in IR, it is immediately apparent that IR scholarship is far from monolithic in terms of approaches and methods. In fact, for the purpose of simplicity, it can be argued that IR scholarship can be grouped into two broad epistemological traditions that advance competing claims as to what should be regarded as acceptable knowledge within the field: empiricism and interpretivism. This dichotomy replicates a divide that is evident across the social sciences and coalesces around the question of what knowledge is of disciplinary value and what knowledge should we strive to produce? Two broad responses have been advanced to these discipline-defining questions. One approach argues that natural science methods should be applied to study the social world, while the other posits that the social world is not amenable to study through scientific methods and **experimentation**. These two responses can be grouped under the labels of empiricism, empirically grounded explanatory research in IR, and interpretivism, reflexive research that rejects the application of natural science methods to the social world and instead interrogates ideas, norms, beliefs and values that underlie international politics.[5] Thus, despite the wide body of research that falls within the scope of IR, most research can be situated in one of these two traditions. In fact, IR scholars have described this division between these two traditions as 'a fundamental division within the discipline' (Burchill, 2001: 2).[6]

Although various authors have used different terms to describe the empiricist-interpretivist epistemological divide, the application of different terminology to essentially the same divide should not confuse students from the underlying division or obscure this divide between the two perspectives (see Table 1.1). In addition, rather than seeing empericism vs. interpretivism as strict dichotomy, it is helpful to approach this divide from the perspective of a choice that will inform how you will approach your own research and that reflects your own research interests.

Table 1.1   Empirical and Interpretive

Empirical	Interpretive
Naturalism	Constructivism
Behavioralism	Reflexivity
Explanation	Understanding

The aforementioned dichotomy does not neatly correspond to theoretical divides within dominant approaches to IR, such as between Realism and Liberalism or Constructivism. For example, there is a broad body of IR Constructivist research that falls within an explanatory empiricist tradition.[7] It is therefore instructive to take a step back from the theoretical debates, which students are likely to attempt to engage with in their own research essays, and approach questions of methodology and methods from the perspective of research purpose, as opposed to theoretical approach. This will in turn guide the formulation of a research question, and later research design. However, before moving on to research purpose, let us first establish the core features of empiricism and interpretivism.

Empiricism

As mentioned earlier, empiricism is drawn from the importation of natural science research practice into the social sciences. It is based on the broad assumption that knowledge can be accumulated through experience and observation and is also often referred to as **positivism**. For those who see IR as a social science, IR should be studied in a systemic, replicable, and evidence-based manner.[8] For empiricists, the study of the social world is analogous to the study of the natural world. Theories of IR can be generated and tested through careful observation and experimentation. There is a rich tradition of empiricist research in IR that parallels that of political science and traces its roots back to founding figures of the discipline, such as Hans Morgenthau, who argued international politics was governed by 'objective laws', and Kenneth Waltz, who crafted a system structure image of international politics in his *Theory of International Politics*. Likewise, neo-liberals adopted the same positivist methodology to studying international politics; however, they reached differing conclusions in relation to conflict and cooperation in international politics than their neo-realist cousins. In sum, theories of International Relations with which students may be most familiar fall within the empiricist tradition. These theories seek to observe and explain state behavior while also testing **falsifiable** hypotheses derived from observations of empirical facts.

There are three core characteristics of IR empiricism: (1) that international politics can be studied as an objective reality that is a world 'out there' and distinct from the researcher; (2) theories are held to the standard of predictive validity; and (3) hypotheses tested in IR research should be falsifiable. An additional sub-characteristic that applies to a significant body of empiricist research is that it aspires to be of policy-relevance and to inform action by decision-makers.

At the outset of designing your own research, it is necessary to understand what side of the divide your own research interests gravitate toward. If you wish to explain events, developments, or the behavior of actors in international politics, then empiricist research methods will provide the means to do so as they will unlock tools that allow for causal claims and explanations of developments and practices of international politics.

Interpretivism

Interpretivism also draws upon a rich tradition in IR among scholars whose aim is not necessarily to explain events, developments or trends. Instead, interpretivism, also referred to as **reflectivism** or **post-positivism**, focuses on understanding social meanings embedded within international politics. Unlike empiricists who aim to advance cumulative knowledge through observation and hypothesis testing, interpretivists aim to unpack core assumptions that underlie the positivist image of the world in an attempt to counter the perceived empiricist orthodoxy in IR. Interpretivist research agendas seek to understand identities, ideas, norms, and culture in international politics. Examples of interpretivist literature in IR include groundbreaking contributions by scholars such as Richard Ashley and Robert Cox who cautioned the empiricist epistemological position that limits acceptable knowledge in the field to empirical observation, which fails to question the underlying social and power structures of international politics.

The principal claim advanced by interpretivists is that the distinction between the researcher and the social world, implied by empiricists, should be rejected. This is because, interpretivists argue, that the researcher intervenes in, or creates, observed social realities through their own role in knowledge production and thus alters the object under study. In other words, the researcher and the research subject are mutually constituted through **intersubjective** understanding, and therefore the object of research does not have its own objective existence outside this mutually constituted relationship (Klotz and Lynch, 2007: 12). The experimental environment of the science laboratory in which control experiments can be carried out to understand the interaction between two or more physical objects cannot be replicated in the social world where the researcher interacts, and develops a relationship with, the social objects under study. As such, concepts at the center of empiricist research agendas, such as explanation and causality are rejected in favor of research agendas dominated by attempts to understand social meaning in international politics.

Now that the distinction between empiricism and interpretivism has been established we can begin to use this divide to better understand which research methods tools we can make use of in pursuit of our own research. Given IR's focus on international politics, most student research papers attempt to engage with topical events or issues in the world today. The topics of events often tell us something about world politics that is relevant beyond the topic or event at hand. How do we get from a description of a given topic or event to larger claims about world politics?

From Theory to Method: Research Choices

IR's disciplinary focus on great debates, or contested theories of international relations, has the unfortunate unintended consequence of obscuring serious attempts to critically reflect upon research design and methods. IR's grand theories, such as neo-realism and neo-liberal institutionalism, operate at a high level of abstraction that aims to elucidate general patterns of behavior decoupled from space and time, and therefore may seem hard to penetrate from the perspective of a student wishing to write on a topical occurrence in world politics. To be sure, while students of IR acquire a strong grasp of core theoretical tenants and controversies within the discipline through introductory texts (Baylis et al., 2010; Burchill et al., 2001), the discipline's internal gap between theory and policy forms a barrier to those attempting to make their own initial contributions to IR research (Walt, 2005).

However, at the same time, often relatively straightforward questions or policy debates in international politics reflect underlying theoretical contestations in IR literature. When we think about a particular event in world politics, such as the wars in the former Yugoslavia during the 1990s or the 2003 Iraq War, there are a host of theoretical approaches to IR, which would lead us to widely divergent policy recommendations. In relation to the former Yugoslavia, those who saw the war as the result of the aggressive behavior of a select few autocratic leaders, such as Slobodan Milosevic, argued for international intervention to bring about an end to the bloodshed – and later demanded regime change to bring about a sustainable peace in the region. On the other hand, those who saw the conflict as the product of deep-seated ancient ethnic animosities cautioned against intervention, as they saw little hope for internationally driven peace-building efforts in the aftermath of an inter-ethnic armed conflict. Likewise, in relation to the 2003 Iraq War, competing theoretical perspectives on both whether or not Saddam Hussein could be deterred from aggressive behavior and on democratization and democratic peace offered divergent policy prescriptions and forecasts for the likely aftermath of the initial US-led invasion.[9] Thus, if we approach theory from the perspective of a causal conjecture of what is likely to occur under certain conditions, then the bridge between topics of interest and theoretical debates becomes more visible.

Now that a relationship to theory has been established the question of method arises. In order to simply start thinking about methods, it is helpful to recall that research methods are 'techniques for collecting data' (Bryman, 2008: 31). These can include quantitative methods to interpret large **datasets** or **qualitative methods** to allow research to delve deeper into specific events, places, organizations, or personalities. However, before embarking upon data collection it is imperative that the researcher has a clear idea of what data to collect. This is especially the case now given the massive body of data that is within easy reach of students of IR.

Data in IR is widely available and rapidly growing. In relation to secondary sources alone, there are an increasing number of online traditional and non-traditional media resources, electronic databases, and libraries that are all easily accessible to the researcher. As such, knowing where to begin data collection is as important as knowing what techniques are available, through which data can be interpreted. Data collection and data analysis thus require the researcher to make choices in terms of research topic, research question, research design, and research method. In short, what data we collect is always contingent upon what questions we ask.

Research is about making choices. From the very outset of the research process students are confronted by choices that will inform what kind of research essay they will write. Although students of IR have no trouble identifying topics of interest, such as international terrorism, human trafficking, civil conflict, the gap between student interest in, or detailed knowledge of, a particular phenomenon, event, or geographic area and the process of distillation of interest and knowledge into a methodologically cogent and theoretically informed research paper often results in essays which fall into the gaps of either over-generalizing – 'I have studied a particular case and my findings therefore will explain a certain behavior across all cases' – or making unsubstantiated claims – 'I argue X, but have not presented relevant empirical data, or scholarly secondary sources, to substantiate this claim.'

Poor research choices result in essays and dissertations that are either unable to support key observations posited by the author or fail to make a contribution to scholarship at all. Often these poor research choices are the result of students taking short cuts in the research process. As mentioned earlier, essay or thesis writing often begins with the prospective author deciding to write on a topical event or trend in international politics. For example, a student's interest could be in the Arab Spring uprisings that began in Tunisia in January 2011 and set off a chain of on-going revolutions across the Arab World. The student, having followed closely media reports on the Arab Spring, already has a general idea of the topic at hand; however, this broad body of descriptive data does not provide guidance as to how to shift from collecting information on the Arab Spring to producing a cogent research essay that makes a contribution to scholarly literature. In short, at this stage the student remains unsure regarding what questions to ask, what type of research design to adopt, and what methods could be effectively used.

First, it is essential to narrow down the topic at hand. While Chapter 2 will assist in formulating a research question, before we can think about our research in terms of research questions, we need to first establish where the project is grounded in relation to the two epistemological perspectives outlined earlier: empiricism and interpretivism. In order to arrive at an answer, you should ask yourself what is your interest in a given topic? What do you want to know about it? What kind of knowledge do you want to create? Your response to these questions will help you make coherent choices in relation to research design and method. Do you aim to explain the causes of revolution? Are you interested in elucidating how authoritarian regimes that were perceived as resilient collapsed in the face of popular protests? Or what role opposition movements played in the Arab Spring revolutions? Perhaps, you are interested in the consequences of revolution. For example, what role will Islamists play in transitional processes? If these are topics you wish to explain, then an empiricist approach will allow you to select a research design and methods that will help you to begin to tease out causal relationships and explain events and outcomes.

Or is your interest more reflective? Are you interested in exploring the symbolism of the Tunisian fruit vendor, Mohammed Bouazizi's self-immolation in December 2010 that set off street protests across Tunisia? Are you interested in Western interpretations of the Arab Spring? Or perhaps, your interest is in discourses of revolution in the Arab Spring? Or would you like to explore evolving regional or ethnic identities in the context of political transformations? If so, you will find that an interpretivist approach to your research, and research method selection, will prove most helpful.

Table 1.2 Researching the Arab Spring: Empirical or Interpretive?

Empirical	Interpretive
I want to explain the causes of revolution.	I want to understand how revolution transformed local identities.
I want to explore the political role of Islamist movements before and after the revolutions.	I want to understand the symbolism of self-immolation in the context of the Tunisian Revolution.
I want to examine the constitution drafting processes in post-revolutionary Tunisia or Libya.	I want to understand Western perceptions of the Arab Spring and how these have been shaped by recent transformations.

Table 1.2 helps to integrate how your interest in a given topic, or the questions you want to answer, will inform your choice in terms of what kind of research you will pursue. At this point, it is then necessary to both interrogate more deeply the topic area and attempt to explore what has been written already in the scholarly literature. While guidance on carrying out a **literature review** is provided in Chapter 4, here it is important to emphasize why a wider awareness of the field is a necessary precondition for any effective data analysis. For example, a student wanted to write an essay that would explain the causes of conflict in the former Yugoslavia. In the end the student argued *the wars in the former Yugoslavia were caused by ancient ethnic hatreds*. Such an essay, explicitly empiricist and focused on making a causal argument about the causes of civil conflict, represents a large number of student research projects in that it is an attempt to explain a salient question in international politics. Indeed, the essay aimed to be policy relevant through presenting to decision-makers an explanation of the causes of internal conflicts in the aftermath of the Cold War, and thus aspired to inform policy responses to internal conflicts.

However, while the student was aware of the empirical focus of this research and explicitly set out to explain the causes of a particular conflict, the student narrowly collected data from select media reports and editorials published during the 1990s, and did not make use of more recent literature that forms the foundation of a scholarly consensus in the field, that the conflict was elite-driven, or in other words was caused by political elites seeking to solidify their hold on power. Forthcoming chapters on writing a research design, writing a literature review, qualitative, and case study research will together offer a guide to avoid such research pitfalls.

On the other hand, another essay on the same topic: *what are the causes of the war in the former Yugoslavia*, failed to make an argument at all. Instead, rather than investigating causality, a summary of the conflict in the form of descriptive essay was provided. Thus, it was little more than a timeline of the war in the former Yugoslavia. While both of these examples aim to impart knowledge of the conflict in the former Yugoslavia to the reader, neither was an effective research essay. The first was an attempt to explain the conflict while the latter constituted little more than a descriptive essay. While both essays are rich in detail, neither succeeds in making an argument, either causal or interpretive. This is not because of a lack of knowledge of the subject matter, but instead because of a failure to effectively apply methods tools presented in the forthcoming chapters.

In sum, in order to avoid falling into the trap of making unsubstantiated causal claims or writing an essay that is little more than a description of an event, students must bridge the gap between interest and knowledge on the one hand and methods on the other. One way to do this has been presented in this chapter: *research interests* and *purpose* should be first located along the aforementioned empiricist–interpretivist divide. This will allow research essays to carry out two functions. The first is to add to empirical knowledge about a given topic and the second is to contribute new insights to scholarly debates within the discipline. Only once the purpose of the research essay is understood can a research question and research design be constructed that will allow the student to write a coherent research essay, and thus select relevant research methods presented in the forthcoming chapters.

Thinking about Methodology, Epistemology and Ontology

Methodological debates within IR have long been at the heart of theoretical contestations within the discipline as scholars and students of IR attempt to either explain events and trends in international politics or understand world politics. Methodologies, *or the means through which we acquire knowledge*, are closely related to two related concepts: **epistemology** and **ontology**. While epistemology was discussed earlier in the context of our discussion of the two epistemological approaches, the question of ontology remains to be addressed. It should be emphasized that all three concepts, methodology, epistemology, and ontology, are important for establishing at the outset the why, how and for what purpose we are undertaking our research project. Ontology frames the object of study. For interpretive research agendas, ontology is often at the center of inquiry as interpretive authors attempt to deconstruct the meaning of entities that we take for granted as existing in international politics, such as states or organizations. The second is epistemology, or the study of knowledge and knowledge production. Empiricists and interpretivists make epistemological claims about what forms of knowledge have value. Are valuable contributions to scholarship those that involve rigorous testing of variables to explain a certain outcome? Or are they those that question the ontology of actors in international politics, such as states? Taken together, methodology, or the means of knowledge acquisition; epistemology, what knowledge we should acquire; and ontology, the study of being, constitute a core foundation upon which we will build our research agendas. Therefore, a basic awareness of methodological traditions in IR will help unlock appropriate research designs and methods for your particular research project. An awareness of what is under study and how to go about studying presupposes ontological and episte-mological assumptions about International Relations.

Ontology, Epistemology, and Methodology

Ontology: the study of being, the nature of social entities

Example: Do objective entities that we take for granted in international politics, such as States, have an external reality? Or more simply, what is a state?

Epistemology: the study of knowledge, how is knowledge produced

Example: Are certain forms of knowledge privileged? Do we focus on explanation?

Methodology: ways through which we acquire knowledge

Example: How do we know, or the underlying logic of knowing.

Back to Basics: Thinking Critically about International Relations

For many students, engaging with theoretical debates within the field can prove daunting at the outset of a research project. One way to bridge the gap between theoretical debates within the discipline and your own research interests is to examine how the particular issue that interests you relates back to wider theoretical dilemmas. Another means of arriving back at these debates is a simple thought exercise aimed at evaluating claims advanced by states, international organizations, non-governmental organizations, or even scholars. What do international organizations claim to achieve? What about states? Are they effective? How do we know whether or not they are effective? There are a host of questions that come to mind simply by taking a cursory look at any number of these international organizations' websites. The box on the next page presents an example drawn from the United Nations' International Criminal Tribunal for the former Yugoslavia.

Thinking Critically about International Relations

States, International Organizations, Non-Governmental Organizations, and Multinational Corporations all make empirical claims about how they shape international politics or developments. As students of International Relations, our research should provide a means to test many of these claims. Take for example the claim put forward by the International Criminal Tribunal for the former Yugoslavia on its website:

'… by removing some of the most senior and notorious criminals and holding them accountable the Tribunal has been able to lift the taint of violence, contribute to ending impunity and help pave the way for reconciliation.' (International Criminal Tribunal for the former Yugoslavia)

A firm grasp of research methods will allow you to immediately recognize that two **causal mechanisms** are argued to lead to three major outcomes.

Causal Mechanisms

- Removing senior criminals
- Holding senior criminals accountable

Outcomes

- Lifts taint of violence
- Contributes to ending impunity
- Helps pave the way for reconciliation

Students with an interest in international justice may attempt to interrogate the claimed causal relationship between holding persons accused of war crimes accountable before an international criminal tribunal and the promotion of reconciliation. Already, you should note that independent and **dependent variables** can be identified.

While the terminology presented above might not yet be entirely clear, there is a common-sense evaluation of claims that can be made at the outset. What does the Tribunal claim to achieve and how does it claim to achieve it? Alternatively, the question could be posed: what does the Tribunal mean by reconciliation? Or reconciliation among whom? Individual victims, ethnic groups, states? At this point you should be able to identify that the first question would lead the researcher down a route of observation and testing: empiricism. While the second question focuses on the meaning of a complex social practice, reconciliation, which requires the researcher to investigate the very concept of reconciliation and how it is used by the Tribunal: interpretivism. Finding responses to these questions will already serve as a basis for thinking about and developing research questions, design and methods that will be presented in the forthcoming chapters. Think back to Table 1.2, which mapped a series of potential research questions against the backdrop of the Arab Spring. Now try to do the same in relation to the Yugoslav Tribunal in Table 1.3.

Table 1.3 International Justice in International Relations

Empirical	Interpretive

Now that you have completed Table 1.3 you can go on to thinking about how to translate these questions into research questions that can serve as a basis for a research essay or dissertation.

Chapter Summary

IR is a field of study defined by contested methodologies and methodological plurality. As such, there is a diversity of theoretical approaches to explaining or understanding world politics alongside a diverse range of research methods available to the student and practitioner of IR. When embarking upon undergraduate or postgraduate essay or dissertation writing there are a number of questions that should be asked even before thinking about a research question. These questions are:

- What is your topic of interest?
- What is the purpose of your study?
  - Is it to explain a certain event, trend or phenomena in world politics?
  - Is it to interrogate the meaning of a particular discourse or practice in world politics?
- Where do you fall along the empiricist/interpretivist divide?

Your response to the first question should be fairly straightforward. The second requires you to think about what it is you want to do. What kind of knowledge do you want to add to a particular issue? Once you have settled on a response to this question you are then able to situate your own research along the two broad traditions in IR research presented in this chapter.

In order to disentangle this divide between contested research agendas, that often fail to communicate with one another, the empiricist–interpretivist episte-mological debate in IR was presented to help understand and evaluate the util-ity of each set of methods tools presented later in this book. It was emphasized that questions of methodology and epistemology are best approached from the perspective of your own interests and research topic. Start from your topic and purpose and ask yourself do you want to explain events in the world 'out there'? Or do you want to question the social meaning of a particular practice in inter-national politics? Once you have established your research topic and purpose, you can then go on to thinking about your research question with an awareness of how the question you pose will in turn determine which methods are most appropriate for your research.

Suggested Further Reading

Scott Burchill, Andrew Linklater, Richard Devetak, Jack Donnelly, Terry Nardin, Matthew Paterson, Christian Reus-Smit and Jacqui True (2013) *Theories of International Relations,* 5th edition. Palgrave Macmillan: New York. See the Introduction, pp. 1–31.

Martin Hollis and Steve Smith (1990) *Explaining and Understanding International Relations*. Clarendon Press: Oxford. This book provides a more in-depth exploration of the supposed dichotomy between explanatory approaches and approaches aimed at understanding.

John Gerring (2012) *Social Science Methodology: A Unified Framework,* 2nd edition. Cambridge: Cambridge University Press. In particular for an overview of an empirical perspective on science see 'Chapter 1: A Unified Framework', pp. 1–23.

Jonathon W. Moses and Torbjorn L. Knutsen (2012) *Ways of Knowing: Competing Methodologies in Social and Political Research,* 2nd edition. For an overview of methodological perspectives see Chapter 1 (pp. 1–18). For an introduction to the empirical, or as Moses and Knutsen refer to it, naturalist, approach see Chapter 2 (pp. 19–51). And, for an overview of an interpretivist, or as Moses and Knuten refer to it, constructivist, approach see Chapter 8 (pp. 169–203).

Notes

1   Chris Brown argues that International Relations, prior to its emergence as a field of study after the First World War, was previously a subset of other disciplines, namely, his-tory, international law, economics and political theory. See Chris Brown, *Understanding International Relations*, 2nd edition. New York: Palgrave, 2001, p. 20.

2   Among the few texts that attempt to engage with research methods for students of IR are Frank P. Harvey and Michael Brecher's *Evaluating Methodology in International Studies*.

Ann Arbor, MI: University of Michigan Press, 2002. Another, yet narrower text is Detleft F. Sprinz and Yael Wolinsky-Nahmias' *Cases, Numbers, Models: International Relations Research Methods*. Ann Arbor, MI: University of Michigan Press, 2004. For a qualitative methods specific text see Audie Klotz and Deepa Prakash (eds), *Qualitative Methods in International Relations: A Pluralist Guide*. New York: Palgrave, 2008.

3   For an illustrative collection of essays see Robert J. Art and Kenneth N. Waltz (eds), *The Use of Force: Military Power and International Politics*. New York: University Press of America, 1993.

4   This continuum is analogous to Klotz and Lynch's use of the term spectrum to differentiate between what they described as positivist and post-positivist epistemological positions. Audie Klotz and Cecelia Lynch, *Strategies for Research in Constructivist International Relations*. Armonk, NY: M.E. Sharpe, 2007, p. 11.

5   Hollis and Smith distinguished between the two with reference to empirical approaches, which aimed to explain, and reflective approaches, which aimed to understand. Martin Hollis and Steve Smith, *Explaining and Understanding International Relations*. Oxford: Clarendon Press, 1990. Andrew Linklater, 'The question of the next stage in international relations theory: a critical-theoretical point of view', *Millennium*, vol. 21, no. 1, 1992.

6   This divide has been described under numerous terms that all reference the same schism: causal vs. constitutive, naturalist vs. constructivist, explanatory vs. constructivist. Scott Burchill refers to this divide as a fundamental division within the discipline.

7   See Martha Finnemore and Kathryn Sikkink, 'Taking Stock: The Constructivist Research Program in International Relations and Comparative Politics', *Annual Review of Political Science*, vol. 4, no. 1, 2001, pp. 391–416. Although some authors use constructivism synonymously with interpretivism when discussing research methodology, the term interpretivism is used here to avoid confusion over the use of constructivism as a theoretical tradition in IR, which also includes explanatory studies of norm evolution.

8   For examples of research methods texts which adopt a scientific approach to disciplines related to IR see Gary King, Robert O. Keohane, and Sydney Verba, *Designing Social Inquiry: Scientific Inference in Qualitative Research*. Princeton, NJ: Princeton University Press, 1994, or John Gerring, *Social Science Methodology: A Unified Framework*, 2nd edition. Cambridge: Cambridge University Press, 2012.

9   Stephen Walt makes a parallel argument in relation to both the former Yugoslavia and Iraq. See Stephen M. Walt, 'The Relationship between Theory and Policy in International Relations', *Annual Review of Political Science*, vol. 8, 2005, p. 28.

2

RESEARCH QUESTIONS AND RESEARCH DESIGN

Now that you have chosen your research topic, understand your research purpose, and know where your research is situated along the empirical–interpretive spectrum you can start thinking about how to frame your research question, and what kind of **research design** is best suited to help you answer your question. Undergraduate and postgraduate students of IR are expected to produce research papers that go beyond simple descriptions or rich anecdotal insights into particular events. Academic papers in IR should not resemble *Wikipedia* entries. Instead, as a student of IR you are encouraged to pursue what can be described as **question-based research**. Question-based research refers to research in which you pose a question that will be responded to during the course of an essay, thesis or dissertation.

As we know from Chapter 1, IR is a field of study defined in part by its plurality of approaches to explaining and understanding the world around us. This means that there is no single template for research questions. Questions can assume many different forms, and different questions can produce different kinds of knowledge for different purposes.

For example, you might wonder *why* states go to war in the hope that a better understanding of the causes of international conflict might serve to mitigate the outbreak of conflict. Alternatively, your interest might be in *how* international courts function in a world of states. Your interest in international courts could emerge from a sense that if international dispute settlement mechanisms were strengthened then states would be less likely to fight and more likely to adjudicate. These two examples illustrate how our research questions often reflect a broader quest for knowledge that goes beyond simple responses to our questions. However, it is this broader quest for knowledge that sometimes complicates our task of honing our research interests into concise questions.

Question-Based Research: A Definition[1]

Question-Based Research

Question-based research is research in which the researcher poses a question that typically attempts to explain an uncertain relationship between two or more variables (empirical research) or that problematizes our understandings of an existing variable (interpretive research).

This chapter provides you with a practical guide to research question formulation and research design in IR that highlights the plurality of research agendas and traditions within the discipline. Therefore, the transition from topic selection to research question development will be discussed first, with special attention to how distinct questions demonstrate an affinity for distinct types of research methods. The interaction between methodological presumptions and research design will also be illuminated by examples that will guide you through the research process with an emphasis on how research purpose is closely linked to choices that you will later make in relation to research methods.

In addition to understanding how your research question will locate your work along the empirical–interpretive spectrum, you should keep in mind that your research question will also inform what kind of research skills you will need to use during the research process. Will you be working with a big picture question that requires you to interpret information derived from large **datasets**? An example of a topic that would assume a certain degree of quantitative literacy would be a project that sought to explain under what conditions an inter-state crisis will escalate into armed conflict taking into account all major inter-state crises in the 20th century. Or will you be reading primary documents looking for changes in official discourse over time? For example, do you want to look at how Just War rhetoric, or the discourse used to justify armed conflict, was used by particular leaders in a particular conflict such as the US-led Global War on Terror? Alternatively, will your research require you to go out into the field and access research sites in a foreign country? Among the many things that you will need to consider, which are addressed in Chapter 9, is the question of whether or not you have the linguistic ability to communicate with your potential research subjects in their native language, or whether or not they will be able to communicate with you in English.

These are questions you will need to reflect on while thinking about your research question. In some cases, you might find it helpful to play to your strengths. And, if pressed for time, do not pose a question that will require you to invest significant amounts of time to acquire a particular skill that you have not yet encountered.[2] For example, if your question lends itself to working with and interpreting large datasets, yet you are not comfortable with advanced mathematics you might consider rethinking your question. Perhaps instead of attempting to look at all inter-state crises and attempting to gain insights from such a large dataset, you can look at one or two crises to draw knowledge out of the processes that led to either armed conflict or the de-escalation. However, before discussing the skills needed to respond to your research question in greater detail, let us first turn to how to bridge the gap between interest in a particular topic and formulating a research question.

From Research Topic to Research Question

Chapter 1 concluded with a demonstration of how you can generate a research topic from a broad area of interest. Here, we will move from your research topic to a research question. First, finding an empirical research question will be discussed with a special focus on strategies for formulating a research question followed by a discussion of research questions and research design. Second, there will be a discussion of interpretive research questions, which will also be followed by an exploration of research questions and interpretive research design.

Empirical Research Questions

One effective tool to arrive at an empirical research question is to uncover a puzzle within your topic. Usually something within your topic area puzzles or confounds you. In essence that is what makes your topic interesting. It appears to cut against common sense, or the scholarly consensus, on the topic. For example, before the Arab Spring scholars focused on explaining *authoritarian resilience* in the Arab world (Brownlee, 2007; Pratt, 2007). In other words, scholars focused on explaining the strength of autocratic regimes and their ability to snuff out potential sites of resistance and political challengers. Yet, in January 2011, a relatively non-violent protest movement in Tunisia was able to send Tunisia's long-time autocrat, Zine al-Abidine Ben Ali, into exile in Saudi Arabia with little warning. To be sure, few had predicted Tunisia was on the cusp of revolution.

Puzzles might not only come from past events that defied general predictions, we can also think of the fall of the Berlin Wall in 1989, or the collapse of the Soviet Union in 1991. They can also be generated by intense policy debates on a particular question. For example, should NATO continue its eastward expansion to include more countries that were once part of the Soviet Union? Should

European Union enlargement processes continue and allow for states in the Western Balkans, such as Bosnia-Herzegovina, Serbia, Montenegro, Macedonia, or Kosovo to become full members? Here, instead of attempting to explain a puzzling past event, we project our understandings of current events and trends into the future. Here the puzzling question juxtaposes the lessons of the past against the shadow of the future. Will NATO and EU expansion contribute to widening the geographic area of Europe that enjoys pacific relations or will expansion contribute to a renewed Cold War by antagonizing Russia?

Table 1.2 (see page 23) presented the various focal areas of research derived from varying interests and distinguished between research interests that would lend themselves to empirical and interpretive research. If we revisit these focal areas here in the table below, we can begin to think about the transition from topic to research question. In Table 2.1, by using the thought exercise of identifying something that puzzles us, we can easily generate a number of questions that lend themselves to research within the discipline.

Table 2.1   Researching the Arab Spring: Empirical Research

Topics of Interest	Research Questions
I want to explain the causes of the Arab Spring revolutions.	What factors explain the 2011 Tunisian Revolution?
I want to explore the political role of Islamist movements before and after the revolutions.	What explains Ennahdha's (an Islamist political party) electoral success in Tunisia's October 23, 2011 elections?
I want to examine the constitution drafting processes in post-revolutionary Tunisia or Libya.	What was the role of religion in the drafting of Tunisia's draft constitution?
I want to understand what role international actors played in the Arab Spring.	What factors explain the United Nations Security Council's decision to intervene in the Libyan civil conflict?
I want to explore whether or not revolutionary movements in the Arab Spring learned from one another.	What impact did protest movements in Tunisia have upon protest movements in Egypt?

Let us first reflect on topic areas that showed an affinity for empirical research. In the table above the first topic issue was 'I want to explain the causes of the Arab Spring revolutions.' Here, the student has a broad interest in the Arab Spring revolutions, but at this point the topic remains far too broad to simply restate as a research question. The Arab Spring affected a wide range of countries from Tunisia in North Africa to Yemen on the Arabian Peninsula. Furthermore, in some cases transitions occurred with relatively little violence, such as in Tunisia, and in other cases revolutionary movements set off pro-tracted civil conflicts, such as in Libya in February 2011 and the Syrian civil war which began in March 2011. In addition, in some cases, there were protests, but no regime change, such as in Bahrain. It is clear that our initial topic the 'Arab Spring' contains within it a myriad of potential essays, but in itself is too broad to attempt to tackle as a whole. In order to get from interest in a topic to a research question, you need to attempt to decompose your topic into smaller parts that lead themselves to empirical study.[3]

Given the wide geographic area and political and cultural contexts in which the protests, which were labeled the Arab Spring, occurred, we must dig more deeply into this highly complex topic area in order to generate a question-based research question that we can respond to within the scope of an academic essay. One way to arrive at a research question is to think in terms of countries and narrow down your area of interest to one or two states. Once you have identified a particular country or countries upon which to focus, then identity a particular issue area or debate that is of interest. Then try to identify a particular debate, controversy, or puzzle so you can turn your interest into a research question.

For example, you might have read a lot on the role of social media and revo-lution, with some authors arguing that social media played a crucial role in protest mobilization and others arguing that its role is overstated. In order to assess these two competing claims, or hypotheses, you may want to pose a ques-tion along the lines of 'What role did social media play in protest mobilization during the Tunisian Revolution?' This question has a clear **dependent variable**, or an object that requires explanation, the Tunisian Revolution. It also has an **independent variable**, something that is conjectured to cause the dependent vari-able. Your response to this single question will juxtapose two competing claims encountered in the literature against each other.

H1: Social media played a significant role in protest mobilization during the 2011 Tunisian Revolution.

H2: Social media did not play a significant role in protest mobilization dur-ing the 2011 Tunisian Revolution.

Now that you have a research question and two testable hypotheses, or con-tested responses, you can begin thinking about research design, which is discussed in the next section of this chapter.

But, what if your interest is broader? You don't have a narrowly defined vari-able through which you can approach the Arab Spring, such as social media. Instead, you are looking to explain the causes of revolution itself. You also have a broader interest that is open to a number of potential variables, political and economic. In other words, your stated interest is: 'I want to explain revolution.' Your purpose is to observe a range of factors that have been offered as potential

explanatory variables instead of isolating a single factor, such as social media. Nevertheless, given the diversity of regimes that were affected by the Arab Spring across the entire Middle East and North Africa, and given widely divergent standards of living, cultural contexts, and ethnic and religious communities, it would be very difficult to explore common factors across these cases in a single essay.

Because question-based research assumes that we will be able to arrive at some sort of meaningful answer that will shed some light on an apparent puzzle, we should articulate our research questions in a way that allows for us to most effectively test conjectured relationships. In the case of the Arab Spring revolutions, the statement, 'I want to explain revolution' can be rearticulated in question form with a narrower country focus: 'What explains the Tunisian and Egyptian revolutions?' Or simply, 'What explains the Tunisian Revolution?' In relation to these questions, your hypotheses won't necessarily be opposing positions on the impact of single variable such as social media, but instead, they will constitute propositions about a number of variables that you have selected as potential explanatory variables, or variables that explain a specific event. Given the wide universe of potential explanatory variables, one way to begin generating hypotheses that you can test in your research is to begin thinking in terms of categories of explanation.

Explanatory Categories: The Agent–Structure Debate

You might have come across scholarly debates in which authors debate the effects of structure versus individual agency. This debate essentially boils down to divergent views on the scope individuals have to effect change in their societies. Is individual action conditioned by institutional or socio-economic structures? Or can individuals radically alter the political trajectories of their countries through their policy choices?

In the case of the Tunisian Revolution, you can think in terms of explanations that are more long term and structural versus explanations that put emphasis on the role of particular individuals during the transitional process, such as Mohamed Bouazizi, who self-immolated in an act of protest on 10 December 2010, or the decision of the head of the Tunisian Army to not fire on demonstrators and support the transitional process under a civilian leadership.[4] Long-term, or structural, explanations can be economic in nature, such as socio-economic inequality, or persistent high levels of youth unemployment. Structural explanations can also be found in institutional structures, such as a kleptocratic political system, or a political party system. These can be juxtaposed against explanations that are more short term, and emphasize the role of individual agency, such as those that point to the self-immolation of Mohamed Bouazizi in December 2010 touching off a nationwide wave of demonstrations and Tunisian President Ben Ali's initial inability to grasp the gravity of the situation.

Thinking in terms of explanatory categories will also help guide you through the literature, and later the data, that you will collect during the course of your research project.

Thinking about Variables

In empirical research your focus is on explaining the relationship between two objects in order to uncover wider patterns or inform our understanding of a specific object. You will therefore be thinking in terms of variables in order to explain relationships.

The dependent variable is the object under study, or the object you wish to explain: for example, **democratization**.

The independent variable is the object that you hypothesize has a **causal relationship** with the dependent variable: for example, **economic growth**.

Given the above two variables you could hypothesize that: **economic growth** leads to **democratization**.

Of course, how you test this **hypothesis** will require you to design your research in a way that would allow you to either affirm or falsify the above statement.

Below are two examples of hypotheses that can be drawn from the Tunisian Revolution. Try to identify the dependent and independent variables and also try to identify whether or not they point to structural causes or emphasize the role of individual agency.

H1: *The causes of the Tunisian Revolution were economic (socio-economic disparity, youth unemployment).*

H2: *The causes of the Tunisian Revolution were political (the inability of Ben Ali to respond quickly to the demands of demonstrators, the role of the head of the Tunisian Army).*

As a student of international politics, your interest may point you in another direction. The variables that you identify may not be internal to the country or countries under study. In this case your interest in the *international politics* of the Arab Spring might lead you to pose questions about revolutionary diffusion among countries affected by the Arab Spring, or what effect did protest movements in one country have upon protest movements in another country. Or your interest may lead you to examine the role of an outside state or international organization during the revolutions. For example, if your interest was in

European Union external policy, you could pose the question 'What role did the European Union play in democracy promotion in North Africa before and after the Arab Spring revolutions?' Or you might have a broader interest in, 'What role can external actors play in facilitating Libya's democratic transition?'[5]

While the Arab Spring is an example of a topic area that is naturally bound in time, beginning with the Tunisian Revolution in January 2011, some topic areas might not be. For example, if your interest in explaining inter-state armed conflict, without a particular conflict in mind, you should consider the period of time you wish to examine. For example, inter-state conflict after the Second World War, inter-state conflict after the end the Cold War? Doing this allows for you to both maintain a broader focus, if you wish to avoid exploring only a single case, and allows for you to limit the period of time, and thus the number of inter-state armed conflict under study.

Before moving to interpretive research it is important to point out that empirical research questions can also be approached from the perspective of what kinds of questions are being asked. For example, while all the examples above are explanatory, your explanation can be used to elucidate a past or on-going event or process, or *predict* what is likely to occur given certain existing circumstances or trends. Both descriptive and predictive questions will inform both policy and theory.

Interpretive Research Questions

Now let us turn to questions that would derive from an interest in interpretive research. Earlier an example was given in relation to Just War theory. Just War theorists do not seek to explain the outbreak of war, but rather focus on the moral justifications for the resort to the use force (O'Driscoll, 2008). Because interpretive researchers turn to language, and not empirical observation, to provide answers to their questions, we do not encounter datasets or testable hypotheses within the toolbox for interpretive research. Rather, to use the example of Just War theory, scholars examine the language used by policymakers to justify the resort to force. Do we see references to self-defense, or pre-emptive self-defense, or to religion? In the case of O'Driscoll's study of Just War in the context of the 2003 US–UK-led war in Iraq, O'Driscoll (2008) used speeches by US President George W. Bush and UK Prime Minister Tony Blair to understand the moral justifications for the Iraq war offered by these two leaders.

As noted in Chapter 1, interpretive research focuses on ideas, identities, norms, and culture in international politics. Thus, while empirical researchers focus their efforts on explaining events, which taken together are referred to as the Arab Spring, interpretive research aims to illuminate social representations, discourses and meanings that underlie these events. Here we can also use the strategy of attempting to unearth a puzzle in order to bridge the gap between a research topic and research question. Let us turn to the example of Islamism, or Political Islam.

In the West, discourses of Political Islam have been dominated by fears and images of terrorism and groups like Al Qaeda or more recently the Islamic State, but the Arab Spring saw Islamists enter government in countries like Tunisia and Egypt, although they were removed from office in the case of the latter in July 2013. Nevertheless, one can ask has the electoral success of Islamist parties transformed Western perceptions of Political Islam? Here, unlike in our empirical questions, the focus of interest is in the meaning of a particular term, Political Islam, for a particular audience, the West.

The focus is therefore not on explanation but on generating knowledge aimed at deepening our understanding of a particular vocabulary that frequently appears in discussions of the Arab Spring (see Table 2.2). What discourses surround the term Political Islam? Is the term used to evoke the image of an anti-modernistic other? Is it juxtaposed against political movements labeled as secular? Or is the meaning of the term more evidently more nuanced? In order to respond to these questions the interpretive researcher can turn to a number of linguistic artifacts such as speeches, **official documents**, television programs, Internet news sites, or blogs to find answers to the aforementioned questions.

Table 2.2   Researching the Arab Spring: Interpretive Research

Research Topics	Research Questions
I want to understand how revolution impacted local identities.	Has Libyan Berber identity been transformed by new opportunities for cultural expression in the aftermath of the Libyan Revolution?
I want to understand the symbolism of self-immolation in the context of the Tunisian Revolution.	How were images of the self-immolation of Mohammed Bouazizi represented during the Tunisian Revolution?
I want to understand Western perceptions of the Arab Spring and how these have been shaped by recent transformations.	Have Western discourses on political Islam been transformed by the Arab Spring revolutions?

The interpretive researcher will not necessarily want to explain events through the identification of specific causes of revolution or explain the role of an external actor such as the US or European Union during the revolutions, but rather the focus will be on understanding basic *ontological assumptions* that underlie empirical research. Arguably, the empirical researcher takes these ontological assumptions, or categories for granted.

Interpretive Research and Critical Theory

There are a number of ways to arrive at an interpretive research question. Sometimes, interpretive research will appear to come close to conjecturing a relationship between variables. Indeed, critical theorists routinely argue that discourse is used to maintain a particular power relationship. These critical theorists, while often not using the empirical research terminology or independent or dependent variables, approach discourse as a form of explanatory variable that makes a certain range of policy options possible. Take Bartolucci's (2010) study of Moroccan elite discourse on terrorism. Bartolucci argued that the Moroccan government used its discourse on terrorism to target specific political opponents.

Interpretive Research and Symbolic Politics

Another common strand of interpretive research focuses on the representations of symbols or events. To begin, you will want to think in terms of unpacking meaning from events, symbols, or even individuals that have assumed taken-for-granted quality in popular culture or society. In relation to the Arab Spring, your interest may be in individuals who have assumed a certain symbolic status in contemporary national mythology. Take for example Libya's Omar Mokhtar, a revolutionary anti-colonial leader from the early 20th century, who has now become a 21st-century symbol of national unity in post-revolutionary Libya. Or you can look to a more modern figure, such as Mohammed Bouazizi, whose self-immolation touched off the Tunisian Revolution in December 2010. In relation to the latter, Rozen (2014) explored the contestation of revolutionary death **narratives** in post-revolutionary Tunisian classrooms.

Summary: Empirical or Interpretive?

While interpretive research would focus on the social meaning of terms frequently used in international politics, such as Just War and Political Islam, or on the hidden power relations maintained by particular discourses, or on the discursive representations of events, symbols or individuals, empirical research is focused on, for the most part, on explanation. In relation to international conflict, if your interest is explaining why wars occur and how wars can be avoided then your interest is empirical. If your interest is understanding the social meaning that underlies the practice of warfare, and not explaining why wars occur, then your interest is interpretive. Likewise in relation to Political Islam, if your interest is in understanding why Islamist parties experienced electoral successes in the aftermath of the Arab Spring, then your interest is empirical. If, on the other hand, you want to understand what the term Political Islam means and how this has evolved, then your interest is interpretive.

Once you have chosen your research question, either empirical or interpretive, you can now begin thinking about research design.

From Research Question to Research Design

After choosing your research question, you will be confronted with questions about research design and methods. Looking back at the aforementioned research questions it is apparent that each question would imply distinct research designs. Some questions sought to examine developments in a single country, others in two or more. Many would imply case study research design whereas others would require **quantitative methods**. In addition, just as it was helpful to remember where your interests were located on the empirical–interpretive spectrum when thinking about your research question, it is also necessary to keep this in mind when thinking about research design.

You can think of research design as setting out the steps you need to take in order to complete your research essay. Table 2.3 lists seven steps that will guide you through the entire research process that are presented in the forthcoming chapters.

Table 2.3   The Research Process and Research Design

1. Choose a topic area that interests you (Chapter 2)

2. Formulate your research question (Chapter 2)

3. Contextualize your research in existing literature – how have others answered your research question or related questions? (Chapter 4)

4. Situate your research question along the empirical–interpretive spectrum and select appropriate methods (Quantitative, Case Study, Mixed?) (Chapters 1, 2, 5, 6, 7, and 8)

5. Are there ethical considerations you should consider before undertaking research? Conducting interviews? Surveys? Questionnaires? Traveling to the field? (Chapter 3)

6. Empirical data collection and analysis or interpretive data collection and analysis (Chapters 5, 6, 7, and 8)

7. Writing up (Chapter 10)

However, before turning to methods, or data collection and data analysis techniques, let us first explore empirical and interpretive research design in greater detail.

Empirical Research Design

Empirical researchers draw some form of proposition out of a relationship between two or more variables. In fact, for empirical researchers, this proposition defines **positive theory**. Van Evera's (1997: 7–8) definition of theory is a useful illustration:

> Theories are general statements that describe and explain the causes or effects of classes of phenomena. They are composed of causal laws or hypotheses, explanations, and antecedent conditions.

In short, theories describe or explain causes or effects. For International Relations students trained in political science, this is likely how you will approach the question of theory. Theories, from the perspective of an empirical researcher, lend themselves to empirical testing and are **falsifiable**. There are two broad strategies that you can employ to test your theory: **observation** and **experimentation**. The most frequently used strategy in IR is observation. When designing your empirical research as a study grounded in observation, you have two further choices: you can observe a large number of cases, or just a few. When looking at a large number, this is referred to as **large-n** research. When looking at just a few, this is known as case study research.

Experimentation is less common in IR, and assumes that you can test a proposed relationship by exposing one of two equivalent groups to a particular stimulus in order to affirm or falsify a predicted, or hypothesized, relationship. Most hard sciences rely heavily on experimentation; however, in IR, outside of computer assisted simulation modeling,[6] we are unable to easily experiment upon our objects of study (Van Evera, 1997: 28–9).

Thus when embarking on research design you will first revisit your research question. For example, you could start from the general question: 'What role does social media play in protest mobilization during revolutions?' From this you will infer a relationship: social media plays a significant role in protest mobilization during revolutions. Now you need to think about how you will subject this relationship to testing. For narrow questions, that attempt to explore an event in a particular country or geographic setting, adopting a case study will allow you to explore in rich detail how your variables relate to one another and uncover underlying causal processes (see Figure 2.1). In short, if your interest is in understanding the how and why of an event of phenomena, case study research is well suited to helping you respond to your research question (for more on case study research see Chapter 8).[7]

Research Design: Research Question to Case Study

Figure 2.1   Research Design: Research Question to Case Study

If, on the other hand, you are examining a wider category of events, such as what explains the outbreak of war, which has long been a central question within the field, you will need to engage with a large dataset that can help you observe **correlations** between variables over a large number of cases. In these types of studies your interest is not in a particular armed conflict per se, such as explaining the Vietnam War, but rather is in explaining the outbreak of war itself. Such big picture questions do not fit well against the backdrop of a single case study because of limitations on your ability to generalize beyond a single case. Instead, you will rely on some form of large dataset that attempts to catalogue all events that fall under the scope of your study. You will notice that many of these studies have temporal boundaries because of the inability to either interpret massively large datasets or the inability to collect reliable data beyond a certain date.

Table 2.4 lists some questions that have been explored in IR that lend themselves to quantitative research (for strategies for quantitative data collection and analysis see Chapter 6).

Table 2.4   Research Design and Quantitative Research: Explaining the Big Picture

Research Question	Example(s)
Relationship between war and structure of the international system?	Daniel S. Geller and J. David Singer, *Nations at War: A Scientific Study of International Conflict* (Cambridge University Press, 1998)
Relationship between regime type (democracies) and war?	Stuart A. Bremer, 'Democracy and Militarized Interstate Conflict, 1816–1965', *International Interactions,* 18 (1993): 231–49
Under what conditions do strategic rivals choose to support non-state armed groups that target their rivals?	Zeev Maoz and Belgin San-Akca, 'Rivalry and State Support for Non-State Armed Groups (NAGs), 1946–2001', *International Studies Quarterly,* 56 (2012): 720–34
Do alliance choices made by states spill over into other cooperative networks such as trade and institutions?	Zeev Maoz, *Networks of Nations: The Evolution, Structure and Impact of International Networks, 1816–2001* (Cambridge University Press, 2011)

In sum, empirical research design will help you explain a puzzle, either in relation to a single case such as the outbreak of revolution in Tunisia, or the decision of the US to go to war in Vietnam, or in relation to a wider phenomena, such as explaining the outbreak of war more widely or explaining why states cooperate. Now that we have established two broad strategies for research design in empirical research, which will be further elucidated in the forthcoming chapters, we can now turn to interpretive research design.

Interpretive Research Design

Interpretive research design does not start from a cause-and-effect puzzle, but rather engages with a very different type of puzzle that can be described as an **ontological puzzle**. Indeed, as noted in Chapter 1, the very purpose of interpretive research diverges from that of empirical research. Here Clifford Geertz' claim that social science should not be 'an experimental science in search of law, but an interpretive one in search of meaning' is instructive (Geertz, 1973: 5).

Interpretive research therefore often relies upon case studies that focus on the use of particular discourses in a given context, or representations of particular individuals or events. For example, if you want to explore the symbolism of particular public individuals, such as individuals indicted for war crimes by the International Criminal Tribunal for the former Yugoslavia (ICTY), you could select one or two indicted war criminals who are of significant public stature. Such a research design, however, would not be aimed at **process-tracing** or making some form of **causal inference**.

An interpretive research design's focus, using the example above, would not be on explaining why states cooperate, or do not cooperate with the Yugoslav Tribunal. Instead, we would turn to understanding how particular notions taken for granted are constituted and contested. A focus on narratives, or constructed memories of past events such as wars or political struggles, can be helpful in illustrating contested notions such as justice (see Pavlakovic, 2008). For example, Pavlakovic (2010) argued that the case of Croatia's indicted General Ante Gotovina highlighted how Croatia's relationship with the EU became bound up in a highly emotive debate on contested narratives of the past that did not coincide with rational models of decision-making.[8]

Another example of interpretive research could be a researcher's exploration of evolving, or contested, conceptions of international justice. If your interest is in the dispute between the International Criminal Court and the African Union over the Court's exercise of jurisdiction over the continent, your interest might not lie in explaining the relationship between the ICC and the AU, but instead you might want to unpack the language of justice. Does international justice mean different things in different social contexts? Likewise, is sovereignty a concept with malleable meanings that can be explored from a number of perspectives?

Given that your focus is on understanding social meaning, tools designed to explain relationships between variables, such as quantitative research methods, will offer little insight into the types of questions asked. Instead, qualitative research methods provide a rich array of tools that you can use, such as **discourse analysis** that will allow you to further investigate contested notions in IR.

In addition, interpretive researchers have a different conception of what constitutes a theory from empirical researchers. While empirical researchers view theories as general statements that explain cause and effect, interpretive researchers see theory as statements concerned with understanding the properties of those objects that we study. These differential views on what constitutes theory have also been described as a divide between explanatory or causal theory (empirical) and constitutive theory (interpretive) (Smith, 1995; Wendt, 1998).

These divergent views on theory lead researchers from empirical and interpretive perspectives to adopt distinct forms of research design, although at times overlaps in method are visible. For example, one can look to explanatory or causal studies that view discourse as a causal or explanatory variable.[9] Table 2.5 presents two examples of research questions and categorizes them in terms of empirical or interpretive and in terms of what kind of theoretical traditions with which they are likely to engage. Having now almost completed this chapter try to add your research question to Table 2.5.

Table 2.5 What is Your Question? Empirical and Interpretive Research Questions and Research Design in International Relations

Research Question	Empirical or Interpretive?	Causal (Explanatory) Theory or Constitutive Theory
Example: What are the causes of European integration after the Second World War?	Empirical	Causal (Explanatory)
Example: How do political actors make use of narratives of the Second World War in the 2014 war in Eastern Ukraine?	Interpretive	Constitutive Theory
Your research question:		

Research Proposals

Normally, for longer pieces of work, your supervisor will ask you to provide a research proposal in which you are expected to present your research topic, research question, and research design. When crafting your proposal, you will start by demonstrating why your research topic is of interest to the field of IR. Is your topic at the center of a major theoretical debate? Is your research question of pressing policy relevance? Would a policy response to your research question potentially impact a large segment of the world's population? In short, the first few lines of your research proposal should be devoted to providing some form of justification for your topic.

Your research proposal will also require you to demonstrate that your project is *feasible* within the timeframe your supervisor expects you to complete your research and writing. This means that your research question is explicitly stated and is consistent with the example research questions noted above for either empirical or interpretive research. If your question is overly broad or effectively unanswerable, you will be asked to go back to the stage of research question development. This also means you have taken into consideration what kind of data you will need to collect in order to answer your research question. Is there an existing dataset which you can make use of? Will you be collecting primarily textual documents that are readily available? Or, will you need to conduct significant fieldwork? For shorter research projects, asking a question that requires you to collect primary data through fieldwork will require you to be extra careful in terms of time management.

What is a Research Proposal?

A Research Proposal is normally a short document. Often for undergraduate work it can be only about 750 words (2 pages), but for more substantial projects, such as postgraduate theses, it can be considerably longer.

A Research Proposal is a document in which you clearly and concisely provide an overview of your thesis project to your supervisor. After reading your BA Thesis Outline, your supervisor should know why you have chosen your research topic, be familiar with what scholarly or policy debates your thesis engages, know what research question(s) you aim to answer, and understand how you will go about answering your research question(s).

Once you have clearly stated your research question, you will need to discuss your research design. Ensuring your research design is an appropriate fit for your research question is perhaps the most challenging task facing you when writing a Research Proposal. You will need to set for yourself a strategy for answering your research question. As noted in the preceding discussions of empirical and interpretive research design, the focus and therefore your strategy for answering your research question is contingent with the kind of question you have posed. You will want to consider, among other questions, things such as will you be using a case study design? If so, is it a single case study, or a comparative case study? What do you hope you will find in your case study? Will it affirm or disprove conjectured hypotheses? Will it help you explain an event through process-tracing?

Next your thesis proposal should make explicit how you will collect data and how you will analyze the data you have collected. Chapters 5, 6, and 7 will help you think about which methods' tools are most helpful in regards to data collection and analysis in relation to your own research question. Questions you will want to consider may include questions such as, will you be relying on large datasets and will you be using statistical tests to interpret your data? Or, will you be relying on textual documents, such as policy papers and speeches, to provide a discourse analysis of your topic? Make sure you are clear about what kinds of sources you will be using for your thesis.

Once you have justified your topic, stated your research question, set out your research design, and strategies for data collection and analysis, you should provide your supervisor with a list of references consulted during your Research Proposal preparation process. This will help give your supervisor a better understanding of where you are coming from, in terms of literature, and whether or not there might be gaps in your reading on the topic. Furthermore, as will be noted in Chapter 4, this will help you to get started in writing your **literature review**.

Chapter Summary

This chapter traced the process of generating a research question and establishing research design. You were introduced to strategies for developing both empirical and interpretive research questions and research design. As mentioned in Chapter 1, research is about making choices. In this chapter you were confronted with choices about your research question. Will you pose a question that is empirical or interpretive? Will your question be narrow or wide in scope? Whether or not you ask an empirical or interpretive question will open up distinct strategies for research design and also direct you toward a particular set of methods tools for data collection and data analysis. For example, if your research question is narrow and focused on explanation, such as explaining the US decision to go to war in Vietnam, it is empirical and lends itself to being answered through a single case study. If, on the other hand, your interest is in explaining US decisions to go to war in general, your work will remain empirical, but you will need to engage with a larger body of case studies to respond to your question.

However, if your research question is interpretive, or focused on ideas, concepts or meaning, you will eschew research designs suited towards hypothesis testing and instead your research will focus on particular cases that allow for in-depth qualitative analysis. Interpretive research requires you to engage deeply with the question of meaning, often in relation to ontological givens that we take for granted such as sovereignty and justice.

In sum, research questions and research design are closely intertwined and should be addressed in relation to each other. Once you have established your research question and settled upon a research design you can begin thinking about tools for data collection and data analysis; however, before going on to discuss these tools there are two important steps remaining. The first is thinking about research ethics and this will be addressed in the next chapter, and the second is your literature review, which will be discussed in Chapter 4.

Suggested Further Reading

Laura Roselle and Sharon Spray (2012) *Research and Writing in International Relations,* 2nd edition. New York: Pearson. See 'Chapter 1: Topic Selection and Topic Development', pp. 5–14. This chapter provides a concise overview of questions related to topic selection and topic development with specific reference to IR.

Charles Lipson (2005) *How to Write a BA Thesis: A Practical Guide from Your First Ideas to Your Finished Paper.* Chicago, IL: University of Chicago Press. See 'Chapter 4: Refining Your Topic, Writing a Proposal, and Beginning Research', pp. 66–86. This chapter is a good introduction to the beginning stages of your research project, and also contains tips on writing a research proposal.

W. Phillips Shively (2013) *The Craft of Political Science Research* (9th edition). New York: Pearson. See 'Chapter 1: Doing Research' pp. 1–13. This chapter provides an introduction to empirical research in IR.

Stephen Van Evera (1997) *Guide to Methods for Students of Political Science.* Ithaca, NY: Cornell University Press. See 'Chapter 1: Hypotheses, Laws and Theories: A User's Guide', pp. 7–48. This chapter provides an overview of the core elements of empirical research in IR.

Notes

1   Roselle and Spray offer a narrower definition of question-based research: 'question-based research papers seek to unravel the puzzles associated with not readily apparent cause-and-effect relationships.' While this definition nicely captures empirical research its focus on cause-and-effect is too narrow to also include interpretive research. Laura Roselle and Sharon Spray, *Research and Writing in International Relations.* New York: Pearson, 2012, p. 8.

2   Of course, when undertaking longer research projects, it makes sense to pursue the academic training necessary to acquire these skills. In fact, this is part of the core curriculum of most postgraduate programs. Furthermore, any project that requires a significant amount of fieldwork will require you to become adept in a wide range of data collection or analysis techniques. Indeed, time-intensive skills, such as acquiring a foreign language, are often both unavoidable and essential.

3   For strategies on decomposing a broad number of cases into a few cases for comparative or individual study see Chapter 8, which discusses case study research.

4   For an exploration of the role of the Tunisian Army before, during and after the Tunisian revolution of January 14, 2011 see Badra Gaaloul, 'Back to the Barracks: The Tunisian Army Post-Revolution', *Sada – Middle East Analysis*, Carnegie Endowment for International Peace, November 3, 2011. Available at: http://carnegieendowment.org/2011/11/03/back-to-barracks-tunisian-army-post-revolution/fduu. Of course, this decision too can be argued to have a more long-term or structural explanation, the relative weakness of the Tunisian Army *vis a vis* other institutions in comparison to other armed forces in the Arab world.

5   See for example Mieczyslaw Boduszynski, 'Comparing Western Democratic Leverage: From Tirana to Tripoli', *Croatian Political Science Review*, vol. 50, no. 5, 2013, pp. 189–203.

6   See Agent-Based Modeling in Chapter 7.

7   Note that case studies come in many different forms and carry out many different functions. These will be set out in Chapter 8.

8   Also see in the same issue as Pavlakovic (2010), Christopher K. Lamont, 'Compliance or Strategic Defiance: The Croatian Democratic Union and the International Criminal Tribunal for the former Yugoslavia', *Europe-Asia Studies*, vol. 62, no. 10, 2010, pp. 1683–705.

9   See Chapter 5 on Qualitative Methods for more on this overlap. At times this overlap has caused confusion in relation to how we define constructivist research, as there are constructivists who adopt empirical, or positivist, methods to argue that norms and ideas have explanatory power in International Relations.

3

RESEARCH ETHICS

Research ethics are an essential component to every step of the research process. While much of the discussion surrounding ethics in research arises in the context of questions asked about how we as researchers interact with people, or as they are often referred to in the context of research ethics, **human subjects**,[1] this chapter will emphasize that research ethics are a much broader area of concern. Failure to reflect upon ethics, or engagement in unethical behavior on the part of a researcher, can result in at best considerable embarrassment and an irreparably damaged professional reputation, or at worst significant harm to those who have participated in our research or to the researcher.

Often, when thinking about research ethics, the first question that comes to mind is where do we draw the boundary between ethical and unethical research practices? In the social sciences more broadly, and in International Relations in particular, we will find that while some ethical transgressions, such as the falsification or distortion of data, always fall outside the scope of acceptable research conventions, other practices, such as securing **interview** consent, may not be in all cases the most appropriate course of action.[2]

When first you pick up a text on research ethics or do a quick literature search on the topic, often you will flip through pages of examples drawn from the medical sciences, where medical doctors or psychiatrists carried out experiments under circumstances where even the most casual observer would raise serious ethical objections (Brandt, 1978; Herrera, 2001). While many of the more notorious of these cases of research malpractice are often trotted out as examples of gross misconduct, here the focus will be on ethical questions of most direct relevance to the student of IR. In order to explore the wide range of ethical dilemmas you are likely to encounter, this chapter will look at ethical dilemmas that arise when you embark upon your research, at the data collection and analysis stage of your project, and when you are writing up your research. Thus, first, we will reflect upon ethics as it might relate to research questions and research funding. Second, we will examine clear ethical transgressions, such as **plagiarism** and data falsification. Then, we will briefly touch on research ethics as they relate to human subjects. As you will note from the following sections in this chapter, many of the ethical dilemmas you are likely to encounter are interlinked and require you to critically evaluate, and constantly reassess, the ethics of your work.

Ethics, Funders, and Asking the Wrong Questions

At this point, you might still wonder how ethical questions or dilemmas relate to you, a student of International Relations. Here it is helpful to remind ourselves that as students of International Relations, our research interest in the social world around us will always require us to reflect on the ethics of how we pursue research and how we communicate our research to a broader audience. If we take a step back from our research project, we might ask ourselves a question drawn from a more critical perspective on IR, which advance value-laden critiques of IR with strong ethical, or normative undertones. For example, in 1981, Robert Cox laid down the charge in the journal *Millennium* that IR '[t]heory is always *for* someone and *for* some purpose' (p. 128). While Cox went on to juxtapose problem-solving approaches to IR, or those that sought to find practical problems encountered in international politics, with critical theory, which questioned the underlying power relations and institutions in international politics, our interest in the question is perhaps more forthright. Is our own research *for* someone or *for* some purpose? More recently, Ackerly and True (2008) argued that IR feminism's reflexivity creates a research ethic standard that allows researchers to resolve ethical dilemmas in their own research.

When thinking about this issue, we might question from whom we are willing to accept funding to conduct research and whether or not there is a conflict of interest between research funders and our potential research findings. Here, tobacco companies funding research on the potential health consequences of cigarette smoking serves as one example.[3] Another example might be large oil companies funding research questioning the link between carbon emissions and human-induced climate change. Of course, these are clear-cut examples of conflicts of interest between the research funder and the researcher. But, what about when this particular dilemma is more nuanced? For example, often scholars of IR rely on various government-funded research bodies for research funding. In the United Kingdom, you have the Research Councils, while in the United States, government funding, which is dispersed through numerous agencies or contractors, makes its way into the academe.

If we have a look at the rigorous debate that the US Army *Human Terrains System Project*'s funding of social science research in places like Iraq and Afghanistan[4] provoked within the American Anthropological Association, we can see the manifold risks that are present for researchers and their human subjects when conducting research in on-going conflict zones.[5] We will return to this question when discussing human subjects and research ethics later in this chapter.

The aforementioned ethical questions related to research funding lead us back to questioning the purpose of our research. Our response to such a question requires us to reflect upon questions such as, what is the purpose of knowledge creation? Do we privilege certain groups while failing to give voice to others? These are questions, which in turn, link back to some of the more fundamental philosophy of science questions touched upon in Chapter 1.

It should now be evident that even though you might not perceive yourself as likely to confront ethical dilemmas, ethical questions need to be addressed even at the very outset of your research. As a researcher of the social world around you, research questions and **research design** are often entangled with questions of ethics. In particular, as a student of IR who aims to contribute to our understanding of international affairs, you will be confronted with ethical dilemmas at every stage of the research process.

It is therefore important to keep in mind that even if you restrict yourself to desk research, this does not relieve you of reflecting on the ethics of your research activities. This is because, as outlined above, many ethical dilemmas go beyond questions of how to engage with people during the course of research. The next set of dilemmas go beyond funders and research purpose, but relate to questions of how we use and present data gained from documentary sources in research. Thus, we are moving on to the data collection and communication phase of the research process. This next section aims to provide guidance on these complex questions, and point you to professional research ethics guidelines that may be useful in resolving ethical dilemmas you may encounter as part of the research process.

Plagiarism and Academic Dishonesty

While ethical dilemmas that confront researchers during field research, such as the principle of do no harm and interaction with interview subjects, will be explored in more detail later in this chapter in our discussion of human subjects and research ethics, and also in Chapter 9, this section focuses on ethical dilemmas that students will most likely encounter in the context of desk research or writing up a research project.

The ethical violations that students are most familiar with are likely to be that of plagiarism and falsification of evidence. Let us take on the question of plagiarism first as this is an example of unethical behavior that you have often been warned not to commit. Nevertheless, despite warnings against plagiarism being ubiquitous, often students still have questions as to exactly where the line can be drawn between plagiarism and sloppiness. This question is particularly pressing given the consequences of plagiarism are often severe within academic institutions.

Research Ethics and Plagiarism

Plagiarism is the act of taking someone else's words or ideas and presenting them as your own. Often this is done by copying and pasting text from other sources and placing them directly in your own essay without attribution. Other times, this includes attempts to submit work, as your own, that has been written by others. As will be discussed below, plagiarism can also result from a simple failure to provide references. A related offense, self-plagiarism, includes the republishing or resubmitting of work that you have already written as a new piece of work. Examples of this include submitting the same research essay, or substantial parts of the same essay, for assessment for two different classes.

It is important to remember that plagiarism can be both intentional and unintentional. It can result from an intentional effort to deceive, or it can result from sloppy note taking and inadvertent mistakes during the writing-up process. In order to guard against the risk of accidental plagiarism it is important that you always record a bibliographic reference along with any notes you might take from a piece of research or any other source of information. It is helpful to include the full bibliographic information, so you do not have to search for this information again later. You may decide to record this information on paper, notecards, or through the use of widely available bibliographic software. This will significantly reduce your risk of committing unintentional plagiarism. After all, any research project entails reading large amounts of texts on a subject and, without careful note taking, it is very easy to reproduce someone else's words or ideas in your own text without providing a reference. Therefore, whenever you read a scholarly article, book, news article, or blog post relevant to your research, always take notes. With careful note taking, it is easy to cross-reference your notes for ideas that appear in your own work. You may even choose to catalogue readings into distinct perspectives on a given topic, in addition to by author. For example, you can create a bibliographic reference list of authors who have taken a particular theoretical approach to a question. In sum, coming up with your own system to organize your notes, whether on paper or digitally, is necessary to ensure that you give appropriate credit in your own work to the ideas and words of others.

Despite plagiarism often being unintentional, plagiarism is one of the most serious offenses that you can commit as a researcher. Indeed, in the words of one of the largest professional association of IR scholars, the *International Studies Association*, plagiarism constitutes, 'a serious breech of professional and academic ethics' (ISA, 2014). Furthermore, the *American Historical Association* points out that the consequences of plagiarism go far beyond harming the academic endeavor of expanding our knowledge of the world:

In addition to the harm that plagiarism does to the pursuit of truth, it can also be an offense against the literary rights of the original author and the property rights of the copyright owner. Detection can therefore result not only in sanctions (such as dismissal from a graduate program, denial of promotion, or termination of employment) but in legal action as well. As a practical matter, plagiarism between scholars rarely goes to court, in part because legal concepts, such as infringement of copyright, are narrower than ethical standards that guide professional conduct. The real penalty for plagiarism is the abhorrence of the community of scholars. (American Historical Association, 2011)

In sum, the consequences of plagiarism are manifold. However, resources such as the Internet have made both the act of plagiarism, and its detection, easier. As was noted in *The New York Times*:

Digital technology makes copying and pasting easy, of course. But that is the least of it. The Internet may also be redefining how students – who came of age with music file-sharing, Wikipedia and Web-linking – understand the concept of authorship and the singularity of any text or image. (Gabriel, 2010)

Indeed, with websites such as Wikipedia, which offer instant access to multi-authored summaries of key theories, concepts, events, individuals, the temptation to rely on such resources for independent research is great. However, as will be pointed out in Chapter 4, the reliability of information that you can access on the Internet is far from consistent, as barriers to scholarly publication, such as **peer-review**, are absent. One rule of thumb for digital research is that nothing, except maybe a direct quote taken from a reliable source, should be copied and pasted into your essay. It is also important to remember to provide the full URL address for any web-based sources, and also include the date you accessed this information. All standard referencing styles will require you to include this information in your bibliographic information.

Referencing and Quoting

As mentioned earlier, the best way to avoid inadvertent plagiarism is to take good notes and provide in-text references. When expressing another author's ideas or argument in your own words, referencing is essential. There are a number of standard referencing styles available to students of IR, and as a rule of thumb, you should consult your course guide, or your publishing outlet, for their preferred referencing guidelines. Two that are most commonly used are in-text, or what are commonly referred to as *Harvard style* references, or footnotes, which often follow the *Cambridge style*.

Harvard and Cambridge Referencing Conventions

Harvard (in-text) references

Example of a direct quote in-text: 'The states that emerged from the former Yugoslavia followed divergent paths of regime change in their first decade of post-communist transition, only to converge on the road to Europe in the second' (Boduszynski, 2010: xi).
  Then the full reference is provided in your bibliography:

  Boduszynski, M. (2010) *Regime Change in the Yugoslav Successor States: Divergent Paths to a New Europe*, Baltimore, MD: Johns Hopkins University Press.

Cambridge footnotes

  'The states that emerged from the former Yugoslavia followed divergent paths of regime change in their first decade of post-communist transition, only to converge on the road to Europe in the second.'[1]

  [1]Mieczyslaw P. Boduszynski, *Regime Change in the Yugoslav Successor States: Divergent Paths to a New Europe* (Baltimore, MD: Johns Hopkins University Press, 2010), p. xi.

What if I reference the same source twice in the same paper? Do I need to provide the full reference again in my footnotes?

Boduszynski argues that although the states of the former Yugoslavia all had different experiences of regime transition after the fall of communism, later these countries shared the goal of joining the European Union.[2]

Instead of providing the full reference again, you can use the author name and the relevant page numbers:

[2]Bodusznyski, *Regime Change*, p. xi.

Remember, if you are making use of a direct quote, referencing is not enough. For short quotes, of three lines or less of text, quotation marks must be provided to indicate to the reader that the words that are quoted are not yours. For longer quotes, you may indent the quoted lines to again make explicit to the reader that the text that is indented is not your own.

Falsification and Distortion of Evidence

Alongside plagiarism another ethical transgression of an equally egregious character is the distortion of data. In some extreme cases, researchers have even falsified or fabricated data. While it goes without saying that falsifying evidence is a serious breach of research ethics, in recent years there has been a number of cases involving academic dishonesty on the part of scholars in both the social and natural sciences. For example, stem cell researcher Hwang Woo Suk's scientific achievements were later proved to be fraudulent (Bhattacharjee, 2013). While this example is an extreme one, it is illustrative of the fact that as a scholarly community, we must be alert to the risk that some members of this community may attempt to abuse the trust of fellow scholars to falsify data or produce fraudulent evidence. In the Netherlands, fraudulent research has also recently made headlines, and forced the resignation of prominent scholars.

Although simply inventing data or falsifying results is clearly an outrage against the scholarly community, sometimes researchers inadvertently alter their research data through sloppy note taking during interviews or through coding errors. In relation to interview data, one tool to ensure your transcripts are accurate, and to provide for an additional level of transparency, is to secure the consent of your interview subjects to have the interview recorded. If you would like to record an interview, always secure permission to do so in advance. If this is not possible, written interview consent forms will provide evidence that you have actually conducted your interview. In the absence of a consent form, make sure you record as much information about your interview as possible. Things like the location, date, and time of the interview, in addition to recording with whom the interview has taken place, all serve to provide you with evidence that your interview actually took place, should you be asked to produce such proof.

Finally, in addition to misrepresentation of data occurring as a result of out-right fraudulent behavior or sloppy record keeping, sometimes students might find themselves tempted to distort another author's argument. Often this takes place early in the essay or article when constructing a theoretical framework or setting the stage for your own theoretical contribution. It can be tempting to over simplify an argument to construct a 'straw man' opposing perspective.[6] While this might help the readability of your essay, this kind of distortion does nothing to advance theoretical debates and only undermines your credibility.

Human Subjects: Institutional Review Boards and Ethics Committees

For researchers in North America, Australia or the United Kingdom, even before the research process begins, researchers are asked to receive ethical clearance from their institutions before carrying out research on human subjects. The need to receive ethical clearance is increasingly common in IR. With more and more students and scholars of IR going into the field, including regions torn by con-flict, questions of research ethics, and how they interact with different codes of ethics from personal ethics to institutional and professional ethics, require greater attention to research ethics within the discipline that goes beyond questions of plagiarism and academic dishonesty.[7]

There was a renewed focus on ethics in research that involved human subjects after the Second World War as the horrors of Nazi-era scientific experiments carried on people were widely publicized in the context of the Nuremberg Trials (Shuster, 1997). Indeed, the trial of medical doctors for experiments carried out on human subjects resulted in the drafting of the Nuremberg Code for medical research ethics, which was described as 'the most important document in the history of the ethics of medical research' (Shuster, 1997: 1436). Furthermore, within the medical sciences, the ethics of using data from Nazi experiments continues to cause controversy decades after Nuremberg (Moe, 1984; Bogod, 2004).

The Nuremberg Code's focus on medical ethics did not prevent many of the core principles found within it from making their way into social science codes of research ethics. As will you will note in the next section, many of the core principles of the Nuremberg Code, such as informed consent and do no harm, are included in most codes of research ethics in the social sciences. Of course, the focus of these codes are on experiments carried out upon human subjects. In Chapter 1, it was noted that the social sciences diverge from the natural science model of scientific methods in respect to the fact that what is of interest to the social scientist is the social world, made up of, and experienced by, people – a community which the researcher is part of. This is opposed to the natural world – from which the researcher is detached. For example, when we observe the interaction between two chemical elements, we can watch and record our observations as a detached observer. When two countries go to war with each other, images of this event broadcast on television or seen on websites evokes a number of emotions, which preclude us from merely watching as a detached observer. Some social scientists use this to argue that experimental methods, such as those conducted in the natural sciences or even medicine, have no place within the discipline. For example, we cannot instigate a war between two states to see whether the outcome would match what we have hypothesized.[8] Nevertheless, Moses and Knutsen point out that in the social sciences, 'experimentation today has become increasingly mainstream' (2012: 54). One example is Mintz et al.'s 2006 work on understanding the representativeness of experiments in their study in which they conducted experiments within two population groups, university students and military officers. Given the fact experiments involving human subjects are increasingly mainstream within International Relations, the Nuremberg Code's emphasis on informed consent on the part of research participants is of increasing relevance to the field of International Relations.

Thus, while it goes without saying that laboratory experiments that would have us instigate an armed conflict are not doable, either in an ethical or material sense, qualitative researchers often conduct small-scale experiments with targeted groups of people in order to improve our understanding of specific populations. For example, Roman David (2011) did just that in order to better understand the social impact of divergent approaches to dealing with the shared legacy of an authoritarian communist past in three countries in Central and Eastern Europe. In sum, experiments are increasingly common. In particular, experiments help us to understand reactions to certain fictional or non-fictional scenarios. Nonetheless, no matter how benign we may perceive our experiments to be, as researchers in IR, we have a responsibility to fully disclose to participants in our research and not to harm those with whom we interact.[9]

In addition to **experimentation**, data collection methods and fieldwork techniques evolve rapidly and challenge some of the core ethical principles such as informed consent that guide social science research. One recent case that involved Facebook saw researchers manipulate data to see if the emotional state of that social networking site's users could be effected by the content of what users were viewing (Kramer et al., 2014). This research design provoked widespread criticism as it entailed the manipulation of user content for the purpose of an experiment without the knowledge or consent of participants (BBC News, 2014). However, what about simply gathering data from publicly available data that people generate through social networking sites: can we use statements extracted from these sites for our research without the consent of those who maintain personal or professional profiles on these networks?

For researchers following Arab Spring activists, Facebook profiles may provide a potentially rich resource for those seeking to understand activist communities. But, just because a Facebook friend has posted something you might wish to use in your research does that mean this friend has consented to having this post, intended for a community of friends, reproduced in your publicly available research? Could this bring harm upon the said activist? These are questions you should ask yourself; however, keep in mind, to always ask those whose words you are using, if derived from a private or restricted medium, whether or not you can use their social media activities for research purposes.

In short, the digitalization of research has expanded the realm of interaction with human subjects. However, keep in mind that even if we aren't conducting interviews or relying upon data generated by users of social media sites, we are always interacting with people during the course of our research. As the American Anthropological Association notes in its *Statement on Ethics: Principles of Professional Responsibility*, 'As a social enterprise, research and practice always involve others – colleagues, students, research participants, employers, clients, funders (whether institutional, community-based or individual).'[10]

Given the complexity of research ethics, a number of professional and funding bodies have drafted codes of research conduct to provide researchers with guidance on some of the dilemmas and challenges they might face during the course of their research. In the following section, this chapter will turn to some of the ethical codes of conduct for researchers that students and scholars of IR might

turn to when seeking guidance on some of the more nuanced dilemmas related
to ethics in IR research.

Ethical Codes of Conduct

There is no shortage of ethical codes of conduct out there that you can turn to
for guidance on research ethics. For example, this chapter has referenced the
International Studies Association and American Historical Association's statements on plagiarism, and the American Anthropological Association's statement
on ethics.[11] Given the wealth of codes of ethics, it is helpful to distill key points
that these often lengthy documents address. One major research funder in the
United Kingdom, the Economic and Social Research Council (ESRC), does just
that through what it sets out as six key principles of ethical research that are
quoted below, with some explanatory notes added for clarity:

- Research should be designed, reviewed and undertaken to ensure integrity
  and quality. (*Transparency in sources, does not contain plagiarism.*)
- Research staff and subjects must be informed fully about the purpose, methods, and intended possible uses of research, what their participation in the
  research entails, and what risks, if any, are involved. *Some variation is
  allowed in very specific and exceptional research contexts for which detailed
  guidance is provided in the policy Guidelines.*[12] (*You must disclose to those
  who are participating in your research, the purpose of your research, what
  you are asking them to do, what you will use the information for, and any
  risks that might result from their participation.*)
- The confidentiality of information supplied by research subjects and the
  anonymity of respondents must be protected. (*If a participant asks not to be
  referenced by name in your research, you should make sure that you protect
  their anonymity and not 'out them' in any published work or submitted theses or dissertations.*)
- Research participants must participate in a voluntary way, free from any
  coercion. (*You cannot threaten or intimidate people into participating in
  your research.*)
- Harm to research participants must be avoided. (*You should make sure that
  participants are not harmed during the research process or as a result of your
  research.*)
- The independence of research must be clear, and any conflicts of interest or
  partiality must be explicit. (*Who is funding your research? What is your
  affiliation? These facts should be disclosed to research participants.*)

At first glance, these six principles may appear to be an inviolable set of rules,
analogous to the *Ten Commandments* in Judeo-Christian tradition. However, in

point two, you will notice that some exceptions are permitted in 'very specific and exceptional research contexts'. Yet, how do we define what these specific and exceptional contexts are? What is important to remember for now is that many professional associations draw their own ethical redlines on such questions in slightly different places. Therefore, it is of utmost importance that you familiarize yourself with the ethics codes or norms of your university or place of employment. However, as mentioned earlier, there are certain practices that are always prohibited and generally these include anything that could result in physical or mental harm to the researcher or the research participant.

Perspectives on Ethics

Often institutions, in addition to having distinct ethical codes of conduct, also have distinct cultures in relation to how they implement their respective ethical guidelines. Bryman set out a useful typology of ethics cultures – the universalist, situationalist, violationalist, and anything goes approaches. This typology provides a useful roadmap to chart these divergent approaches to implementing codes of ethics (Bryman, 2008: 116–17). They are also useful to help you critically reflect on your own ethical choices that you will be confronted with in your own research. After reading descriptions of the following perspectives try to establish where you would place yourself.

The first perspective on ethics that Bryman describes is *universalist*. Universalist is the perspective that you will most likely encounter as a starting researcher in IR enrolled in an undergraduate program. In the absence of years of experience working with research participants, and being new to the research process, faculty members you encounter will probably insist that you adhere strictly to ethical codes imposed by your institution. Indeed, when you first venture out into the field to conduct interviews, your first few interviews will constitute an important learning process where you familiarize yourself with the realities of interviewing. Because you are still learning how to interact with human subjects, it is unlikely that you will need to assume risks during the process.[13] In addition, in most cases, starting researchers lack the appropriate training to work directly with vulnerable or traumatized groups of people, such as victims of war crimes or minors. Universalist approaches to research ethics are often applied to protect the institution for which a researcher is conducting research from potential legal liability for harm or to protect the researcher from doing harm to themselves. Universalists thus hold firm that ethics codes cannot under any circumstances be violated.

If, however, you are a more advanced researcher, and you are being asked to present your proposed research to an institutional ethics review board, you might find yourself encountering a more *situationalist* approach to research ethics. In such cases, you will be asked to justify your proposed research in writing and submit what may look like an application to conduct your research project to a panel of researchers who will evaluate the ethical implications of your proposed course of action. Situationalist approaches emphasize a case-by-case evaluation of potential transgressions and may even consider whether or not significant new knowledge will be created through your proposed research. And, perhaps, would that new knowledge outweigh harm? In these cases you may find some allowance for practices such as deception that are normally prohibited by ethical codes of conduct.[14]

The next two approaches to research ethics are worth mentioning, but are approaches that you are not likely to encounter when seeking institutional ethical clearance to conduct research. Nevertheless, they are worth mentioning because they help in our critical reflection on research ethics. A *violationist* approach assumes all research includes some minor violations. In short, such an approach assumes social science researchers are unable to avoid engaging in behavior that can be defined as unethical. For those who adopt a violationist approach, ethical codes of conduct are of little value because compliance with such codes is viewed as either impossible or impractical. In a similar vein there is the *anything goes* approach put forward by Douglas in 1976. Those who subscribe to such an approach argue that the kinds of deception that we can engage in as social scientists can hardly be considered serious when taken against the backdrop of the types of activities routinely engaged in by the state police or security services (Bryman, 2008: 116). Such an approach to ethics imagines social science researchers as agents who can potentially challenge the state's monopoly on power and knowledge; however, at the same time very little concern for potential research participants is evident.

In short, what you have been presented with thus far are both diverse codes of ethics and diverse ways that these codes can be implemented that range from strict adherence to the rules, to the allowance of deviance from them, to the outright rejection of the rules. When thinking about the ethics of your own project it is imperative to comply with the ethical guidelines of your own institution and to also engage in your own ethical self-reflection. Below are some questions you might want to consider asking yourself.

Self-Reflection on Ethics

1 Are there any underlying ethical questions posed by my research question?
2 *(In the event you are conducting funded research)* Is there a potential conflict of interest between my research funders and my research?
3 Is there a potential conflict of interest between me, the researcher, and my research question?
4 Does my research design require me to interact with human subjects?

There are probably very few research questions that would allow you to answer 'no' to question one in the self-reflection. Indeed, as noted earlier in this chapter, more critical approaches to IR often critique research agendas in the discipline as being carried out 'for someone and for some purpose' to quote Cox once again. However, one does not have to be a critical theorist to reflect upon the underlying ethics of their research. Question two is a question you should ask yourself in the event your research is funded by a third party, while question three is something that one should always keep in mind. Sometimes a researcher might find themselves emotionally too close to a particular topic to write or research it dispassionately. Finally, if you answer 'yes' to question four, you should try to think about what kind of people you will be interacting with, such as members of a particular profession, employees of a particular organization, members of a certain political party. More guidance on how to provide informed consent and how to protect participants from harm will be provided in Chapter 9. If you are likely to find yourself working with children or vulnerable adults, you should consult closely with your institutional ethics committee to ensure that you have the appropriate permissions and training to carry out your research.

Chapter Summary

Research ethics inform every step of the research process, and should be approached holistically on the part of the researcher. Each step of our essay or dissertation writing process poses potential ethical dilemmas that we should be aware of. Most importantly, we should be especially careful when interacting with human subjects. We also need to remember that transgressions such as plagiarism and data falsification need not always be intentional and can easily result from sloppy note taking or a failure to accurately transcribe interviews.

Second, research ethics are particularly important when considering conducting research that requires the participation of human subjects. Any time we depend on people to participate in our research we should take into consideration whether or not we have secured their informed consent and also whether or not there is a prospect for harm that can either effect us or our research participants.

Now that we have reflected upon the ethics of what we will do during the research process, we can begin our essay or dissertation writing in earnest. The next chapter will help us to begin this process by introducing the **literature review**.

Suggested Further Reading

Brooke Ackerly and Jacqui True (2008) 'Reflexivity in Practice: Power and Ethics in Feminist Research on International Relations', *International Studies Review*, 10 (4): 693–707. This article provides a concise introduction to questions of power and ethics in research.

Alan Bryman (2008) *Social Research Methods, 3rd edition*. Oxford: Oxford University Press. See 'Chapter 5, Ethics and Politics in Social Research', pp. 112–36.

Charles Lipson (2005) *How to Write A BA Thesis: A Practical Guide from Your First Ideas to Your Finished Paper*. Chicago, IL: University of Chicago Press. See 'Chapter 3: Taking Effective Notes and Avoiding Plagiarism', pp. 37–65.

Greg Scott and Roberta Garner (2013) *Doing Qualitative Research: Design, Methods, and Techniques*. Boston, MA: Pearson. See 'Chapter 4: The Ethics of Qualitative Research', pp. 51–66.

Notes

1 See for example Alan Bryman, *Social Research Methods*, 3rd edition. Oxford: Oxford University Press, 2008, Chapter 5, pp. 112–36; Karen Jacobsen and Loren B. Landau, 'The Dual Imperative in Refugee Research: Some Ethical and Methodological Considerations in Social Science Research on Forced Migration', *Disasters*, vol. 27, no. 3, 2003, pp. 185–206.

2 In fact, there are numerous examples where cultural contexts would make securing written consent inappropriate. To reference one, Bestor et al. note that in Japan an attempt to secure written consent from interview subjects could call into question the researcher's understanding of the local cultural context and even their trustworthiness. Theodore C. Bestor, Patricia G. Steinhoff and Victoria Lyon Bestor, 'Introduction: Doing Fieldwork in Japan', in *Doing Fieldwork in Japan*, edited by Theodore C. Bestor, Patricia G. Steinhoff and Victoria Lyon Bestor. Honolulu: University of Hawaii Press, 2003, p. 14. Also see Chapter 9 for more on informed consent in interviews.

3 Gardiner Harris, 'Cigarette Company Paid for Lung Cancer Study', *The New York Times*, March 26, 2008, available at: www.nytimes.com/2008/03/26/health/research/26lung.html?pagewanted=all&_r=0

4 See the *US Army Human Terrain System* website: http://humanterrainsystem.army.mil

5 *American Anthropological Association's Executive Board Statement on the Human Terrain System Project*, October 31, 2007 [released on November 7, 2007]. Available at: www.aaanet.org/pdf/EB_Resolution_110807.pdf

6 This will be discussed again in Chapter 4.

7 For more specific guidance on the question of ethics in field research also see Chapter 9.

8 Moses and Knutsen make a similar observation when stating, 'While we can assume that many generals long for a better understanding of the nature of war, ... it would be neither cheap nor appropriate to explore these topics through research projects that apply the experimental method'. Jonathon W. Moses and Torbjorn L. Knutsen, *Ways of Knowing: Competing Methodologies in Social and Political Research*, 2nd edition. Basingstoke: Palgrave Macmillan, 2012, p. 53.

9   An oft referenced case where the line was arguably crossed in relation to these are the Milgram experiments, where Milgram attempted to study destructive obedience through a laboratory experiment which had some participants harm others. See Stanley Milgram, 'Behavioral Study of Obedience', *The Journal of Abnormal and Social Psychology*, vol. 67, no. 4, 1963, pp. 371–8.

10 The statement goes on to note that the American Anthropological Association also considers 'non-human primates and other animals, among others' to be considered 'research participants'. *Statement on Ethics: Principles of Professional Responsibility*. Arlington, VA: American Anthropological Association, 2012.

11 The American Anthropological Association provides the most guidance in terms of ethics, research funding and fieldwork. This is because unlike the International Studies Association, the American Anthropological Association has faced vigorous internal debates on anthropological research funded by armed forces. I would like to thank Dr. Timothy Wittig for this observation.

12 Students often ask about the ethics of covert observation or the use of deceit to secure a participant's participation in research. On this matter the ESRC states in its policy guidelines, 'The primary objective is to conduct research openly and without deception. Deception (i.e. research without consent) should only be used as a last resort when no other approach is possible. This principle also requires that research staff need to be made fully aware of the proposed research and its potential risks to them.' *Research Ethics Framework (REF)*, London: Economic and Social Research Council.

13 Some fieldwork choices that entail greater risk will be described in Chapter 9.

14 For an example of this see Chapter 9.

4

WRITING A LITERATURE REVIEW

Now that you have settled upon your research question, thought about your **research design**, and reflected upon the ethics of your research, you are almost ready to embark upon the data collection and analysis phase of your research project. Scholarly research is much more than a barrage of monologues on the part of scholars, although sometimes you might feel this might be the case. Scholarly literature is always part of a wider dialogue among scholars. In order to have a dialogue we must acknowledge what others have said before us when we make our own interventions. Absent this acknowledgment, those who we wish to engage in dialogue with might say, 'but you haven't heard what I have said' or 'you weren't listening to me'. As scholars, we need to ensure that we communicate our engagement with those who have already 'spoken' on our topics of interest. Therefore, at this point, one crucial element of the research and writing process remains missing – the **literature review**.

Literature reviews constitute a sometimes underappreciated, yet essential component to any research essay, thesis, dissertation, or scholarly publication. Indeed, a thorough literature review is the foundation upon which your data analysis, either empirical or interpretive,[1] and your conclusions will be built. To be sure, many of the early stages of the research process, such as research topic selection, research question development, and questions of research design, will require you to turn to existing literature on your topic; however, the literature review requires you to approach existing literature systemically so that it can be organized in a manner that communicates how your research project relates to extant scholarship. The literature review also demonstrates, the relevance, importance, or novelty of your research question. Without a literature review none of these things will be visible to your readers.

You are most likely already familiar with literature reviews as they are part of almost every **peer-reviewed** journal article that you will have read up to this point.

In fact, if your instructor has assigned review essays in your course reading lists, you will have read what amounts to a lengthy literature review. Alternatively, if you have read a scholarly monograph, you will notice that one of the first chapters always dwells on how others have approached a particular topic in the past. You might also have noticed that literature reviews assume many different forms and can be organized in a number of different ways. Indeed, given the breadth and extent of literature on pretty much any topic of interest in International Relations, and the diverse forms that literature reviews sometimes assume, the task of condensing potentially massive bodies of literature into a concise literature review may at first appear to be daunting.

Despite the literature review's crucial importance, you may encounter difficulties in knowing just what to include, or leave out, when writing your literature review. You might also be troubled by the question of where to begin the process of background reading for your literature review. Here, it is helpful to point to two essential purposes of a literature review that can help guide you in negotiating the aforementioned questions. The first purpose is simply to *situate your research question in the context of existing scholarly literature on your topic*. Abstractly, you might want to think about research traditions that have attempted to grapple with your research topic, and how have they done so in the past. For example, if your interest is on understanding Just War theory, you will likely need to identify, and demonstrate your familiarity with, canons in the literature such as Michael Walzer's *Just and Unjust Wars* (1977). The second purpose is to justify *why the question you posed remains at the center of a scholarly debate or why it is of policy interest*. For the second purpose, you should go back to the initial puzzle that triggered your research question. How did you learn of this puzzle? Why did it remain puzzling even after a cursory survey of scholarly literature?

Background reading for your literature is of crucial importance to your ability to conduct research on your topic. Absent adequate background readings, you might not be able to collect data using the most effective means or sources. Has the data that interests you already been gathered by someone else? Has your particular case study already been explored in the context of your research question? What research methods have researchers working on your topic used? You should be able to answer all of the above questions before going on to the data collection and analysis phase of your research project.

Furthermore, you should always be aware that the task of a literature review is both *organizational* and *analytical*. Thus when exploring how authors have addressed your research question, start making lists that will help you organize literature into particular categories or theoretical traditions. The more thorough your background readings are, the more you can be sure that you will be able to set out for the reader the major perspectives that exist in terms of responses to your question.

Dual Purposes of a Literature Review

1. Situate your research question in the context of existing scholarly literature on your topic.
2. Justify the importance of knowing the answer to your research question, and its implications for existing scholarly debates.

Responding to these questions in a well-organized and analytically coherent literature review early in your work is necessary to prevent the reader from dismissing your piece as uninformed at the outset. Keep in mind, the literature review, while often placed early on in your essay, is distinct from the *Introduction* of your essay, which will be dealt with in Chapter 10 on Writing Up.[2] A well-written literature review will help your reader place your academic writing in the wider context of literature on your topic, will demonstrate your familiarity with existing scholarship, and it will help you to avoid simply reinventing the wheel in your essay through exploring a question that has already been addressed at length in a manner that does not add a new perspective to the particular question. Now that we have addressed the nuts and bolts of the literature review, we can move on to the task at hand: conducting a literature review.

Literature Review: What is it? And What is it not?

A literature review is an analytical overview of existing scholarly research on a certain topic of scholarly interest that establishes, organizes, and identifies gaps in existing concepts and theoretical frameworks for the reader. It provides your reader with a concise snapshot or *state of the art* of existing scholarly engagement with your research topic, and establishes major theoretical debates of relevance to your research question and the methods others have used to respond to your research question. It is a component part of every piece of scholarly writing. Depending on the length of your research project, it may constitute a few paragraphs after the Introduction, but before you go into justifying your methods, or it could be its own stand-alone chapter in a large thesis or dissertation project.

The best way to understand the elements of a good literature review is to attempt to look at literature reviews written by scholars in your field. Table 4.1 will ask you to find a literature review in a peer-reviewed journal article and determine whether or not the core elements of a literature review are present.

Table 4.1 What is a Literature Review?

Article reference information: author, title, journal, volume & issue, year published, page numbers	How long is the literature review? Paragraphs, page number(s)?	Does the literature review provide an analytical and theoretical overview of how the topic has been addressed in existing scholarship?	Does the literature review provide any sense of what methods were used in existing scholarship?

Often, when tasked with writing a short essay your literature review will need to be particularly concise, so you should not dwell on describing in detail the arguments of others, but distill their contributions into one or two key sentences that highlight their perspectives to the extent they are relevant to your own research question. When undertaking a more lengthy piece of writing, your literature review should provide a more comprehensive overview of how scholars have addressed your wider topic area, in addition to highlighting how their works interact with your own. However, when in doubt about expectations, in terms of length, for your literature review, always consult with your supervisor or course instructor.

One resource that you should make use of are introductory textbooks on your topic area for a survey of relevant literature, but as a word of warning, you should not rely on these textbooks in themselves for your literature review, but you should use them as a point of reference for key literature that you will locate and read. You can also use books written on your topic area as a resource, because often, if scholarly, they will preface their own main arguments with a literature review. For example, if you are writing an essay on International Political Economy, you could organize competing approaches into liberal, realist or Marxist approaches.[3] You will be familiar with the main authors from each theoretical perspective, and you can sum up their arguments in a few short concise sentences. Or, if writing on international justice or international human rights, one could contrast realist-based explanations that see international human rights commitments as only being taken to the extent that they reflect underlying national interests, or constructivist norm-based approaches that reflect changing underlying norms of appropriate behavior.[4] One characteristic you should glean from other scholars' treatment of their literature reviews is that a literature review is not a literature summary. You are expected to organize the existing literature and not simply provide short article summaries of various works that you have read.

In fact, the importance of your literature review to your essay, thesis, or dissertation cannot be overstated. In addition to a literature mapping exercise that introduces you to scholarly literature on your topic, and familiarizes yourself with major debates or points of contestation, the literature review provides a conceptual framework that will allow your reader to understand the research choices you have made. Indeed, an effective literature review should set the stage for your discussion of methodology through establishing how your particular question has, or has not, been addressed in existing scholarship. Sometimes you will find that applying a different research method or research design to a question that has been addressed at length in the scholarship can yield new insights.

Furthermore, a poorly constructed literature review will give your reader the impression that you lack familiarity with existing scholarship. Poorly constructed literature reviews usually are the result of the author falling into one of two common traps. The first common error that students make is that they present a list of literature on their topic with no analysis. The purpose of a literature review is not to provide readers with a list of everything you have read on the topic. You should analytically engage with existing scholarship through organizing the literature into analytical categories. The section on how to organize your literature review presented later within this chapter will provide you with further guidance on how to place literature into analytical categories.

The second common mistake is to provide a detailed summary of a few articles or books that have been written on your topic. In this case the literature review will come to resemble a review of a particular set of articles or books, but provide little analytical support for the arguments that are developed later in the work. The best way to avoid falling into this mistake is to ask yourself whether or not your literature review has established clear analytical categories that places your research question, and if applicable, your hypotheses, in the context of existing literature. And, if so, does your literature review provide an analytical framework through which points of contestation within your field have been effectively presented to the reader? If your response is negative, then you might have written a concise literature summary rather than a literature review.

A Literature Review is NOT

1. A *list* of everything written on your topic
2. A *summary* of articles and books written on your topic

Before moving on to discuss how to go about researching and writing your literature review, two additional points of clarification are necessary. First, given a literature review's scholarly focus, you should target your background reading toward scholarly research outlets such as peer-reviewed journals, scholarly edited volumes, research monographs, and other peer-reviewed academic publications.[5] Before you start writing your literature review, it is essential to first come up with a reading list on background literature for your topic. The techniques noted above, looking back to textbooks or scholarly monographs for guidance, should provide assistance. When you begin your background readings, keep in mind that you already have some familiarity with the literature, particularly if you have been asked to write a research proposal for your project.

what to read

A research proposal is often a required part of the research process that serves as a bridge between you becoming interested in a potential research topic and the research process itself. A research proposal is usually no more than 1–2 pages. While requirements for what you should include in a research proposal differ across academic programs, all research proposals should include your main research question, why it matters, how – in terms of methods – you will go about answering your research question, and some form of indicative reading list. For more on research proposal writing turn back to Chapter 2.

really ??

The Literature Review: Getting Started

When beginning your literature review process, keep in mind that the research process is not always a linear step-by-step process. As noted above, you will have started reading on your topic long before you have consciously started with the literature review writing process. In fact, in good research proposals, you might even foreshadow elements of your literature review at the proposal stage. Nevertheless, the next two sections will go over two important skills that you will need to hone to write an effective literature review: conducting effective literature searches and taking good notes.

Searching the Literature

The first step in searching the literature is to first identify key works on your topic. As mentioned earlier, often you can find these works on your course syllabi or you can find references to them in course textbooks. Sometimes when beginning a literature review, the useful aforementioned starting point of first turning to prominent scholars who have addressed your topic or the seminal works in your field, might not be an option because you have chosen to write on a relatively narrow topic, or a relatively new phenomena such as cyber warfare, which lacks a long history of scholarly debate due to the relative newness of the phenomena under study.

Keyword Searches: Google Scholar and E-Journal Databases

Being able to conduct effective keyword searches is an essential skill for any researcher. Using the example of cyber warfare try to conduct your own keyword search using *Google Scholar*. *Google Scholar* is a valuable electronic resource that catalogues a wide range of scholarly articles of varying quality from a broad range of sources. Often access to these articles will be restricted, but if using a computer on a University network, of if subscribed to major electronic journal and book databases through your Library, you should be able to access works you find on *Google Scholar*. Nevertheless, a word of caution is in order. Unlike electronic journal archives such as *JSTOR*, or *EBSCOhost*, you cannot be sure what you are accessing through *Google Scholar* is indeed scholarly. Second, e-journal databases that your University library subscribes to often contain more options to narrow down your search, and therefore produce results that are often more relevant to your research topic. On the other hand, you might find yourself looking through a large number of search results on *Google Scholar* that have little relevance to your topic.

Try to practice your own keyword search for scholarly literature. You can start by using the keywords provided on cyber security: cyber security, cyber wars, cyber warfare, cyber terrorism, cyber attacks, and cyber defense.

Now think about your own topic. What other keywords can you think of that might help guide a keyword search of the literature?

When, as in the case of cyber security, the topic is both entirely new to you, and you are not familiar with those scholars who have written on your topic, there are also numerous online electronic journal databases that you can search by *topic* or *keyword*. Make sure that you don't give up, or formulate your final reading lists on the basis of a single keyword search. Different authors might have used different terminology to describe the same phenomena. So, for example, when searching for literature on cyber security, you might search for, in addition to cyber security, cyber wars, cyber warfare, cyber terrorism, cyber attacks, or cyber defense.

In the past, one technique that was often used by students searching for literature was to go to the journal stacks in a library and take out the most current and back issues of journals in your field and flip through the tables of contents of the journals to see what has been published in the leading journals in your field on your topic. While resources such as *Google Scholar* might provide shortcuts to finding articles, you should still survey the tables of contents of scholarly journals in your field of interest. For example, for many essay topics addressed by students of IR, *International Organization, International Studies*

Quarterly, Foreign Policy Analysis, World Politics, and *International Security* are a few examples of journals in the field that might contain articles relevant to your research.

Don't forget that your supervisor or course lecturer is also a resource that you should not hesitate to approach for assistance if you find yourself lost in the literature review process. To be sure, it may be that the best place to start your search, and to seek consultation, is your research adviser or course lecturer. Indeed, your adviser or lecturer will often prepare you early on for your literature review. In fact, you might find yourself asked to include an indicative bibliography in your research proposal so that your lecture or supervisor can provide suggestions for further readings or see if there are any significant omissions in your reading list that they can point out.

Finally, in the event you are writing on a topic dealt with in a lecture or seminar class, your class reading lists will be a good starting point for your literature review. From this point, by using the technique of mining the references from these readings, you will be able to quickly identify other relevant readings. You also should have a good sense of the overarching scholarly debates on your topic.

Taking Good Notes

Now that you know where to go to find literature, you will be faced with the task of reading a wide range of literature and condensing often lengthy and complex arguments into a few key points that will form a sort of organizational compass for your literature review. Given the breath and of background reading for your literature review, it is important to ensure that you take careful notes. Taking good notes for your literature review will also help you develop good note taking skills, which are essential for the research process as a whole.

As mentioned in Chapter 3, good notes serve multiple important functions. First, good notes guard against unintentional plagiarism. In addition, good notes ensure that you accurately represent arguments you come across in your readings. It is essential that once you begin writing your literature review you accurately relay key arguments raised by other authors. It is also important that you do not oversimplify these arguments into a *straw man* that you tear down in the course of your essay, thesis or dissertation. The deliberate misrepresentation of an opposing view on a topic not only harms your own credibility before the reader, but also devalues your own contribution, as it will do nothing to advance scholarly debates in your field of interest. Of course, creating a straw man representation of existing literature is not always a deliberate act of misrepresentation, but can also be the result of sloppy work, in which you make reference to a piece of scholarship, which itself contains a straw man representation of an opposing view. The best way to avoid this is to always read an author's argument before making reference to it in your literature. Never rely on summaries of an argument provided by others.

Things to Avoid: Straw Man Argumentation

A straw man in scholarship is a reference to the misrepresentation of another scholar's argument in order to make it easier to undermine or disprove. Given that in the literature review you are confronted with the task of summarizing complex arguments in relation to your research topic, it is important that you do not oversimplify another scholar's work to the extent that you leave out important characteristics or key observations.

Now that we have established taking good notes is important, how do we know we are taking good notes? In fact, you might be asking yourself at this point what are good notes? Good notes come in many different forms that can range from notes taken on notecards to notes written in notebooks, but they all include a few common key characteristics. The first is the full bibliographic reference of the work cited. This includes full citations and relevant pages numbers.[6] Then, for the purpose of your literature review, record the author's key arguments, perspective and how they went about responding to the question. This will give you a baseline on the work itself that will help you in organizing the literature. Then look for how the author(s) positions their work in relation to other scholars. Is there someone, some perspective that the author(s) take issue with? This question will help you identify the next important component of good notes, record keeping on how the work relates to your own piece of writing.[7] And, it will also help you to begin thinking analytically about the literature you are reading.

Writing a Literature Review

Once you have completed your readings and taking your notes, you will be able to begin writing your literature review in earnest. A thorough and well-organized literature review establishes a strong foundation for the rest of your research paper. Once you have familiarized yourself with the relevant literature, you will need to begin to organize scholarly works into contrasting perspectives on your research topic. In some cases, after reading the literature, you might also find that the question you posed initially might be too broad. It could be that the concept or phenomenon in IR that you wish to explore might need further refining. For example, you might have started your project with a desire to explain the causes of conflict. However, once you began your background readings, you discovered that conflict has been addressed in the literature on two distinct levels: inter-state conflict and intra-state conflict. Explanations for intra-state conflict point to a number of different **independent variables** than explanations for inter-state conflict. These include, for example, state failure, internal ethnic divisions, resource allocation. Or perhaps you wanted to write on cyber security. Once you started your readings you might have discovered there are distinct bodies of literature that deal with inter-state cyber warfare, cyber terrorism by non-state actors, and cyber-crime. Each of these have triggered their own distinct set of policy responses, and you might find that focusing your essay on a particular subset of issue areas within the broader issue of cyber security will help you to more effectively write a cogently argued piece of academic writing.

Organizing your Literature

You can organize your literature review in a number of ways. However, there is a basic structure common to most literature reviews. This includes an introduction, or for shorter literature reviews an introductory sentence or two. The body of the literature review, that reflects the organizational structure you have decided upon, and a conclusion. The conclusion of your literature review differs from other conclusions you may have written in the past in that it both provides a summary of the major points of contestation in the literature, or theoretical debates, that you have presented, but also once again highlights to the reader the importance of your research question, and how a response to your question will impact existing debates, or in some cases policies.

If writing a longer literature review, you will need to provide an introductory paragraph in which you clearly set out the focal area of literature for your review, and how this relates to your topic. For shorter literature reviews, which are part of research essays or journal articles, you will provide this information in a sentence introducing the review. For example, if writing an essay that aims to explain why states voluntarily signed the Rome Statute, which established the International Criminal Court, you should introduce your topic in a manner that makes clear to the reader that the target of your readings address existing scholarship on this question:

> Scholars have long sought to understand why states submit to the jurisdiction of the International Criminal Court.

Now using your own research question try to come up with a topic sentence for your literature review.

Once you have introduced your literature review, you will move on to the body of the review. All literature reviews reflect some form of organizational structure that is derived from characteristics scholarship either has in common or on significant points of divergence. In relation to the example noted above that aims to explain why states entered into the Rome Statute creating the International Criminal Court, you could transition into the organizational structure component of the literature review by making reference to a major point of disagreement within scholarship. For example you could state:

> Scholars have long sought to understand why states submit to the jurisdiction of the International Criminal Court. Rationalists argue that states join the International Criminal Court because it reduces transaction costs incurred when establishing ad hoc tribunals, whereas, constructivists argue that the norm of international justice, rather than material interests, has led states to join the Court.

In most cases, like the example above, you will find that your research question addresses a topic or issue that allows you to nicely organize literature into competing theoretical perspectives on a your topic. However, you might, depending on your research question, find another organizational criteria for your literature review such as contestations over methods, methodologies, interpretation of data, or conclusions.

For example, using the example of a research question closely related to explanations of why states join international criminal courts: *what explains the causes of cooperation or non-cooperation with international criminal tribunals*, we find that IR theory offers three potential explanations for why states cooperate. These could range from more realist approaches that would argue that states cooperate because they are coerced to do so by more powerful states, to liberal approaches, which argue states cooperate out of self-interest rather than coercion, to constructivist approaches, which emphasize the role of norms of appropriate behavior dictating compliance. All three of the above explanatory pathways make reference to their own distinct bodies of literature to which you can make reference.[8]

Another common second strategy for organizing a literature review is to attempt to discern how others might have attempted to answer your question in the past. Are there substantial disagreements in terms of method? For example, if your interest is in democratic peace theory, you might find that depending on the methods used, scholars arrive at different conclusions. Has one group of scholars relied primarily on **large-*n* datasets**? Has another used more qualitative case study methods?

Once you have mapped the body of your literature review, you will provide a conclusion that will constitute the core analytical take home message for your reader. Highlight here your own evaluation of the existing literature. There are two opposing tendencies that students sometimes fall into when evaluating existing literature. The first is being over generous towards existing scholars and offering only platitudes. The second is being over dismissive and suggesting that you are the first who has anything worthwhile on your topic. In relation to these two tendencies, with regard to the first, there will always be room for criticism, no work is perfect, and with regard to the second, it helps to be humble and recognize the achievements of those who have gone before you.

In sum, your literature review should conclude by making responses to the following questions explicit to the reader: What key points of contestation have you identified? What have we learned about your topic thus far? What points have been clarified by existing scholarship, and what points remain obscure? And, most importantly, what gaps remain in the literature?

important points of conclusion

Chapter Summary

The literature review is an essential component of any piece of academic writing. The literature review is, in a way, analogous to an organizational map for the reader that provides an overview of key concepts, theoretical debates and major works on the topic at hand. It also demonstrates why scholars should take note of your work and clarifies what body of literature you see your contribution to be in dialogue with. The purpose of your literature review thus is to provide scholarly background so as to help situate your work, but it is also analytical because you are expected to evaluate existing scholarship and make judgments as to contributions made by scholars.

The literature review research and writing process will in the end help improve your ability to critically evaluate scholarly literature. Through your critical reflection on how scholars have addressed your topic in the past, and through your evaluation, or weighing, of arguments advanced by these scholars, you will approach the literature with a much more critical eye. You will no longer read and just harvest information from texts, but you will also critically evaluate those texts, which you are reading.

Finally, the literature review process helps you guard against rehashing stale debates or collecting data that has already been collected. On the other hand, it also helps you identify important gaps in the literature, and if your research question is well thought out, you may find that the research project that you have embarked upon will serve to fill an important gap in the scholarly literature.

framework for your data

Suggested Further Reading

Laura Roselle and Sharon Spray (2012) *Research and Writing in International Relations,* 2nd edition. New York: Pearson. 'Chapter 2: Getting Started on Your Literature Review', pp. 15–31. This chapter provides some useful tips for searching the literature.

Alan Bryman (2008) *Social Research Methods,* 3rd edition. Oxford: Oxford University Press. See 'Chapter 4: Getting Started: Reviewing the Literature', pp. 80–111, for a thorough overview of many different kinds of literature reviews.

Bruce L. Berg and Howard Lune (2012) *Qualitative Methods for the Social Sciences,* 8th edition. New York: Pearson, pp. 26–36. Berg and Lune provide a short section on literature reviews within 'Chapter 2: Designing Qualitative Research'.

Notes

1 In fact, some interpretive research papers might have the feel of an elongated literature review in the sense that they might engage with how a particular piece of work has been interpreted by other authors.

2 Chapter 10 will provide a detailed description of component parts of research essays.

3 See Robert Gilpin, *Global Political Economy: Understanding the International Economic Order*. Princeton, NJ: Princeton University Press, 2001, for a mapping of major approaches to IPE.

4 See for example Christopher K. Lamont, *International Criminal Justice and the Politics of Compliance*. Farnham, UK: Ashgate, 2010, Chapter 1.

5 Similarly, Roselle and Spray note that a literature review '... should focus on scholarly resources – resources considered to be highly reliable by academic scholars and research professionals in the field of international relations.' Laura Roselle and Sharon Spray, *Research and Writing in International Relations*, 2nd edition. New York: Pearson, 2012, p. 17.

6 For two common citation styles, Harvard and Cambridge, see Chapter 3.

7 Berg and Lune make a similar observation when they pointed out that notes should be taken both to create a record of the content of the work itself, its main arguments, and a record of its use, or as Berg and Lune state, 'how does this relate to me?' See Bruce L. Berg and Howard Lune, *Qualitative Research Methods for the Social Sciences*, 8th edition. New York: Pearson, 2012.

8 For an example, see Chapter 1 of Lamont, *International Criminal Justice*.

5

QUALITATIVE METHODS IN INTERNATIONAL RELATIONS

The next three chapters will address three strategies, or sets of tools, for data collection and data analysis. Chapter 5 will examine **Qualitative Methods**. **Quantitative Methods** will be addressed in Chapter 6, and Mixed Methods in Chapter 7. These three approaches to data collection, and analysis, include specific research tools and techniques that are frequently used by students, researchers, and scholars of IR alike. However, one brief word of caution is necessary before moving on to these next three chapters. We should not conflate qualitative, quantitative, or mixed methods research with a particular theoretical tradition, or sub-field within IR. For example, **constructivism**, as a theoretical approach to IR, often relies upon qualitative techniques to advance constructivist claims about norms, but there are also constructivist authors who rely on quantitative methods to make similar observations.[1] On the other hand, IR realist scholars have also made use of a wide range of both qualitative and quantitative methods in advancing theoretical claims on power politics in international affairs.[2]

With this potential for theoretical and methodological cross-fertilization across traditions in mind, we can now turn to qualitative research methods in International Relations. Qualitative methods have been deployed within a broad body of scholarship that spans from empiricist explanatory studies of norm evolution that came to occupy a central position within IR scholarship in the 1990s (Klotz, 1995; Risse et al., 1999) to other more interpretive studies that reflect on social meaning and how the social world is constituted or produced (Campbell, 1998). This chapter will explore qualitative methods used in both traditions. In fact, as pointed out by Klotz, when the divide between interpretive and empirical research is approached from the perspective of practical questions of methods, or how to collect and analyze data, we find a significant degree of overlap between the two epistemological positions.[3]

This chapter will first define qualitative methods in IR. It will then explore the advantages and limitations of their use within the context of a diverse body of empiricist and interpretive qualitative research traditions. It will also contrast the utility of qualitative methods against that of quantitative methods, which are explored in Chapter 6, and demonstrate how qualitative methods allow researchers to answer questions that seek to explain complex social processes and understand meaning. Then, following on from this, you will be provided with a practical guide to major qualitative data collection and analysis techniques used within the field of IR.

Qualitative Methods in International Relations: What are they? And Why use them?

Qualitative methods refer broadly to data collection and analysis strategies that rely upon the collection of, and analysis of, non-numeric data.[4] Qualitative methods are used in order to better understand how we make sense of the world around us, and as such require us to focus on meanings and processes that make up international politics.[5] Often this is done through in-depth studies of particular events, phenomena, regions, countries, organizations, or individuals. While qualitative methods in International Relations is sometimes conflated with case study research design,[6] which will be addressed separately in Chapter 8, qualitative methods is meant here to describe the diverse set of tools and resources that we can draw upon to collect and analyze data that comes in the form of the spoken or written language and is not formalized into numbers.

Qualitative methods often rely on inductive reasoning. This is because qualitative researchers commonly generate theoretical propositions out of our empirical observations (Bryman, 2008: 366). For example, an in-depth case study on political party system development in Poland can generate new theoretical propositions about the development of political party systems in post-communist Europe. As mentioned in the introduction to this chapter, it is important to keep in mind that qualitative methods are *not* wedded to a particular epistemological position in IR. Thus, although Bryman presents qualitative methods as a form of interpretive research, and contrasts qualitative methods against 'a natural scientific model in quantitative research' (2008: 366), qualitative methods actually encompass a wide range of methods, which have been used by scholars from a wide range of research traditions.

Qualitative Methods

Qualitative methods are data collection and analysis techniques or strategies that rely upon the collection of, and analysis of, non-numeric data.

In fact, qualitative researchers include empiricists, such as King, Keohane, and Verba, who argue the logic of scientific inference, or what has been referred to in Chapter 1 as the empiricist tradition, unites qualitative and quantitative approaches to research (King et al., 1994). Qualitative researchers also count within their numbers interpretive researchers who reject the logic of scientific inference and instead seek to understand the meaning of social action. The data collection and analysis methods described in this chapter will include collection and analysis methods that will encompass both the empirical and interpretive traditions in quantitative methods.

Collecting Qualitative Data

Principle strategies for collecting qualitative data that have been used by scholars of IR include interviews, focus groups, Internet-based research, and archival or document-based research.[7] It should also be noted that qualitative data can also include non-textual forms of work such as monuments, maps, art or other social artifacts. Indeed, more recently, scholars of IR have turned to visual methods to help illuminate how we perceive and understand the world around us (Shim, 2014). When gathering qualitative data, it is useful to triangulate your data collection techniques in order to cross-reference your findings. This can be useful to guard against misinforming your readers on the basis of an interview in which the participant knowingly provides misleading answers.

For example, when I conducted field research in Croatia, from 1999 until 2008, a period of time which included the country's turbulent transition years, I interviewed members of political parties on their electoral strategies. However, relying on interview data alone would have given me a distorted picture of the party system as party officials were aware that they were talking to an outside researcher and wanted to present their parties in the best possible light. In this case, triangulation proved an effective strategy in assessing the validity of my interview data. Often, when the contents of the interviews were compared with media reports or other official party documents, inconsistencies emerged that would not have been visible in the absence of triangulation of data collection.

In addition to a diverse range of data collection tools available to the researcher, there are also a number of qualitative tools available for data analysis. Some of the most frequently used are content and discourse analysis. However, before moving on to data analysis, we first must turn to how we collect qualitative data. The next few sections will explore three common collection strategies used in IR: archival or document-based research, interviews, and Internet-based research.

Archival and Document-based Research

Archival or document-based research is perhaps the most common strategy used by students for research in IR. Very few research agendas would not include some aspect of archival or documentary research. Any attempt to study international conflict, international organizations, environmental politics, or human rights requires us at some level to engage with documents. Whether these documents are treaties, official reports, policy statements, legislation, or media reports, we almost always reference documents in our research. These documents come in two different forms. For the most part, our research requires us to access primary source documents. Primary source documents are the original documents, authored by individuals who had direct access to the information that they are describing, or directly experienced a particular event. For example, if we use the analogy of a criminal trial, a primary source would be the equivalent to a witness statement from someone who directly observed the event in question. Secondary source documents are those documents, which make reference to, and analyze, primary source documents. So, for example, if you cite directly US President Barack Obama's 2014 State of the Union address, you would be engaging with a primary source document, whereas, if you have instead referenced an article about the speech, you would be relying upon a secondary source. Or going back to the analogy of a criminal trial, often prosecutors commission expert reports that analyze contested evidence or to assist in the interpretation of evidence. These expert reports, which make use of primary sources, in the context of a criminal trial would in themselves be secondary sources.

Official Documents and Archival Research

Often we rely on a particular kind of primary source document, official documents. Official documents are documents, which are published, or are publicly released, by a state, organization, or business.[8] Official documents come in many different forms. They can include lengthy research reports, policy statements, interview or speech transcripts, records of memoranda or official emails, budgets, staffing, or personnel files. Official documents can give us a detailed insight into a particular organization; however, in most cases, you will not have unlimited access to an organization's documents. While most organizations archive their records, access to these archives is often restricted.[9] In fact, in the field of IR, it is rare to have full access to an organization's official records, although this is more common for the historian investigating organizations that no longer exist, or researching an event that happened long ago.

For the student of IR this lack of access can pose a challenge. Our interest in foreign policy and salient questions in international politics means that we will be seeking to collect documents from states or organizations that have an interest, or need, to conceal much of their internal day-to-day activities and decision-making processes in the context of a world populated by competitive external actors who might use that information to accrue some form of advantage.

A student wanting to explore the US' *Global War on Terror*, would for example, not be able to access many documents that would contain important factual details, actors, and decision-making processes. At the same time, there is a wide range of documents that are publicly available, from primary official documents to a wide range of in-depth secondary sources. Yet, these documents are dispersed across a number of organizations, media outlets, non-fiction books, biographies, and autobiographies. Therefore, primary document-based research requires us to invest time in discovering where to look for documents that may be relevant to our research.

In the absence of access to a central authoritative archive on our topic of interest, which you could methodically and systematically go through to conduct an exhaustive search for documentation on your particular topic, we should guard against focusing too narrowly on a few documents that could give us a distorted picture of the topic under study. One way to do this is to be transparent about the documents you have used and those that you have not used. Clearly define the scope of documents you set out to collect and those that you have examined.

Media and Secondary Source Collection

Media reports can constitute a valuable research resource. In fact, we often rely upon media sources to alert us to a particular topic of interest, or provide us with basic background information on our research topic. When using media sources, it is important to distinguish between international media sources, such as reporting by major global networks, such as CNN or BBC, and newspapers, such as *The New York Times* or the *Guardian*, and local news sources that have an exclusively local circulation or audience. When relying upon local news sources from an unfamiliar field site, you should consult with local academics or colleagues about whether the sources you are consulting are focused more on niche audiences or are nationally read. You should also familiarize yourself with whether or not your local media sources cater to a particular ideological or political grouping.[10]

For example, if you were researching the effect of international criminal trials on domestic Croatian politics, and you referenced a news story from *Hrvatski list*, you should be aware that this paper is a small circulation publication that appeals to a nationalist audience, and certainly would not be counted among Croatia's major national newspapers. As such, news stories critical of international criminal trials found in this particular source would offer a certain perspective on your research question, but should not be extrapolated to suggest a wider national sentiment.

Limitations of Document-based Research

Document-based research, while a commonly used method of qualitative data collection, has a number of limitations of which the researcher should be aware. First, as mentioned earlier, it is very rarely the case that a researcher would have access to the full and complete archives of a given organization or state. Even when complete access is possible, documents only give you a glimpse into those items that were recorded into an organization's institutional memory. There are many aspects of social interaction that remain invisible to the researcher. For example, even after a thorough document review, whether media or archival, you might be left with questions about how a certain outcome came about or how a decision-making process worked. Here, interviews can provide a valuable tool for expanding your knowledge on a given topic.

Media Sources and Generating Hypotheses

Sometimes a review of media coverage on your topic can help signal to you potential explanatory hypotheses. For example, why did states adopt measures aimed at punishing former members of a ruling regime in the aftermath of political transitions? A media search can help you come up with potential explanations, but these sources in themselves will not allow you to test these hypotheses, which would rely on you gathering more in-depth data on elite motivations for decision-making.

Brian Grodsky's *Costs of Justice* (2010) is an example of a study that relied upon this method of establishing a general history of key events and generating hypotheses that would later be proven or disproven against data derived from elite interviews.

Second, you should always question the veracity of what is written in documents, whether official, media, or other private sources. In some cases, consultations with local academics can give you a perspective on how a media source is perceived within a particular country. You might find that the national paper from which you collected data is known for promoting a particular perspective on a given issue, and therefore you might want to also expand your search to other national newspapers in order to check the veracity of your collected reports. In other cases, you may find that official reports published by a particular governmental agency are historically known to contain information that has proven unreliable. In this case, you would want to begin to reach out to explore whether or not other sources might have produced more reliable reports. In sum, the more you know about your document-based sources, the better you will be able to make clear to your readers what kinds of sources you have relied upon for data collection, and how that may, or may not, impact the veracity of your findings.

Interviews

Interview data can provide a rich resource for qualitative analysis and provide new insights into just about any aspect of International Relations. Researchers conduct interviews to gain factual data about a particular phenomena, event or object, to elicit the opinions or perspectives of an interview participant, or to learn more about their behavior.[11] The section will present you with the basic interview formats and their uses. For more on questions of how to gain access to interview participants once you are in the field see Chapter 9.

Interview Formats: Structured, Semi-Structured and Unstructured

Interviews normally are sub-divided into three different categories. These are structured, semi-structured, and unstructured. The first category of interview, the **structured interview**, produces quantitative data but will nonetheless be discussed here as it is related to the other two sub-categories of interviews, and sometimes is combined with other qualitative data collection methods, such as focus groups.[12] The second category of interview is the **semi-structured interview**, and is what we commonly think about as an interview when discussing or teaching interview techniques. This is because it operates with a degree of flexibility, but allows the researcher to maintain a basic structure across interview participants. The final category is less common in IR, and is essentially an unscripted free flowing conversation with the interview participant.

Structured Interviews

Structured interviews are used to produce quantitative research data, and include a menu of responses from which the participant selects a response that

is recorded by the interviewer. In many respects a structured interview is analogous to a questionnaire delivered orally rather than in written form. Structured
interviews are usually carried out by teams of interviewers, who are provided
with pre-written interview questions and categories of responses. These interviewers then conduct their interviews, but are extremely careful to stay on
script. Any deviation from the interview script on the part of those conducting
the interview can distort the findings because the data collected will no longer
be structured. Due to the highly scripted nature of structured interviews, there
is generally no need to create an audio record of these encounters. Responses
can be recorded swiftly by the researcher either in numeric form or through
simply checking a particular response among set of pre-selected responses.

Semi-Structured Interviews

Semi-structured interviews are the most common interview format used by
researchers in IR. Given the research topics that are of interest to many scholars
of IR are related to explaining international political events, the foreign policies
of states, the behavior of international organizations, multi-national corporations, or non-governmental and civil society organizations, most semi-structured
interviews target elites, and are therefore also referred to as elite interviews.[13]

Elite Interviews

Although elite interviewing is common, students often ask who qualifies as an elite? Because
the definition of an elite within a particular society is highly subjective, responses to this question
often vary. For example, do we use a more restrictive definition, where we focus on those who
have special standing such as members of Congress or Parliament? Here we use a broader
definition that sees elites as anyone who occupies a position of influence or importance within a
particular organization that is under study.

For example, if your research project requires you to conduct interviews with representatives of human rights organizations in Banda Aceh, those activists who you will interview are
considered elites.

Semi-structured interviews are commonly used because there is a degree of
structure that allows for cross-referencing across interview participants, but
there is also scope for more in-depth probing on issues of interest to the
researcher. We also avoid the pitfall that is apparent in structured interviews
whereby we limit the scope of responses through our pre-selected menu of
questions and answers, and thus potentially miss some important insights that
the interview participant may offer.

Unstructured Interviews

The third common interview format is the **unstructured interview**. The unstructured interview is often compared to an ordinary conversation that you might have with friends or colleagues. Unstructured interviews are aimed at eliciting the unfiltered perspectives of interview participants. They usually begin with simple, but broad, open-ended questions. For example, if trying to understand the experiences of ordinary citizens during the armed conflict in Croatia, one might ask, 'Can you tell me about your most memorable experience from 1991?'[14] You could then phrase this question differently among research participants. Keep in mind that your role in an unstructured interview is more like that of a participant in the sense that you are participating in a conversation with your interviewee, not necessarily leading it. Finally, due to the nuanced, complex and unexpected responses generated during an unstructured interview, these types of interviews do not lend themselves to note-taking on the part of the researcher, so they should be recorded either in audio or video form (Scott and Garner, 2013).

Conducting Interviews: General Tips and Guidelines

Gaining **access** to the interview subject is generally the most difficult part of the interview process. Particularly, when attempting to get in touch with elites, who themselves have busy schedules and might not see the utility in talking to a researcher, we must expend a significant amount of time. While Chapter 9 will provide some advice on gaining access to interview participants, here some more general tips and considerations will be provided. However, before moving on, as noted in both Chapters 3 and 9, you must, if possible, attempt to secure the informed consent of interview participants.[15]

Once someone has agreed to an interview, there are a few things you should always do in preparation for the interview. The first is to make sure you have thoroughly researched the interview participant. If the participant is an elite, they will have likely made statements or granted interviews to the media, authored relevant reports, or delivered testimony before an official body. It is essential that you are familiar with what your interview participant has said on your topic in the past so as not to give the impression that you are uniformed and more importantly so you can avoid wasting time collecting data on views that are already in the public domain, and instead make use of the interview to triangulate data with the other sources. Second, make sure that you are explicit as to the amount of time you will require, and make sure in advance that your interview questions, whether structured, semi-structured, or unstructured, can be completed in the allocated time.

At the interview itself, you should maintain a professional appearance. You should be transparent about the purpose of your research, how the interview data will be used, and whether or not you can protect the confidentiality of the research participant. This information is normally provided in an interview consent form, which is discussed further in Chapter 9. Also, be careful not to transmit a sense of disapproval or approval through verbal or body language. Such reactions will result in your interview participant being able to manipulate the interview to provide you only what you want to hear. Finally, make sure that you meticulously document your interview, either through detailed notes or through audio or video recording. If you are going to record the interview you must ask for permission from the interview participant to be recorded.

In addition, it must be noted that new communications technologies are changing how many researchers conduct interviews. Expensive fieldwork visits to foreign countries can sometimes be supplemented with interviews via remote communications software such as Skype. This provides an easy and inexpensive way to conduct a follow-up interview with your interview participants. In some cases, some researchers have used Skype for the initial interview as well. In fact, in relation to a recent study of youth activists in the former Yugoslavia, Kurze noted:

> ... that the subjects were immersed in a web of social media online and all of them were at ease with using Internet technology as an indispensable communication tool not only for work, but also with friends and family. Skype, Facebook and Twitter, thus turned into essential analytical tools for this project. (Kurze, 2013: 6)

Kurze's observation that research participants were at ease 'in a web of social media' highlights rapid changes to how we communicate that are also impacting how researchers access potential research participants. As social media and remote communications continue to expand, we can expect more interviews to be conducted in this virtual sphere. However, just because we are not conducting a face-to-face interview does not mean that any of the ethical standards or formats described above are more relaxed. In fact, we should keep in mind that when using data gathered from social media, or when interviewing research participants via Internet communications software, we have secured their informed consent.

Once the interview is completed, always, if possible, send an email or note to the participant thanking them for their time. While this may seem trivial, it will help open the door to potential follow-up interviews that you will conduct. Often we end up building long-term professional relationships with our research informants, and the best way to do this is to remain in touch with them after the interview. You may also want to send them any quotes that you will use in published research in order to get their confirmation that they are not being misquoted on a particular issue. Once your work is published, it is also polite to alert your interview participants to this.

In sum, interviews are an important window into the social world around us, and can provide us unique insight into how individuals perceive specific phenomena, events, objects or other individuals. Just as we acquire a lot of knowledge about the world around us through conversations, our interview informants can potentially provide us with a tremendous amount of insight that we cannot gather from official documents or media reports alone. On the other hand, we must always be aware of the need to triangulate interview data. Interviews reflect the perceptions of our interview subjects, and thus we should be careful when using data gleaned from interviews alone as statements of fact.

Focus Groups

Focus groups can be characterized as a form of group interviewing. Focus groups generally involve bringing together groups of six to ten research participants in order to discuss a particular topic or question (Bryman, 2008: 479). Focus groups always include more than just one group as the researcher aims to gather information on how people perceive certain information in the context of social interaction. Bryman notes while the number of focus groups used in particular studies range from eight to fifty-two, generally more studies that make use of focus groups use between ten to fifteen groups (p. 477). Furthermore, focus groups can take on many different forms. All focus groups are led by a moderator, who has a list of issues, or questions, to complete; however, the moderator can choose to be more interventionist, or use a more interpretive approach. Or the moderator can attempt to be less interventionist and more objective for research that aims to be more empiricist (Harrison and Callan, 2013).

Focus groups are rarely used by an individual student researcher because of the time-intensive nature of gathering groups of participants together and facilitating discussions across multiple groups that are recorded by the facilitator. Often focus group research is done in the context of larger funded projects that allow the researcher to hirer research assistants to carry out the task of administering focus groups.

Internet-based Research

In addition to making use of the Internet to access traditional scholarly materials, such as scholarly journal articles and books, often we find ourselves making use of the Internet to gather information about our research topic. Just like any other source from which we gather information, with the Internet we should always check the veracity of the source we are using. Webpages, and their content, can be created by anyone. There are no gatekeepers or peer-review processes which those who publish on the Internet must go through. As noted earlier, the proliferation of social media has also resulted in large amounts of data being generated by individuals. On the one hand, this has created a rich resource in the form of blog entries and social network sites where we can read the perspectives of activists and bloggers on the ground in the country we might be studying. On the other hand, it is difficult to assess whether or not what we are reading is factual or simply represents the views of an individual.

In addition, we have also seen the emergence of virtual encyclopedias from which we can gain a wealth of information on places, individuals, events, theories, and concepts. Wikipedia is a source that students often make use of in order to gain instant access to concise background information on a topic of interest; however, given that Wikipedia relies upon users to generate content, content can be added that is intentionally false or misleading. It is therefore dubious at best to rely upon a Wikipedia entry for an academic essay or thesis. Nevertheless, Wikipedia can still function as a useful starting point from which you can access other sources. In fact, it is recommended that you use references provided within a particular Wikipedia entry to confirm the veracity of the information you have gathered. One use of the Internet is to simply gather factual information on the topic or information about particular events we wish to address in our work. For this we can make use of freely available news sites such as BBC News. Almost all major English language newspapers, such as *The New York Times*, also have websites; however, many of these require you to subscribe in order to access articles or archives.

We can also access governmental websites to gain instant access to official statements or press interview transcripts. With a growing move towards *e-government*, more and more countries are providing access to an ever-greater number of official documents, legislations, reports and policy memoranda online. For example, if you are interested in US foreign policy, a visit to the US State Department website (www.state.gov) can provide you with access to official statements on US policy toward a specific country, region or even issue area. Meanwhile the United Kingdom's Foreign and Commonwealth Office also maintains a webpage that provides access to similar information on UK foreign policy (www.gov.uk/government/organisations/foreign-commonwealth-office). Moreover, all major international organizations maintain detailed websites and online archives that can provide you with direct access to a wide range of documentary material. The United Nations maintains a website that can provide you with a wealth of information on the UN and its subsidiary bodies (www.un.org). If you are interested in international justice, the International Criminal Tribunal for the former Yugoslavia provides you with instant access to a vast archive of legal documents and trial testimony in its online archive, which you can access upon completion of a short registration process (http://icr.icty.org). These are just a few examples – a quick Internet search can direct you to the websites, and often the digital records, of almost any government or international organization.

Qualitative Data Analysis

Once you have gathered your qualitative data you will be confronted with the task of analyzing it. When looking over your interview transcripts, official documents, or web-based resources, you will no doubt realize that qualitative data lends itself to many different interpretations and means of analysis. Unlike quantitative data analysis techniques, which rely on statistical tests or mathematical modeling,[16] with explicit rules and proofs, qualitative data analysis is much more subjective. Qualitative research is often presented in the form of case studies, and there are qualitative analysis techniques used within case studies such as **process-tracing**, which will be discussed in Chapter 8. However, as the focus of this chapter is on qualitative data collection and analysis; here we will be introduced to two common qualitative analysis techniques used by researchers in IR.

One commonly used qualitative analytical technique used by scholars of IR is discourse analysis. Sometimes, it is juxtaposed against **content analysis**, which is commonly described as purely empiricist, or quantitative (Lowe, 2004). This is not the case. As Berg and Lune (2012: 354) point out, 'content analysis is not inherently either quantitative or qualitative.' Content and discourse analysis can assume many different forms. We can look at language to understand and explain the world around us (empiricist), or we can use language to understand how language constitutes or produces the social world (interpretive).[17] The next two sections will address content analysis and discourse analysis respectively and provide some practical guidance on these two methods of data analysis.

Content Analysis

Some scholars view content analysis as the breaking down of textual data into numeric form, or some sort of counting exercise, and therefore, have a tendency to view content analysis as a quantitative method. This is because content analysis allows researchers to examine large amounts of data through categorization and **coding**. However, as noted above, content analysis is neither purely quantitative nor qualitative. Content analysis is best defined as an activity in which 'researchers examine artifacts of social communication' (Berg and Lune, 2012: 353). As such, it can include textual data, photographs, television programs, films, and other forms of art (p. 353).

In order to conduct a content analysis, you should first explicitly specify the scope of your analysis; for example, you may be interested in a content analysis of news coverage of the tragedy of the downing of Malaysia Airlines Flight 17 in Eastern Ukraine on July 17, 2014. Perhaps you want to contrast Western coverage with coverage from Russian news outlets. Given that the number of media outlets that covered the incident is far too large for you to systemically cover, you may choose a couple of representative news outlets. Once you have established some criteria for selecting your news outlets, such as major national networks with international coverage and readership, and with a significant amount of reporting done in English, you can begin to select the sources you will be using for your content analysis. In this case, you could settle upon *BBC News* and *Russia Today*, which both maintain extensive websites, and both covered the event in English. However, even after narrowing your scope to two manageable sources, you also need to create a timeframe, let us say the first month following the incident, so from July 17–August 17, 2014. You would then be able to create a catalogue of news stories from both websites. However, at this point, you still need to categorize news story contents. If you are doing a primarily textual analysis on the basis of textual news stories published on the Internet, there are a number of software packages commercially available, or potentially available through your university, that can assist with content analysis such as *SPSSTextSmart*.

Categorization can be a complex task, and can be approached in two different ways. The first, a deductive approach, would have you create categories in advance on the basis of your pre-existing knowledge and expectations. Given the growing tension between the European Union and the United States on one side, and Russia on the other, over the growing civil conflict in Ukraine during the months preceding the incident, one could expect news coverage to privilege a particular narrative or perspective. Thus, we could create two categories, which reflect these **narratives** that we expect to find, and perhaps a third neutral category for those stories, which appear to privilege neither.

Alternatively, we could take an inductive approach to generating categories by diving straight into the news stories so as to identify particular categories that we discover during the course of our reading. You might find after reading a number of news stories that there are many more nuanced themes, such as stories relating to particular theories or conjecture as to what or who brought down the aircraft, stories focused on civilian casualties from the conflict itself, or stories focused on victims who were on board the downed aircraft.

Once we have generated our categories, either inductively or deductively, we still have to **code** keywords in the text. Coding for context analysis is essentially the process of coming up with words that represent a particular concept of category. For example, we could code terms related to assigning blame, such as responsibility, liability, or accountability, and others related to the causes of the incident, such as surface-to-air missile, ground-to-air missile, or air-to-air missile among others. Context analysis software will allow for you to code a number of terms, such as the examples noted above. However, in many cases students also use basic software packages that are readily available to conduct basic key word searches, which can be done for example using Word, or even most Web browsers.

Key word counting is perhaps the most basic form of content analysis and many different elements within texts can lend themselves to counting. We can focus on a particular word. For example, we might want to simply count references to *he* or *she* in order to get a sense of gender. Alternatively, we can focus on themes, which convey a particular message in sentence form.[18]

Once you begin coding your textual data into categories, you might be able to distinguish the emergence of specific trends or patterns. The more you have thought about your categories the better your analysis will be. At this point you will have generated a large amount of coded data, which you can use descriptively in your writing, or should you choose, you can attempt to discern **correlations** or relationships through quantitative statistical tests, which you will be introduced to in Chapter 6. In short, the principle aim of content analysis is to look for patterns in communication.

Discourse Analysis

Discourse analysis is a form of qualitative analysis that focuses on the interpretation of linguistic forms of communication. It can be either spoken or written, and can include both official and unofficial forms of communication. For discourse analysts, who see the world as constituted by actors whose identities are formed through **intersubjective** understandings, language plays a key role in constituting the objects under study and thus plays a *performative* role, and their principle interest is to understand how and why particular discourses emerge, become dominant, and are used by actors.

Hardy et al. define discourse analysis as 'a methodology for analyzing social phenomena that is qualitative, interpretive and constructivist' (2004: 19). They argue that discourse analysis is more than just a technique for understanding the content of texts, but also brings with it a set of assumptions about how the world is constructed through language (p. 19).

To conduct a discourse analysis, as with content analysis, you will first need to specify the scope of what you will be examining. What particular speeches, documents, or declarations will you examine, and why? What is it that you are looking for or attempting to understand? Are you looking to conduct a discourse analysis on discourses of terrorism in US foreign policy? Remember, discourse analyses do not normally rely upon just a single text, speech, or official document, so you will need to attempt to gather those statements which are the most prominent, or canonical. However, unlike content analysis, where you can code entire sets of documents, such as US State Department daily briefings over a longer period of time, through the aid of computer assisted programs, normally discourse analyses rely on fewer representative texts. When reflecting upon official discourses, it is important that these texts are authoritative, or come from official sources authorized to speak on behalf of the organization under study.

To conduct your discourse analysis, you need to identify and justify your selection of texts. The justification is important because you will be making an argument as to the representativeness of the texts for a broader discourse that serves to constitute and produce something of interest in IR. After you have identified and justified your selection of texts, the processes will depart from content analysis, because you will not be interested in categorizing data into specific coded typologies, but rather you will attempt to discern why and how actors resorted to a particular discourse.

Who is being called a terrorist? What exactly is being considered to be terrorism? For example, is the word terrorism being applied to a broader set of actions that go beyond violent acts to non-violent protest? Does the use of this discourse legitimize a certain course of action? Does the framing of counter-terrorism policies in the context of a Global War on Terrorism make possible certain policy choices or actions? These are questions that would be of interest in a discourse analysis.

In short, despite criticisms of discourse analysis being 'unscientific', it is a useful tool for illuminating the world around us. Discourse analysis' focus is on understanding how language constitutes and produces the world around us. How it creates categories, how it limits our choices, or how it creates new choices. Discourse analysis constitutes a powerful tool for illuminating responses to the above questions.

Chapter Summary

Qualitative methods include a broad range of data collection and analysis techniques that provide researchers with deeper insight into the social world. Major techniques for data collection used by scholars of IR include archival or document-based research, interviews, and Internet-based research. Each of these data collection techniques allows you to unlock vast amounts of qualitative data in order to help you find the data that is necessary to respond to your research question. We also presented two forms of qualitative data analysis – content analysis and discourse analysis. Of course, it is important to remember that this chapter provided you with a broad spectrum of qualitative techniques, and it is up to you to decide which techniques are most appropriate for your own research project. In some cases, we use qualitative data collection techniques to gather factual background information, or the perceptions of elites through interviews, and therefore we choose to integrate this data into our research directly in the absence of content analysis or discourse analysis. In principle, there is nothing wrong with this, as long as you are always transparent about your sources and methods.

Suggested Further Reading

Jack S. Levy (2002) 'Qualitative Methods in International Relations', in Frank P. Harvey and Michael Brecher (eds), *Evaluating Methodology in International Studies*. Ann Arbor, MI: University of Michigan Press, pp. 131–60.

Lisa Harrison and Theresa Callan (2013) 'Qualitative Methods', in *Key Research Concepts in Politics & International Relations*. London: Sage, pp. 116–20.

Greg Scott and Roberta Garner (2013) *Doing Qualitative Research: Designs, Methods and Techniques*. Boston, MA: Pearson. For more on conducting interviews see 'Chapter 18: Interviewing', pp. 280–97.

David Richards (1996) 'Elite Interviewing: Approaches and Pitfalls', *Politics*, 16 (3): 199–204. This article provides a short introduction to elite interviews and provides some additional practical guidance on carrying out interviews with elites.

Jennifer Milliken (1999) 'The Study of Discourse in International Relations', *European Journal of International Relations*, 5 (2): 225–54. This article provides an important contribution to setting out the core tenets of discourse analysis and its use within the field of International Relations.

Notes

1   See Martha Finnemore and Kathryn Sikkink, 'Taking Stock: The Constructivist Research Program in International Relations and Comparative Politics', *Annual Review of Political Science*, vol. 4, 2001, pp. 391–416. Klotz relied upon a wide range of qualitative documentary sources from statements of activists, media reports, to official pronouncements on the part of states in her single case study that examined US sanctions against apartheid-era South Africa. Meanwhile, Hunjoon Kim and Kathryn Sikkink relied upon the quantitative analysis of a dataset that included human rights prosecutions in over 100 transitional countries to argue that human rights prosecutions do have a deterrent effect that is brought about through both normative and material factors. See Audie Klotz, 'Norms Reconstituting Interests: Global Racial Equality and US Sanctions Against South Africa', *International Organization*, vol. 49, no. 3, 1995, pp. 451–78, and Hunjoon Kim and Kathryn Sikkink, 'Explaining the Deterrence Effect of Human Rights Prosecutions for Transitional Countries', *International Studies Quarterly*, vol. 54, no. 4, 2010, pp. 939–63.

2   Christopher Lane used three historical case studies to process-trace causal mechanisms that were advanced by democratic peace theorists to challenge the underlying logic of democratic peace theory. Meanwhile, in an earlier work published in 1960 that sought to further understandings of arms races, Lewis Fry Richardson attempted to model strategic interactions during arms races. See Christopher Lane, 'Kant or Cant: The Myth of Democratic Peace', *International Security*, vol. 19, no. 2, 1994, pp. 5–49, and Lewis Fry Richardson, *The Statistics of Deadly Quarrels*. Pacific Grove, CA: Boxwood, 1960.

3   Audie Klotz, 'Introduction', in *Qualitative Methods in International Relations: A Pluralist Guide*, edited by Audie Klotz and Deepa Prakash. New York: Palgrave, 2008, pp. 2–3.

4   Klotz offers another definition of qualitative methods that argues qualitative methods 'are somehow linked to meaning'. Klotz, 'Introduction', p. 3. Both Klotz' definition of qualitative

methods, and the definition presented here are intentionally broad so as to be able to capture the full range of research that can be described as qualitative.

5   As noted earlier, many definitions of qualitative methods define qualitative methods with reference to their purpose: to help better understand meaning. See also Lisa Harrison and Theresa Callan, *Key Research Concepts in Politics & International Relations*. London: Sage, 2013, p. 116.

6   For examples, although Jack S. Levy pointed out that we should not conflate qualitative methods with case study methods, Levy notes, 'the core of the literature on the methodology of qualitative research in the international relations field focuses on comparative and case study methods.' Jack S. Levy, 'Qualitative Methods in International Relations', in *Evaluating Methodology in International Studies*, edited by Frank P. Harvey and Michael Brecher. Ann Arbor, MI, University of Michigan Press, 2002, pp. 132.

7   Often scholars combine elements of the above in their research rather than relying on a single data collection technique. See for example, Victor Peskin and Mieczyslaw Boduszynski, 'Balancing International Justice in the Balkans: Surrogate Enforcers, Uncertain Transitions and the Road to Europe', *International Journal of Transitional Justice*, vol. 5, no. 1, 2011, pp. 52–74. Focus groups constitute another commonly used qualitative data collection technique; however, its use on the part of scholars of IR is less common. Focus groups provide in-depth information on how participants perceive certain issues or questions and is widely used in the context of marketing, and is more commonly used among political scientists than in IR.

8   Sometimes individuals who hold senior positions within an organization maintain personal libraries and records, such as work diaries.

9   Or, as will be noted in Chapter 9, official documents can also prove unreliable.

10   Brian Grodsky describes, for example, how he selected local media sources for his study of transitional justice in Poland, Uzbekistan, Serbia, and Croatia. He noted that he selected his local media sources on their breadth of national coverage and in consultation with local academics and non-governmental actors. Grodsky pointed out that in some cases local sources proved to be an essential source of data, because there was almost no international reporting of transitional justice issues within some of his case studies, whereas in others, such as Croatia, he was able to rely upon the international press. Brian K. Grodsky, *The Costs of Justice: How New Leaders Respond to Previous Rights Abuses*. Notre Dame, IN: University of Notre Dame Press, 2010, pp. 81–2.

11   For more on the purposes of interview research see Greg Scott and Roberta Garner, *Doing Qualitative Research: Designs, Methods and Techniques*. Boston, MA: Pearson, 2013, pp. 280–1.

12   For example, you might want to collect biographical data on focus group participants and conduct a structured interview with individuals either before or after a focus group. For more on mixed methods see Chapter 7.

13   This is not to say that elite interviews cannot take on a structured or unstructured form; however, given the challenges in securing access to elites, building rapport with your interview subject, and the often limited time elites have available to spend with researchers, semi-structured interviews are often the most effective means of eliciting information from elite interviews. For a further guide on how to conduct elite interviews see David Richards, 'Elite Interviewing: Approaches and Pitfalls', *Politics*, vol. 16, no. 3, 1996, pp. 199–204.

14   1991 being the year that armed conflict broke out in Croatia.

15   An exception to informed consent concerning a highly unusually research design will be noted in Chapter 9.

16 See Chapter 6.
17 Bryman makes an additional distinction between discourse analysis and critical discourse analysis, with the former being primarily interpretive and the latter being informed by Michel Foucault's work on power and discourse. Alan Bryman, *Social Research Methods*, 3rd edition. Oxford: Oxford University Press, pp. 499–511.
18 Other elements that can be coded include: characters, or individuals who appear in documents; paragraphs, in the event each paragraph covers a particular idea or claim; items, or counting the individual texts used; concepts, in the event words can be grouped into particular clusters; and semantics, or how strong or weak a word is in relation to other words. For more on units for counting in context analysis see Bruce L. Berg and Howard Lune, *Qualitative Research Methods for the Social Sciences*. New York: Pearson, pp. 359–60.

6

QUANTITATIVE METHODS IN INTERNATIONAL RELATIONS

Quantitative methods, deeply rooted in North American political science, have been frequently used in IR, yet are inaccessible to many students and scholars who lack advanced mathematics or statistical training. On the one hand, this lack of accessibility is understandable given the specialized technical training needed to conduct more advanced statistical tests or interpret mathematical models. Yet on the other hand, this inaccessibility is puzzling given the fact that the media, politicians, businesses, and non-governmental organizations confront us on a daily basis with information, and arguments, in numeric form. In fact, it is hard to imagine making sense of the world around us without an understanding of mathematics or statistics. For example, economic trends, trafficking crime rates, incidences of terrorism, climate change, all contain numerical information of interest to students, scholars, and practitioners in the field of IR.

We often point to numeric figures because they contain meaning beyond simple descriptive language. While it is without question these figures provide certainty and precision, scholars of IR have used numbers to advance arguments related to a broad range of topics within the field. To be sure, numbers do far more than just provide an accurate tool for **measurement**, numbers help us establish differences between objects of study, visualize trends, and provide us with the data necessary to estimate the degree of relationship between variables, and more broadly even to understand behavior. Indeed, it was the desire to understand the behavior, decisions and choices of actors in international politics that led to the initial **formalization**,[1] or application of mathematic language to strategic studies literature. And, it was the urgent need to understand high stakes strategic choices that confronted policy-makers during the height of the Cold War between the US and the Soviet Union that led both decision-makers and scholars to seek increased certainty in **formal models** of deterrence and crisis management in order to prevent a nuclear exchange between the rival superpowers. More recently, formal methods have been applied to conflict management in the context of intra-state wars,[2] with scholars attempting to model the conditions under which belligerent parties are likely to acquiesce to a peace agreement (Walter, 2002). In addition to creating mathematical models, statistics have also been used to provide empirical tests or to describe developments and trends in international politics. For example, have incidences of human trafficking grown over the last ten years? Is foreign direct investment into a particular country or region growing or decreasing? Is the world becoming more violent? These are all questions to which responses are often provided in numeric form. Therefore, even if we do not consider ourselves to be quantitative researchers, quantitative literacy remains a prerequisite to research in international affairs.

This chapter will provide an introduction to the contributions and utility of quantitative research in International Relations. It also contains a practical guide to quantitative research data collection and analysis tools that are used by scholars in IR. Starting with an overview of the **behavioralist** tradition in IR, this chapter will move on to provide you with a comprehensive introduction to formal methods and widely used statistical methods deployed within quantitative scholarship in IR. Of course, formal methods and statistics require additional specialized training, which is beyond the scope of this text; however, here you will be presented with the basic foundation necessary to unlock these methods. You will therefore be provided with strategies for operationalizing quantitative methods in your own research.

Statistics and formal methods remain widely used in IR and appear frequently in the discipline's leading journals. Indeed, scholars have attempted to model a wide range of issue areas in the study of international relations from cooperation to conflict. Thus, literacy in formal methods, in particular an ability to draw and understand relationships between variables, is increasingly necessary for both students and scholars to access a growing body of IR scholarship.

Quantitative Methods in International Relations: What are they? And why use them?

Quantitative methods refer to data collection and analysis strategies where numeric data is collected in order to determine whether or not a relationship exists between two or more variables. This can be done either through attempting to predict the value of one variable on the basis of another known variable, or through attempts to model interactions among actors. Thus quantitative methods encompass both **statistical analysis** and **formal modeling**.

When attempting to understand the relationship between variables, this relationship is usually deducted from some form of theoretical proposition. Thus, whereas *qualitative* research is often argued to follow an **inductive** logic (Bryman, 2008: 366), whereby empirical observations are used to generate theoretical propositions, quantitative research is argued to be **deductive**, as theoretical propositions are tested against empirical data. All quantitative methods require data to be either gathered, coded, or scaled into numerical form. Either through the **coding** of large bodies of unstructured data, such as the contents of media reports, or through the **scaling** of qualitative data into quantitative numeric form, or establishing the intensity of payoffs when modeling strategic interaction, you will be confronted with the task of moving away from natural languages, such as English, toward formal language, that of mathematics.

Scholars of IR sometimes make use of formal models, which apply mathematical formal methods to the study of IR.[3] According to Michael Nicholson (2002: 24), those who use formal models seek to, '... search for the nature of the logic of various situations.' Thus, quantitative methods encompass much more than the collection of **descriptive statistics**. Quantitative methods also include attempts to infer from collected data for the purpose of making predictive claims about how actors are likely to behave or to put theoretical claims to an empirical test (Moses and Knutsen, 2012: 71). When thinking about quantitative methods in terms of the latter, or decision-making, IR scholarship has long engaged with **rational choice** behavioralist models, which applies econometric assumptions about behavior to states and has been closely tied to the realist tradition within IR (Kahler, 1998).

Advantages of Quantitative Methods

Any serious attempt to use quantitative methods will require you to gain a certain degree of fluency in communicating through mathematics and statistics. For those who lack mathematical training, this is probably something that will take a considerable amount of time. It is thus not surprising that many question the utility of quantitative methods in IR when juxtaposed against the perquisite mathematical and statistical training needed to use these methods effectively in your own research.[4]

Indeed, Hedley Bull (1966) was one of the scholars of IR who feared the advanced technical training needed to sustain quantitative research in the discipline would crowd out more context-based approaches to understanding IR. However, there are a number of advantages that quantitative methods can bring to the table. The first is data aggregation, or that quantitative methods allow us to engage with large amounts of data. Whether gathered through questionnaires or surveys, or coded into large **datasets**, quantitative methods provides us with the tools to interpret large bodies of data. The second is specificity. When using statistical methods we must be explicit about our assumptions and by translating our argument into a common statistical language. Related to the second is the third advantage, that of transparency. Quantitative methods force us to be transparent about our methods from our coding choices to the underlying logic of our arguments and how we arrive at our conclusions (Braumoeller and Sartori, 2004). Furthermore, another important defense of quantitative methods notes that formal language, or mathematics, can assist researchers in making **causal inferences** about relationships among variables. Quantitative methods, or formal languages, also permit us to more effectively communicate long chains of deductive arguments than traditional languages (Nicholson, 2002: 24). Finally, another advantage of quantitative methods is that they are good at providing us with tools to test theories and hypotheses. However, they are less useful when it comes to generating new theories or hypotheses.[5] Indeed, when contemplating the complexity of the social world and the multitude of variables we must account for when even attempting to construct the most basic explanation for an event, quantitative methods provides a communicative tool that allows us to take into account a wide range of variables and communicate our arguments concisely to the informed reader.

Advantages of Quantitative Methods

- **Aggregation**: allows the researcher to make sense of large amounts of data to an extent not possible without quantification
- **Specificity**: allows for the researcher to be *explicit* about assumptions and relationships
- **Transparency**: allows for the researcher to be *explicit about coding* (clear about what is and is not being measured); mitigates only noticing trends consistent with that which is under investigation
- **Causal inference**: can assist in understanding the relationship between variables
- **Theory and hypotheses testing**: permits the researcher to test theories and hypotheses against data (although quantitative methods are not as good at generating new theories or hypotheses)

Now that we have established the basic building blocks of quantitative research and formal methods, and we have discussed some of the merits of quantitative research, we can begin to look at practical ways we can integrate quantitative methods into your research. Let us begin with an examination of just how we can translate phenomena observed in natural languages into numbers.

Often one of the first questions posed by students when they are introduced to mathematical models is, where do the numbers come from? Are the values simply assigned arbitrarily by the modeler? The answer to the latter question is of course no, while the response to the first question will be provided in a brief introduction to formal methods and game theory presented below.

Formal Methods and Game Theory in IR

<u>Game theory</u> refers to the application of mathematical models to understand strategic interaction among actors, and it is precisely here that the contribution of formal methods to the study of IR has been greatest. Bruce Bueno de Mesquita (2002) traces the application of game theory to the study of IR to Thomas Schelling's publication of *The Strategy of Conflict* in 1960.[6] Schelling's attempt to model strategies of conflict generated a growing body of literature on the part of scholars to model strategic behavior during the Cold War. In the context of a superpower standoff, where the actual outbreak of hostilities would reap catastrophic consequences on a global scale, the perceived urgency to provide greater strategic certainty to policymakers sought to deepen our understanding of strategic interact and strategic choices. Furthermore, even after the Cold War, game theory came to occupy a place of increased prominence within the field of IR, and was even argued by Milner (1998) to mark a growing convergence between the fields of International Relations, Comparative Politics, and American Political Science.

Models require a high degree of abstraction. When constructing a model we begin by reducing the phenomena under study to its basic elements. We can model almost any social situation which involves choice and more than one potential outcome. For example, if you are with a group of five friends and are deciding upon which restaurant to go to, you might come up with two our more choices. Let's say that three friends want to go to *Restaurant A*, while the other two want to go to *Restaurant B*. Let's assume you prefer A. A simple ordinal ranking of preferences, or a ranking of preferences in relation to each other, would give you something like this:

Friend 1	=	A>B
Friend 2	=	A>B
Friend 3	=	A>B
Friend 4	=	A<B
Friend 5	=	A<B
You	=	A>B

However, just because more of you initially wanted to go to *Restaurant A*, does not mean that this preference is reflected in the outcome. In fact, let us assume you all ended up going to *Restaurant B* instead. How could you explain this unexpected result? John Von Neumann and Oskar Morgenstern, two of the founding fathers of modern game theory, created a method to rank cardinal preference, or the intensity of preferences. They started by assigning the worst possible outcome for everyone involved 0, then the best possible outcome 100. Now let's take a look at the data with cardinal preferences included.

Ordinal Preference

Friend 1 = A>B
Friend 2 = A>B
Friend 3 = A>B
Friend 4 = A<B
Friend 5 = A<B
You   = A>B

Cardinal Preference

Friend 1 = 60 for A
Friend 2 = 55 for A
Friend 3 = 55 for A
Friend 4 = 100 for B
Friend 5 = 100 for B
You   = 55 for A

The figures above give you some insight into not just preferences, but now also the *intensity of preferences*. Let's assume that the two friends who expressed a preference for *Restaurant B*, would not under any circumstances go to *Restaurant A*, because of a previous bad experience at that restaurant. Those who initially expressed a preference for *Restaurant A* only preferred *Restaurant A*, but would still be willing to go to *Restaurant B*. Thus, in order to keep the group together, *Restaurant B* became the preferred destination. When looking at inter-state bargaining, different states want different things and have different preferences, so explaining bargaining outcomes is a complex task that, much like the restaurant example, can be illuminated by formal modeling.

Simple games are parsimonious and relatively easy to follow. For example, decision trees confront us with a set of choices and expected payoffs. However, decision trees are single player games, and the purported payoffs are not contingent upon the action of another player. Figure 6.1 provides you with a simple illustration of a decision tree. Note that there is only one player, who is presented with two choices.

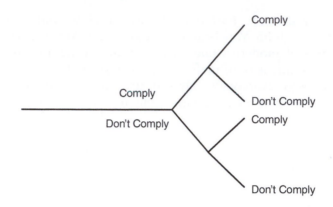

Figure 6.1   Decision Trees

Strategic games, or non-cooperative games, assume that your payoff is contingent upon the strategic choice of another player. Strategic games, at a minimum, require only a handful of characteristics. The first is the requirement that we have two or more players. Each player must also be confronted with choices. Each choice must have a certain payoff for the players, and payoffs are not just dictated by one's own choice, but also the choice of the other player (Nicholson, 1992: 57). These payoffs can be represented ordinally. Rules also govern how the players interact with each other during the game.

Below in Figure 6.2 is a simple diagram that illustrates how two player game matrixes are usually presented.

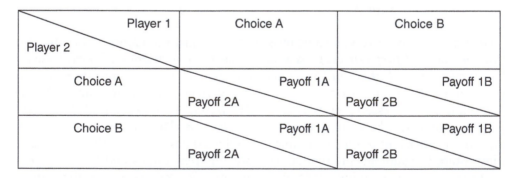

Figure 6.2   A Two Player Game Matrix

When applied to strategic interactions in International Relations, we can insert actors faced with strategic choices for Players 1 and 2. The strategic choices will then take the place of Choices A and B. Then we will use the expected outcomes to calculate the payoffs for each move and for each player. Let us imagine we are modeling the strategic interaction between the United States and the Soviet Union. Both states are confronted with complying with the terms of a nuclear arms reduction agreement that would require both states to drastically reduce their nuclear stockpile. Neither the US nor the Soviet Union is sure the opposing party will comply with the terms of the agreement. Here we have two players, the United States and the Soviet Union. Each player is faced with a strategic choice: either to comply or not comply with an arms control agreement. The expected payoffs are as follows: both sides comply and reap the reward for arms reduction (R), neither side complies with the agreement and neither reaps any reward, but at the same time strategic parity is maintained (NR). Or one side is suckered into complying (S) while the other side gains a strategic advantage (A). Thus the ordinal values of the expected payoffs can be stated as follows: A>R>NR>S. Note that this payoff structure reflects a common game known as the Prisoner's Dilemma.[7] Figure 6.3 demonstrates what such a game would look like.

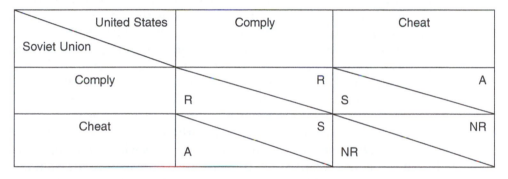

Figure 6.3 US–Soviet Arms Control Prisoner's Dilemma

Think about the choices that confront the United States and Soviet Union and the potential payoffs. *What policy advice would you give in such a situation and why?*

If we assume the players are rational, then we can assume that in the context of the above zero-sum game they will seek to minimize their losses while maximizing their gain. Because being suckered is the least desired outcome (S), both players will attempt to avoid being confronted with this particular payoff. This risk is only present should the player comply with the agreement. The highest value payoff, that of strategic advantage (A), can also be accrued through compliance. The maintenance of strategic parity (NR) means that neither party is better off than before the agreement, but also neither has been suckered into losing strategic parity. Thus, because non-compliance or the 'cheat' option reduces the risk of loss, we can expect both parties to non-comply with the terms of this agreement. Or stated in other words, we would have found the Nash equilibrium because no single player can gain by unilaterally adopting another choice when the other player's strategy remains constant (see Figure 6.4).

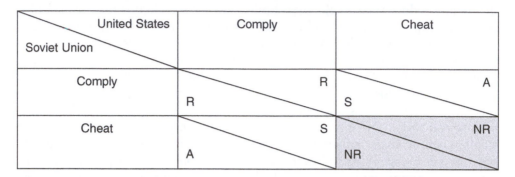

Figure 6.4   Nash Equilibrium

The equilibrium point for both players in this single game is shaded in green. While game theory may seem like a simple tool, you should remember that games come in many different forms. Furthermore, the modeling of strategic behavior of actors in International Relations requires us to take into account that games are not single play games where states encounter one another for the first and only time, but rather they are repeated, or  games. All of these factors, changing payoff structures, repeated interaction, large numbers of players, all serve to increase the complexity of game theoretic modeling.

    It is important to note that the focus of scholarly interest has been on non-cooperative games. Non-cooperative games are not games where cooperation is impossible, but rather cooperative or non-cooperative outcomes result from the strategic interaction of players. Cooperative games refer to those games where factors outside the strategic interaction of players can enforce cooperation or compliance (Milner, 1998: 783).

Quantitative Methods: Datasets and Statistical Analysis

In addition to attempts to model strategic behavior, quantitative methods in International Relations have provided us with tools for the interpretation of large datasets and statistical analysis. The key difference between mathematical models, such as those presented in the previous section, and statistical methods, such as those that are described within this section is that whereas mathematical models hope to predict behavior on the basis of mathematical models (Nicholson, 1992: 59), statistical analysis attempt to predict a certain outcome on the basis of other known elements. In order to run statistical tests we either need to gather our own data, through surveys or questionnaires, or make use of pre-existing large datasets.

Examples of Where You Can Find Datasets

- Correlates of War: www.correlatesofwar.org
- Environmental Treaties and Resource Indicators: http://sedac.ciesin.org/entri/
- Peace Research Institute Oslo: www.prio.org/Data/
- Stockholm International Peace Research Institute: www.sipri.org/databases
- World Bank: http://data.worldbank.org
- OECD: www.oecd.org/statistics/

In the event you are researching a topic for which there is no pre-existing dataset, you will be confronted with the task of generating your own data. While creating a new dataset on a particular topic of interest in IR may be an option, it should be noted that the datasets listed above were compiled by large teams of researchers and require a significant amount of time researching and coding data for entry into the dataset. Coding entails the categorization and quantification of material for analysis. When coding you will be matching values with particular concepts. While coding, for the most part, remains labor intensive there has been a remarkable shift in the field that has brought renewed interest to large dataset analysis in IR. The shift from hand coding by researchers to automated coding by software has sparked a renewed interest in the quantitative study of IR. For an example, Gary King and Will Lowe (2003) evaluated one of these automatic coders, the *Integrated Data for Events Analysis* project, which aims to code social, economic and political events data. King and Lowe found that in comparing a computerized coding program against a Harvard undergraduate student:

> The computer program we evaluated was able to extract information from Reuters news reports on a level equal to trained Harvard undergraduates—and this was for a short-term application. Computer programs do not get tired, bored, and distracted, and so in the long run the program would certainly outdo any human coder that would be feasible for a researcher to recruit. (2003: 619)

Given the growth in datasets available to researchers and the lower costs associated with generating datasets through software, the ability to understand and conduct statistical tests on the part of students of IR, will surely continue to grow.

Survey and Questionnaire Design

In addition to large datasets that record international events, there is another level of analysis that is of increasing interest to researchers in IR, the individual. Another common technique used for generating quantitative data is the use of surveys or questionnaires. If you are interested in the characteristics or perceptions of a particular population, surveys and questionnaires can be a useful tool for generating such data. Balnaves and Caputi (2001: 76) define surveys as 'a method of collecting data from people about who they are (education, finances, etc.), how they think (motivations, beliefs, etc.), and what they do (behaviour)'. One example of a survey that attempts to map global public opinion on a variety of issues is *World Public Opinion*.[8]

However, in some cases, rather than turning to existing sources of survey or questionnaire data, you may find yourself attempting to distribute your own surveys or questionnaires. When doing this you should always be transparent about your **sample frame**, of the wider pool of potential respondents from which you draw your research participants. This helps you demonstrate the **external validity** of your data, or the extent to which your data is representative of the population you are claiming to study.[9] For students of IR, it is not likely that we will be able to survey, or distribute questionnaires to a **random sample** of potential respondents, but instead we will be targeting specific groups; for example, employees of a particular organization that we are studying such as a political party or international organization, or we might be soliciting the perspectives of our peers. Random sampling means that every potential respondent within your target population has an equal chance of being selected for participation in your survey or questionnaire. Of course, as will be pointed out in Chapter 9, there are different strategies for finding research participants, which would fall within the category of non-random sampling. For example, one strategy is opportunistic sampling, where a researcher takes advantage of their existing network to facilitate the distribution of surveys or questionnaires. Brinton's distribution of questionnaires in Japan to explore the sources of a male–female wage gap relied on opportunistic factors such as personal contacts in neighborhoods near Tokyo, in Sapporo, and in Toyohashi. Brinton selected these three locations as fieldwork sites as they were all urban, and personal contacts meant that accessing records in these sites, which was necessary to distribute questionnaires, was possible. In addition, Brinton noted these sites were also selected because while all were urban, they contained variation in terms of geographic location and social classes (2003: 202).

In addition to opportunistic sampling, another non-random sampling technique that you will be introduced to in Chapter 9 is **snowball sampling**.

Common Types of Survey Questions and Scales

Nominal Questions: Nominal questions generate responses that are categorical. Generally these will be closed-ended questions with a menu of categories provided to the respondent to choose from.

Example: What is your gender? Male/Female

Ordinal Questions: Ordinal questions require the respondent to provide a ranking for a series of responses.

Example: Please rank the following international organizations in terms of effectiveness. 1 being the organization which most effectively carries out its mandate with 4 being the least effective.

(__) The United Nations

(__) The Organization of American States

(__) The Council of Europe

(__) The African Union

Multiple Choice Questions: This type of question you are likely already familiar with from multiple choice examinations.

Example: Your position within your organization is: (a) intern, (b) assistant office manager, (c) office manager, (d) director.

Interval Questions: Interval questions ask respondents to place themselves in a particular class of responses.

Example: What is your average grade?

____Less than 60%

____60%–69%

____70%–79%

____80%–89%

____90%–100%

Scales: Scales allow researchers to determine the intensity of preference among respondents. The most common form of scale question is the Likert scale, which asks respondents to indicate their level of agreement or disagreement with a given statement.

Example: Armed humanitarian intervention should be allowed to take place even in the absence of a United Nations Security Council resolution authorizing the use of force.

(1) Strongly disagree, (2) disagree, (3) agree, (4) strongly agree

When designing your own surveys or questionnaires, there are a few guidelines that will help you through the process. First, it is essential to ensure you have secured the informed consent of your research participants. You can turn to Chapters 3 and 9 for further discussion of informed consent. Second, it is important you carefully think about how you will pose your question and what kinds of responses, and by extension what kind of data, you aim to collect. Different kinds of survey questions include: nominal questions, ordinal questions, multiple choice questions, interval questions, and scales.[10] Third, you should also take into account that distributing questionnaires and surveys is time intensive, potentially expensive, and does not always result in the collection of enough data to allow for you to effectively conduct a meaningful data analysis (Brinton, 2003: 203–4). Always check to see if the data you aim to collect may already exist in the form of a national census, surveys carried out in the media, or survey or questionnaire data collected by local or state government. While designing your own survey and questionnaires has the benefit of allowing you to design your questions specifically around your own project, conducting a survey or questionnaire can be a time-consuming endeavor and there is no guarantee that potential participants will prove willing to participate.

In the event you have decided to conduct your own survey or questionnaire, you should pay careful attention to survey design. Well-designed surveys are more likely to generate responses as respondents can complete them with ease. Examples of common question types noted in the preceding paragraph are widely used because respondents find them easy to understand. In addition, you should make sure that you have proofread your questions before distributing your survey. When proofreading, there are some additional factors you should take into account when designing your survey or questionnaire. In particular, make sure that each question contains only one question. This means do not ask two questions within a single question. Second, make sure your questions are not overly ambiguous and your likely respondents have requisite knowledge needed to respond. And third, where appropriate, provide respondents with the option of responding with 'don't know/prefer not to say'.[11]

Surveys and Questionnaires in International Relations

Survey and questionnaire data is often associated with the social sciences, but some students may question whether or not this could be a usable method for data collection in IR. However, for researchers with an interest in sub-fields such as political psychology or comparative politics, survey data features commonly in research and provides a rich source of data for quantitative data analysis.

Statistical Analysis

Once you have gathered your quantitative data, either from a large dataset or through surveys or questionnaires, you are now ready to begin your statistical data analysis. As mentioned at the outset, quantitative methods provide you with a set of tools to do things that go far beyond measurement. Here, our focus will move from descriptive statistics to **inferential statistics**. Descriptive statistics are simply a tool for measurement, which provides us with a basic indication of value for our variables. Inferential statistics refer to statistical tools that help us answer questions about our data. What, if any, relationships exist among variables? What trends can we observe? Most commonly to arrive at inferential statistics we will engage in **hypothesis** testing, looking for **correlations,** or to model relationships.

Perhaps the most common statistical test that is used to model relationships within IR is **regression analysis,** which is a simple statistical tool that allows for us to predict the value of a **dependent variable** on the basis of the value of an **independent variable**. In its most basic form regression analysis relies upon a linear regression model that assumes that you have two kinds of variables, one set, which we will call x, and another variable that is known as y. The values of y are randomly distributed along a mean value deterministically related to x (Lowe, 2004). This means that we can guess the value of y as long as we know the value of x.

There are two common types of regression analysis used by scholars, **bivariate** and **multivariate regression analysis.** Bivariate regression analysis simply provides for a means to see how changes in an independent variable correlate with changes in a dependent variable, or as noted above how changes in the value of x correlate with changes in the value of y. Bivariate regressions include only two variables: one independent variable and one dependent variable. It should be emphasized that when conducting bivariate regression analyses that the purpose of this exercise is to determine whether or not a relationship exists between two variables. In other words, the purpose of the analysis is to determine if there is a correlation between the two variables. If there is no correlation we will see a wide and seemingly random distribution of variables. If there is a strong correlation we will observe variables that appear to be plotted nicely along a line or curve. Nevertheless, while bivariate regressions are helpful in highlighting correlations, they cannot tell us whether or not one variable caused another variable. Regression analysis is not a tool to explain **causation**. For more on tools to understand the processes of causation see Chapter 8 on case studies.

To carry out your own regression analysis, you will need data on your independent and dependent variables, and a software package such as SPSS that can help you plot your data. For illustrative purposes let us take a look at the ficti-tious data gathered below on six states (Table 6.1).

Table 6.1

State	x (independent variable)	y (dependent variable)
State 1	8	6
State 2	11	7
State 3	6	5
State 4	7	6
State 5	2	2
State 6	5	4

Once we have our data we can then create a scatterplot (Figure 6.5). Remember the dependent variable is usually placed along the *y*-axis, while the independ-ent variable falls along the *x*-axis. Bivariate regression allows us to see whether or not there is a correlation between *x* and *y*, or whether or not knowing something about *x* will tell us something about *y*. In order to do this we will try to draw an imaginary straight line across the scatterplot, which minimize the distance between each point on the scatterplot and the line. The mathemat-ical equation for a straight line is $y = a + bx$. It is beyond the scope of this chapter to go into further detail regarding the regression equations you can

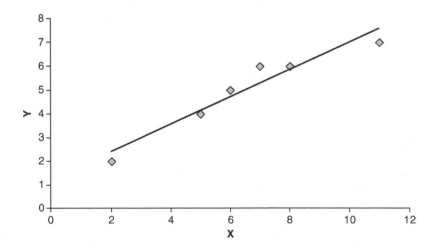

Figure 6.5   Scatterplot for *x* and *y*

use to calculate your straight line that minimizes the distance between each point on the scatterplot. This is because you will be able to easily compute these calculations on statistical software programs in which you will likely have input your data such as SPSS or Excel. The scatterplot below allows you to quickly visualize the distribution of the two variables from Table 6.1 and to make a determination that there appears to be a relatively strong correlation between the two. The regional line serves to further illustrate the presence of a strong positive correlation.

Multivariate regression provides a tool that allows us to examine three or more variables. Multivariate regression analysis can be a powerful tool to test the relationship among variables because it can provide insight into whether or not our bivariate regression analysis produced a **spurious relationship** (Bryman, 2008: 330–1). A spurious relationship is when two variables appear to be related to each other, but the relationship is actually caused by a third variable. For example, let's say we hear about a strong correlation between increased climate change and decreasing rates of piracy (Andersen, 2012). Obviously, this relationship is spurious, and we would need to investigate further so as to ascertain causes for either variable. Multivariate regression analysis would allow us to test the relationships between multiple variables to do so.

Chapter Summary

Quantitative methods in IR encompass a rich a diverse body of literature that continues to grow as students gain access to an ever increasing number of datasets that chart all sorts of phenomena in IR from environmental treaties to armed conflict. Quantitative methods aim, through measurement and formalization, to provide greater precision to a field of study that explicitly takes on the task of improving our understanding of a world defined by uncertainty. Either by coming up with formal models to better understand strategic interaction between rival powers in order to make predictive claims about the strategic choices actors will make under certain conditions, or through the codification of data into large datasets, in order to uncover correlations between variables through bivariate or multivariate regressions, we have been provided with a set of tools that can help us test our assumptions about the world. Furthermore, quantitative methods also equip us with the tools necessary to gather large amounts of data through large populations, such as surveys and questionnaires. With the ever increasing amount of information and data that researchers are expected to process, we can expect the need for students of IR to make use of quantitative methods to continue to grow.

Suggested Further Reading

Hedley Bull (1966) 'International Theory: The Case for a Classical Approach', *World Politics*, 18 (3): 361–77. This reading contains an impassioned critique of quantitative IR.

Stephen M. Walt (1999) 'Rigor or Rigor Mortis? Rational Choice and Security Studies', *International Security*, 23 (4): 5–48.

Bear F. Braumoeller and Anne E. Sartori (2004) 'The Promise and Perils of Statistics in International Relations', in Detleft F. Sprinz and Yael Wolinsky-Nahmias (eds), *Models, Numbers, and Cases: Methods for Studying International Relations*. Ann Arbor, MI: University of Michigan Press, pp. 129–51.

Helen V. Milner (1998) 'Rationalizing Politics: The Emerging of International, American and Comparative Politics', *International Organization*, 52 (4): 759–86.

Notes

1   Formalization refers here to the translation of verbal arguments or statements into mathematical form.

2   For example, James D. Fearon used mathematic models to explore the question of why some civil wars last longer than others. See James D. Fearon, 'Why Do Some Civil Wars Last So Much Longer than Others?' *Journal of Peace Research*, vol. 41, no. 3, 2004, pp. 275–301.

3   This chapter will use the terms formal and mathematical models interchangeably. Michael Nicholson, 'Formal Methods in International Relations', in *Evaluating Methodology in International Studies*, edited by Frank P. Harvey and Michael Brecher. Ann Arbor, MI: University of Michigan Press, 2002, p. 28.

4   For a critical perspective on the amount of time necessary to be able to understand and perform some of the more advanced mathematical models that have been used in IR, see Stephen M. Walt, 'Rigor or Rigor Mortis? Rational Choice and Security Studies', *International Security*, vol. 23, no. 4, 1999, pp. 25–48.

5   Indeed, as noted in Chapters 5 and 8, qualitative methods and case study research design can prove to be an effective tool for generating new theories and hypotheses.

6   Game theory itself emerged within the field of economics in John Von Neumann and Oskar Morgenstern's, *The Theory of Games and Economic Behavior*. Princeton, NJ: Princeton University Press, 1944.

7   For a more detailed explanation see 'Prisoner's Dilemma', *Stanford Encyclopedia of Philosophy*, September 4, 1997 [revised on October 22, 2007]. Available at: http://plato.stanford.edu/entries/prisoner-dilemma/

8   See *World Public Opinion* at: http://worldpublicopinion.org/index.php

9   Internal validity on the other hand refers to the ability of the researcher to draw conclusions about relationship between variables under examination in a particular study. For more on both external and internal validity see Mark Balnaves and Peter Caputi, *Introduction to Quantitative Research Methods*. London: Sage, p. 89.

10 For more on different styles of survey or questionnaire questions, see Balnaves and Caputi, *Introduction to Quantitative Research Methods*, pp. 77–80.

11 For a more lengthy checklist for surveys and questionnaires, see Balnaves and Caputi, *Introduction to Quantitative Research Methods*, pp. 82–3.

7
MIXED METHODS RESEARCH IN INTERNATIONAL RELATIONS

Although research methods curricula are often divided along the lines of quantitative and qualitative research methods, increasingly students are turning to mixed methods, which include elements of both in their research. In fact, Johnson et al. (2007: 112) argue that mixed methods have become recognized as 'a third major research approach' to methods, in addition to quantitative and qualitative research. The embrace of mixed methods research was driven by a desire to abandon methods factionalism, which saw researchers subdivide themselves into distinct camps of scholarship along the lines of methods. After all, if **qualitative methods** help us test theories and hypotheses, but are weak in illuminating processes that link variables, why can't they be combined with qualitative methods?

Mixed methods, as 'a third major research approach', is conceptually not very problematic if we distinguish debates over methods from epistemological commitments about how we acquire knowledge about the social world. In other words, if quantitative and qualitative researchers have a shared aim to illuminate causal inferences, as approached from the perspective of King et al. (1994), then mixed methods research should provide a powerful methods tool that allows for researchers to make their findings more robust.

However, how do we approach the question of mixed methods across the empirical–interpretive divide? It should be recalled that qualitative methods are neither exclusively empiricist nor interpretive, as noted in Chapter 5, and Chapter 6 pointed out that quantitative data can also be of use to the interpretive researcher. Indeed, we should always be careful to note that the claims we make in our research, whether focused on explanation, causality, or understanding, contain underlying assumptions about how we interpret IR, and more broadly the social world. Data collection and analysis are the tools that we use to support our claims, or arguments, and these tools can be employed within the context of divergent perspectives on the philosophy of social science. Thus, in this sense, mixed methods research is not necessarily an exclusively an empiricist project.

To be sure, within the empiricist tradition, it has been argued by scholars such as King et al. and Gerring that quantitative and qualitative research are complementary approaches that both attempt to advance cumulative knowledge about the world around us. King et al. argued that the quantitative–qualitative divide among researchers was a false one. This was because, as they argued in *Designing Social Inquiry*, that 'the same underlying logic provides the framework for each research approach' (King et al., 1994: 3) and moreover, they also noted, 'much of the best social science research can combine quantitative and qualitative data, precisely because there is no contradiction between the fundamental processes of inference involved in each' (King et al., 2010: 183). Furthermore, Gerring (2012: xxi) used the yardstick of *scientific* research to minimize the distance between quantitative and qualitative methods. While this chapter recognizes the internal coherence of mixed methods **research designs** within the empiricist tradition, it also underlines the utility of mixed methods beyond **empiricism**.

Chapter 7 will serve to provide a guide to mixed methods research in International Relations. Mixed methods are those that seek to combine quantitative and qualitative methods in IR. In many cases, mixed methods are used to apply more robust tests to hypotheses or theoretical propositions. If data collected using one technique affirms a **hypothesis**, then would it also be confirmed by using another data collection technique? In other words, would **focus groups** and questionnaires reveal similar attitudes or perceptions toward a given object? Or perhaps you have found that **large-n** analysis affirms a hypothesis, but you do not understand the process that links to the two variables. Perhaps, qualitative case studies can be used to illuminate causal processes that are not apparent from the quantitative large-n study? See, for example, Weller and Barnes (2014). Attempts to confirm findings through multiple methods, **triangulation** among methods, is not new and has been used by students and scholars to provide new insights in the social sciences, in fields such as criminology, and has also been used in other fields such as the medical sciences.[1]

This chapter will start by defining mixed methods research, and survey common usages of mixed methods research within IR. It will include examples drawn from the field to illustrate mixed methods, both research design and operationalization. For example, discursive approaches to understanding treaty compliance bring together both quantitative and qualitative methods along with elements of **interpretivism**.

Mixed Methods Research: What is It? And, Why Use It?

Mixed methods research is commonly defined as research that combines quantitative and qualitative methods (Bryman, 2008: 603; Johnson et al., 2007). Mixed methods have been used for a variety of purposes from complementarity, triangulation, to simply gathering more information on a given topic. In order to effectively make use of mixed methods, at the outset you should have a clear idea as to why you are using mixed methods. Furthermore, in addition to bringing together methods across the quantitative–qualitative divide, we can also include innovative methods within our discussion of mixed methods. Such innovative methods, such as **agent-based modeling,** are hard to place in either quantitative or qualitative methods since they combine elements of both.

Mixed Methods Research and Complementarity

Gerring points out that every single-case or *small-n* qualitative work has the potential to include large-*n* analysis within it (2012: 364). And likewise, every large-*n* quantitative work has the potential to be complemented by a *small-n* study. Often this is achieved through the combination of in-depth qualitative case studies with statistical tools as presented in Chapter 6. This perspective sees quantitative and qualitative research as complementary. For example, if we look at quantitative research we can see that it is effective in demonstrating **correlations** between variables, but is weak in illuminating causal processes. Thus, using **quantitative methods** to demonstrate a relationship exists between two variables, then using qualitative methods to uncover the underlying causal process would generate a much more complete understanding of the how these variables interact.

For example, if we wish to understand state cooperation with the international criminal courts, we would create a **dataset** of war crimes suspects transferred to court custody from a particular state. However, while this dataset would show us trends in terms of transfers, it would tell us very little about the processes that led a state to transfer members of its own armed forces to an international court.[2] Often scholars and policy-makers are interested in not just what happened, or in this case that states transferred war crimes suspects to an international tribunal, but *why* something happened: *what motivated the state to transfer one of its own nationals, who is viewed as a war hero at home, for trial before an international tribunal?* A response to this question is something that can be illuminated by a **process-tracing** case study.

A combination of quantitative data on transfers combined with a qualitative analysis of the discourse of actors involved in the transfer process can provide deeper understanding of how this process plays out and reasons why states may cooperate with an international court. In fact, if we simply count the number of war crimes trials, we may find ourselves making assumptions about the spread of norms of appropriate behavior that do not reflect underlying practices. However, in-depth qualitative studies can raise a number of questions as to the quality of war crimes trials, whether or not these trials target a particular ethnicity or party to the conflict, or whether or not local elites discursively attempt to undermine the legitimacy of trial processes. It is only when qualitative in-depth studies are combined with broader quantitative statistical observations that the combination of these two sets of data illuminates the more complex social processes that are at play, which are obscured by simply taking one or the other approach to data collection. To be sure, an in-depth qualitative study of war crimes trials in a particular setting may flag a number of important findings, but cannot tell us about wider trends or broader contexts. This example of war crimes trials touches upon another useful purpose of mixed methods research that emerge when we encounter conflicting data emanating from each approach.

Another example of a research design that employed both quantitative and qualitative methods in a complementary fashion is White et al.'s study of foreign policy and public attitudes in post-Soviet Europe through a combination of nationwide survey data and 18 focus groups (White et al., 2002). The question the authors hoped to shed light on was whether or not the citizens of the four countries under study perceived themselves as more European, or as members of a distinct civilization (ibid.). Indeed, while surveys proved fruitful in providing researchers with raw data on swings in public opinion on foreign policy, the focus groups provided more nuanced insight into how participants perceived their respective countries' foreign policy choices (ibid.).

Mixed Methods Research and Triangulation

In addition to being complementary, in the sense that the two methods can compensate for each other's weaknesses, mixed methods research can also be used to corroborate finds derived from one or the other, or highlight divergent findings between the two that will themselves require further explanation on the part of the researcher. This is an important function as new theories or hypotheses that emerge from qualitative case studies can find themselves not standing up to the empirical test of large-n studies. Likewise, assumed relationships between variables that are illuminated by large-n studies can prove spurious when scrutinized more closely through a qualitative case study.

If used for this purpose, to test the robustness of causal inferences drawn from our research findings, mixed methods research can be viewed as facilitating a process of methods triangulation. Triangulation was mentioned in Chapter 5, in the context of intra-qualitative methods' data collection strategies, i.e. **interviews**, media reports, and **official documents**, to corroborate findings in relation to a process under investigation; however, here triangulation will be addressed from an inter-methods perspective. To be sure, triangulation is a strategy that can be used both in terms of data collection and data analysis.

What does triangulation mean in this context of mixed methods research? Triangulation among methods is carried out in part because researchers recognize that quantitative and qualitative data collection techniques can result in researchers accumulating different bodies of data in relation to the same phenomena. Sometimes, quantitative and qualitative data collection and analysis results in contradictory findings in relation to the same phenomena. For example, the assumptions underlying democratic peace theory, when tested against large datasets appears to hold up to empirical scrutiny; however, when explored in a more qualitative in-depth case study, sometimes they do not. Or, as will be discussed further below, when quantitative findings related to the causes of civil wars are challenged by researchers using qualitative methods to explore the same phenomenon.

Triangulation requires the researcher to use a different set of methods tools to explore the same question. It requires the quantitative researcher to go beyond statistical tests on large-n datasets and delve into processes, while qualitative researchers are asked to incorporate quantitative strategies for data collection and analysis into their work. For example, researchers could combine qualitative **semi-structured interviews** with quantitative questionnaires to gain a greater insight into an international organization. The data elicited from the interviews could then be corroborated against the questionnaires to determine points of consistency or inconsistency that would have been left obscured by the use of only a single method.

It was precisely this attempt to corroborate insights drawn from quantitative methods with qualitative methods, which led to Collier and Sambanis' edited volume on *Understanding Civil War* (2005). Collier and Sambanis collected these essays to test the *Collier–Hoeffner model* on the economics of violent conflict, which emphasized the link between poverty and conflict and triggered the 'greed or grievance' debate among conflict scholars, with those who criticized the *Collier–Hoeffner model* arguing that the model over emphasized the role of economics and underplayed the role of social and political grievances. Furthermore, an additional criticism levied against the model argued that the quantitative methods used were not suited to understanding conflict dynamics, and instead in-depth qualitative studies of individual conflicts should be carried out.[3]

In response, Collier and Sambanis collected eight qualitative conflict case studies to refine their model and found upon further investigation that the initial greed or grievance debate was misplaced, as both greed and grievance worked together to fuel conflicts. Moreover, case studies provided contextual information that exposed **coding** errors within the initial model. For example, it was noted that in some cases where the model predicted the outbreak of civil war, no war was observed. However, upon closer inspection through a qualitative case study, it was revealed that in the case of Burundi (1965–1969) a war did occur

(Sambanis, 2005: 304). Furthermore, when countries were described as being at peace, despite being predicted to be at a high probability for experiencing civil war by the model, often they still experienced significant forms of domestic violence and turmoil that fell short of civil war, such as coups and violent insurgencies (ibid.). Significantly, the dataset also had problems in terms of excluding civil wars, which after closer scrutiny would certainly merit inclusion into the dataset. These problems all reduced the predictive validity of the model, but arguably coding errors could be corrected through qualitative case studies (p. 305).

Brinton noted another example where research triangulation provided new insights into quantitative data. Brinton found that Japanese official statistics suggested a very high rate of successful job placements for Japan's high school graduates. However, when Brinton interviewed teachers in career planning and guidance offices, she discovered that students who were seen as not likely to enjoy success on the job market were discouraged from conducting a job search and instead were advised to either go into vocational school or take a break from their job search. Of course, with these students excluded from job placement statistics, looking at the quantitative data alone would provide a very skewed picture of post-high school job placement prospects for Japanese graduates (Brinton: 2003: 210).

Mixed Methods Research and Holistic Data Collection

Mixed methods research is also sometimes used for the purpose of generating more data about an object under study rather than for the purposes of complementarity or triangulation. This usually refers to the combination of data collection tools from across the quantitative–qualitative divide. Often, data collection techniques limit the kind of data we can accumulate. Quantitative questionnaires pre-select responses and cannot elicit ideas or insight that the researcher wasn't expecting to find. For example, you may accumulate factual background biographical information, but only in relation to the questions asked. Respondents will not have the opportunity to volunteer more information that might be relevant to your research, but that you have not included in your questionnaire. On the other hand, qualitative techniques sometimes lack structure and can result in a lack of consistency in relation to the data gathered across research participants. This is particularly the case in relation to **unstructured interview**s.

Indeed, it is often the case that much of the necessary background data on our research participants can be effectively collected through quantitative questionnaires; however, just because you have selected a quantitative data collection technique, mixed methods research means that this does not preclude you from also using qualitative data collection techniques. Semi-structured interviews are aimed at eliciting the perspectives and insights of our interview participants;

however, in some cases when interviewing large numbers of people in the same organization, you might want to gather more information about your research participants. You might want to include a questionnaire that records basic facts such as how long an individual has worked for the organization, which are questions that are better placed in a questionnaire than an interview in which you are attempting to initiate a more probing conversation.

A number of researchers have combined these two approaches in their research. For example, Roman David uses both interview data and questionnaire data to explore the social impact of lustration systems in Central and Eastern Europe (David, 2011). In the sub-field of human rights, there are numerous examples of researchers who attempt to explain or understand the complex social processes that constitute human rights through a number of methods aimed at eliciting responses from either practitioners in the field of human rights, or the broader public. Likewise, the combination of data collection techniques has also been widely used in the field of comparative politics. The study of organizations such as political parties, for example, often includes mixed method approaches to gather a more complete picture of these complex social organizations.

Table 7.1 summarizes the major motivations for mixed methods researchers along with examples of scholarly works that make use of mixed methods.

Table 7.1 Motivations for Mixed Methods Research

Complementarity	Triangulation	Holistic Data Collection
This permits the researcher to strengthen the robustness of causal inferences drawn from their study through the use of data analysis techniques from quantitative large-*n* research and small-*n* qualitative research.	This focuses on using mixed methods to corroborate findings from across the quantitative–qualitative divide. This is done because the researcher recognizes data collection techniques can result in the collection of different kinds of data, and data analysis techniques can produce divergent outcomes.	This permits the researcher to combine quantitative and qualitative data collection techniques, such as questionnaires and interviews, in order to gather more data on their research topic.
Example(s): Lamont (2010), White et al. (2002)	*Example(s)*: Collier and Sambanis (2005)	*Example(s)*: David (2011)

Innovative Methods: Simulation Models

There are research tools emerging in the field of IR that lack the ability to be easily boxed into a particular tradition, one of these tools is that of simulation modeling. It may at first appear odd that a form of mathematical modeling can be discussed in the context of mixed methods; however, as this section will note, simulation models do not operate with the same set of assumptions of traditional **formal models** addressed in Chapter 6. Simulation modeling can be conceptualized in two forms. Those which are highly empirical and wish to generate real-world scenarios to those which are highly abstract and focus more on using models to explore the underlying logics of social processes.[4] Pepinsky argues, in an epistemological critique of simulation models as a 'fourth methodology' (Pepinsky, 2005: 383) that, 'the epistemological foundations of simulation emerge as a selective combination, of sorts, of different epistemological traditions that themselves lead to often conflicting conclusions' (p. 376). Pepinsky's critique is for the most part directed at simulation models that aim to reproduce the real, or empirically observed, world in simulation form to test propositions as to how agents will interact within certain environments. While the application of computational models to model interactions between complex agents in a complex environment so as to make predictions as to how agents will respond to particular *stimuli* always, as Pepinsky cautions against, presupposes a number of assumptions about international politics and reduces them to rules and parameters that can be adjusted by the modeler (pp. 367–94), simulation modeling nonetheless has found increasing application in the field.

Agent-based modeling (ABM) is one such method that has found itself increasingly used among scholars of IR, and has been applied to a number of questions such as attempts to understand the processes through which ideas spread within a group.[5] ABM refers to computer assisted mathematically based simulation models that generate data on how agents interact within a given environment that can be analyzed inductively. Robert Axelrod argued that ABM provides 'a third way of doing science' because rather than deduction it does not test theoretical propositions against empirical data, but instead generates data that can be analyzed inductively (Axelrod, 1997: 3–4). While on the one hand it relies on mathematical formal modeling, and thus could warrant classification as a quantitative method, on the other, it does not deductively prove theoretical propositions nor require the application of statistical tests to hypothesis. Instead, it attempts to shed light on the qualities and meanings of social interaction (Hoffman, 2008: 188).

Nevertheless, those who see simulation modeling as importing empiricism into the understanding of complex social processes are wary of attempts to model IR. Pepinsky uses the analogy of an aviation engineer's model of an aircraft under design to illustrate this concern. An aviation engineer makes changes to a model to see how changes to the properties of the aircraft will affect its lift. In order to model this, the engineer must be familiar with both the properties of the aircraft itself and environmental factors, such as the properties of air particles. Furthermore, the laws of physics will provide a set of rules that will govern how the aircraft and environmental factors will interact and the parameters of these rules (Pepinsky, 2005: 373). However, unlike the engineer, the student of IR is confronted with constant and predictable outside laws that govern how the model will interact with its environment. Instead, the student of IR can continuously alter the rules and parameters until a desired outcome is achieved.

While Pepinsky's analogy helps us conceptualize the limits of modeling in its more empirical form, agent-based modeling does not attempt to simply replicate the real world. In the words of Hoffman, agent-based modeling 'is *not* an empirical method' (Hoffman, 2008: 195). In fact, one can create models that are highly abstract to explore fundamental logics, and are not meant to replicate the real world. In this sense, the aim of agent-based modeling is that of a heuristic device into fundamental processes (p. 196).

Creating an Agent-Based Model

ABMs are defined by their simplicity and can be easily generated through the assistance of simulation software. Hoffman emphasizes that the utility of ABM is its allowance for the creation of artificial computer agents. These agents can be endowed with a set of characteristics, an ability to interpret the environment around them, and a decision-making process. After the creation of an artificial agent, environments can be created that can also take on many different forms ranging from social environments with a number of rules that govern agent interaction to environments that allow simply for interaction among agents. Once the agent and environment have been established the researcher can run the simulation and gather data. Once data has been gathered it can be analyzed by the researcher to either deductively test assumptions programed into the model in the form of rules and parameters or to inductively generate new hypotheses on complex social processes through the data generated (Hoffman, 2008: 188–90).

Overview: A Practical Guide to Mixed Methods

As noted above mixed methods research can be used for research complementarity, triangulation, or gathering a more holistic body of data for your research. In addition, innovative methods in the field sometimes combine qualitative and quantitative techniques. Often researchers use mixed methods with more than one of the above purposes in mind. When designing your own mixed methods research it is essential that you understand what you are trying to gain by employing mixed methods. If you are using mixed methods for complementarity, or to buttress each other's weaknesses, you should select those methods that shed light upon each other's blind spots. For example, focus groups can tell you a lot about how the group perceives a certain topic that you have introduced, but survey data can provide additional information about your focus group participants that can help you make sense of that data.

Alternatively, if you are using mixed methods for the purpose of triangulation, or corroboration, you should focus on selecting methods on the basis of which ones are most likely to be mutually corroborative. For example, questionnaires and semi-structured interviews may simply help you to gather *more* data, but won't necessarily help you triangulate data. When attempting to triangulate data, you should look to your **dependent variable,** for example that of civil wars. If you have found a certain correlation in your quantitative data that suggests a particular variable may cause a conflict, but you cannot make an argument of causality on the correlation alone, as it may be spurious, you could look for cases where both variables were present, and conduct an in-depth qualitative study to see what, if any, processes link these two variables.

In sum, whether interpretive or empirical, mixed methods research can provide a set of tools for data collection and data analysis that will allow you to either gain deeper insight into your research topic, deepen your understanding of **causal effects** and processes, to subject your hypotheses to more rigorous tests or to generate new hypotheses. In operationalizing mixed methods research, either through the bringing together of data collection tools or analytical tools or through the use of methods such as simulation modeling, it is important to have a clear idea as what you hope to achieve through the use of mixed methods. In other words, it is essential to have a clearly defined purpose that will guide you through the choices of which methods to select and why.

Mixed methods research can assume many different forms; however, you should establish a clear roadmap for your mixed methods project in order to ensure that the methods you will bring together are logically consistent. The box below sets out some key steps for mixed methods research that will help you design your own mixed methods research strategy.

Mixed Methods Research – A Practical Guide

Mixed methods research while popular among researchers should be used only when you have a clear purpose in mind. Mixing methods without a clear idea of how these methods can help you answer your research question can have the effect of obscuring your overall argument rather than making it clearer to the reader. In order to avoid obscuring your findings try to make sure that you:

1. Justify why you are using mixed methods early in your work.
2. Tell the reader what you expect to find, or discover, through the use of mixed methods.
3. Explain how you have designed your mixed methods study. Are you bringing together data collection techniques? Are you combining tools for data analysis, such as statistical tests with case studies? Or are you using an innovative method, such as agent-based modeling?
4. Present the implications of your findings.

Chapter Summary

Mixed methods research is increasingly recognized as a third pillar in the quantitative, qualitative family of research methods. Researchers who employ mixed methods reject the more rigid conceptualizations of qualitative and quantitative methods as containing mutually exclusive assumptions about how to understand the world. This chapter has demonstrated that mixed methods research can provide a rich resource for exploring topics in greater depth as tools for data collection and data analysis can be operationalized complementarily, or these tools can be used to triangulate data, or simply gather a more holistic body of data. Furthermore, innovative methods have emerged which challenge the assumed boundaries that have been drawn between quantitative and qualitative research, and empiricism and interpretivism. Agent-based modeling was highlighted to provide an example of one such method that draws upon formal modeling tools to allow scholars to generate hypotheses about complex social processes through the use of computer assisted simulations. In sum, mixed methods research is both increasingly common within the field, and has brought about a number of new insights into IR that neither quantitative nor qualitative methods alone could have provided.

Suggested Further Reading

Dirk Berg-Schlosser (2012) *Mixed Methods in Comparative Politics: Principles and Applications.* Houndsmills, Basingstoke: Palgrave Macmillan. This book provides an overview of mixed methods research strategies in comparative politics through chapters that focus on both themes in mixed methods research and case studies.

R. Burke Johnson, Anthony J. Onwuegbuzie, and Lisa A. Turner (2007) 'Toward a Definition of Mixed Methods Research', *Journal of Mixed Methods Research*, 1 (2): 112–33. This article provides a concise introduction to mixed methods research.

John Gerring (2012) *Social Science Methodology: A Unified Framework,* 2nd edition. Cambridge: Cambridge University Press. See Chapter 14 (pp. 379–94) for a defense of mixed methods, or what Gerring refers to as multimethod research from an empiricist perspective.

Thomas B. Pepinsky (2005) 'From Agents to Outcomes: Simulation in International Relations', *European Journal of International Relations,* 11 (3): 267–394. See this article for a critique of attempts to create real world empirical models through simulation modeling.

Alan Bryman (2008) *Social Research Methods,* 3rd edition. Oxford: Oxford University Press. For a detailed overview of mixed methods research in the broader social sciences see 'Chapter 25: Mixed Methods Research: Combining Quantitative and Qualitative Research', pp. 602–26. Bryman's chapters provide a practical overview of mixed methods research strategies in the wider social sciences.

Notes

1   Inter-methods triangulation is distinct from intra-methods triangulation that was described
    in Chapter 5. For more on triangulation, see Alan Bryman, *Social Research Methods*, 3rd
    edition. Oxford: Oxford University Press, 2008, pp. 611–14.
2   For an example, see Christopher K. Lamont, 'Compliance or Strategic Defiance: The
    Croatian Democratic Union and the International Criminal Tribunal for the former
    Yugoslavia', *Europe-Asia Studies*, vol. 62, no. 10, 2010, pp. 1683–705. This article, while
    addressing a relatively small-*n* sample, examines the question of how to reconcile out-
    comes that suggest a cooperative attitude toward the International Criminal Tribunal for
    the former Yugoslavia, with non-cooperative rhetoric from local elites.
3   For more on these criticisms, see Paul Collier and Nicholas Sambanis (eds) *Understanding
    Civil War: Evidence and Analysis*. Washington, DC: The World Bank, p. x.
4   Hoffman argues that agent-based modelers should focus creating models which function
    as abstract heuristic devices that help explore the fundamental logics of social processes.
    See Matthew J. Hoffman 'Agent-Based Modelling as Qualitative Method', in Audie Klotz
    and Deepa Prakash (eds), *Qualitative Methods in International Relations*. New York:
    Palgrave, pp. 196–9.
5   In relation to processes, see David Rousseau and A. Maurits van der Veen, 'The Emergence
    of a Shared Identity: An Agent Based Computer Simulation of Idea Diffusion', *Journal of
    Conflict Resolution*, vol. 49, no. 5, 2005, pp. 686–712. Also see Hoffmann, 'Agent-Based
    Modeling', in particular see Hoffman's modeling of Finnemore and Sikkink's norm life
    cycle, pp. 191–4. See, for example, Lars-Erik Cederman, 'The Size of Wars: From Billiard
    Balls to Sandpiles', *The American Political Science Review*, vol. 97, no. 1, 2003, pp. 135–50.

8

CASE STUDY RESEARCH IN INTERNATIONAL RELATIONS

Case study research is a commonly used research method in International Relations, but paradoxically it is often viewed within the discipline as either methodologically suspect or underdeveloped (Maoz, 2002; Gerring, 2004: 341). In addition to the case study's widespread usage, there is a general absence of conceptual clarity as to what makes up a good case study. Furthermore, the terms case study research, comparative method and qualitative research are sometimes used almost inter-changeably as case studies become ever more present within the field.[1] Given this absence of conceptual clarity and the stretching of the meaning of case studies to encompass a wide range of methods, it is not surprising that students of IR often find writing good case study essays difficult despite the method's apparent simplicity.

As a student of IR, you may have selected a case study method without even being aware you have begun to make methodological choices. In Chapter 1, it was pointed out that student essays are often focused on events, phenomena or actors that are of interest to students. The events, phenomena, or actors in IR often come into focus in the form of case studies. However, most students wish to contribute more to the field than simply describe these events, phenomena, or actors. They want to contribute to our understanding of the world around us and want their findings to be relevant beyond the single case study at hand. Remember the purpose of your research is to move from generating specific knowledge about your area of interest to general knowledge that impacts wider theory-oriented debates.

Yet, while as a student of IR the purpose of your research is theory oriented, it would be a mistake to label case studies as particularly suited to a single theoretical tradition in IR such as social constructivism. Although case studies have been frequently used to test material and ideational variables in social constructivist research agendas (Klotz, 1995), rational choice theorists (Williams and Zeager, 2004), and IR realists have also relied upon case study methods to advance their own theoretical claims. Yet, at the same time it should be noted that theories that are highly abstract, such as Kenneth Waltz' structural realism (Waltz, 1979), do not easily lend themselves to the types of questions best suited to case study research.[2] Likewise, interpretive researchers have used case studies to highlight the power of discourse or to highlight the use of **narratives**.[3]

This chapter will explore why case studies are better at answering certain kinds of questions to generate a rich and detailed understanding about how certain processes work, but are less well suited toward making grand theoretical claims applicable across cases (George and Bennett, 2005). This is not to say that case studies only provide insights into particular cases. In fact, carefully constructed case studies often provide insights into social processes that inform how we understand or explain IR more broadly. In fact, paradigmatic work that has generated new insights into IR has often come in the form of case studies.

This chapter will provide you with the foundational tools necessary to begin to critically approach the question of case study design to ensure that your case study does more than provide an in-depth description, but contributes to our understanding of the world around us. It will accomplish this through providing you with a practical guide to the case study method and case study design. This chapter will also allow you to avoid some of the major pitfalls of the method that are often encountered by both students and scholars who, through neglecting to critically reflect on case study **methodology**, sometimes in the end fail to accomplish little more than to provide the reader with a thick historic description of a particular event.

Indeed, despite the case study method's wide spread usage, many case studies are written without any serious reflection on the methodological underpinnings of the case study method, **research design**, or an understanding of limitations of the generalizability of findings from case studies. In order to avoid making common mistakes, such as overgeneralization or making comparisons with little **causal inference**, it is important that when you choose to undertake case study research that you ask yourself two fundamental questions: *what do you hope to learn from the case study*? And, *why have you selected your case(s)?* These two questions, while seemingly intuitive, will help you set out your case study research design, which as this chapter will demonstrate, is much more than simply about selecting events, places or actors that are interesting. However, before moving on to questions of research design, types of case studies, and their limitations, it is first necessary to pose the question: what is a case study?

What is a Case Study?

There is a lot of confusion over just what a case study is among both students and scholars of IR. Is it simply a historical study of an event? Does the term describe all *small-n* research? Is it another way of describing qualitative research? These are all questions that have been posed in relation to case studies and led Gerring to observe that term case study has become a 'definitional morass'. In fact, this is how he categorizes the most common assumed meanings of the term:

- Qualitative *small-n* research
- Ethnographic, clinical, participant observation of other 'field' research
- **Process-tracing** research
- Research that investigates the properties of a single case
- Research that investigates a single phenomena, instance or example (Gerring, 2004: 341–2)

It should be pointed out that in relation to the first proposed definition, often scholars have used the terms case studies and **qualitative methods** almost synonymously (Levy, 2002). However, as pointed out in Chapter 5, which introduced qualitative methods in International Relations, qualitative methods encompasses a broad range of methods or techniques that allow researchers to examine contextually rich data on their selected research topic. The second proposed definition, which deals with **field research**, is explored in Chapter 9, but again this is more a method or technique for collecting data than a question of research design. Meanwhile, process-tracing, while an important part of case study research is too narrow to define all case studies and the last two definitions focus on the case itself without broader implications or claims to generalizability.

Key Terms

Process-tracing: an attempt to trace the processes that link possible causes with observed outcomes.

Causal Mechanisms: factors that under certain conditions link causes to effects. For example, when applied to democratic peace theory the focus would be on understanding the factors that explain why democracies did not go to war in particular instances. Causal mechanisms can also be considered causal pathways.

Causal Effects: the outcomes brought about by a posited causal variable. For example, when applied to democratic peace theory a focus on causal effects would have us look at conflict and non-conflict outcomes in crises.

When turning to methodological literature on case studies, students may not find the clarity they were looking for. Scholars have posited numerous definitions of case studies. Are case studies 'histories with a point', as described by

Moses and Knutsen (2012), and, thus potentially limited to detailed historical studies of specific events in recent history? Or are they 'detailed investigations of individual events, actors, and relationships' as defined by Lipson, and thus perhaps also seek to establish causal relationships and engage in explanation? (Lipson, 2005) Or are case studies 'the detailed examination of an aspect of a historical episode to develop or test historical explanations that may be generalizable to other events' as argued by George and Bennett (2005)? Or are case studies, as Gerring (2004: 342) suggests, 'an intensive study of a single unit for the purpose of understanding a large class of (similar) units'.

As IR research essays are both question based and theory oriented, the most appropriate definitions that will guide this chapter are those offered by Gerring, George and Bennett. Both of these definitions focus on a crucial task of case study research, to help us generate knowledge that is relevant beyond the case or cases that are under study in a particular essay. The first two definitions, those offered by Moses and Knutsen and Lipson, while illustrative of many case studies, do not quite capture this larger purpose of the case study in IR, which is about more than simply providing rich description of an event or actor.

Table 8.1   Case Study Definitions

Author(s)	Definition
Moses and Knutsen	histories with a point
Lipson	detailed investigations of individual events, actors, and relationships
George and Bennett	the detailed examination of an aspect of a historical episode to develop or test historical explanations that may be generalizable to other events
Gerring	an intensive study of a single unit for the purpose of understanding a large class of (similar) units

The definitions in Table 8.1 highlight the fact that the task of defining case studies is not a trivial methodological endeavor, but rather crucial to assessing what kinds of questions case studies can answer. In fact, responses to questions such as: 'to what extent can we generalize from a case study?' often hinge on the observation depending on how you define or design your case study. For example, in relation to defining your case study, if case studies are simply in-depth studies of a specific historical event or actor, they are of little use for hypothesis testing or theory development, two pillars of the empirical research tradition. This criticism of the case study is often advanced by those, such as King et al., who design social science inquiry around attempts to generate knowledge to answer bigger questions within the field (King et al., 1994: 211). In short, for those who privilege causal effects over causal mechanisms, there is an implicit assumption that the bigger the universe of cases that is being tested the better.

But, there is no reason to assume causal effects are more valuable in scholarship. Case studies do something large quantitative studies cannot. They can help generate new hypotheses. When you conduct interviews or do archival research often you will encounter new primary data that you did not expect to discover when you started the research process. This may lead you to propose alternative causal explanations for your study that are not present in the literature. Furthermore, beyond causal explanation, case study research can be used to illuminate particular narratives that are not visible to the quantitative researcher. For example, how are founding narratives of statehood reproduced? A response to this question could take a state as a case study and through an examination of school history textbooks provide an illuminating insight into official narratives.

At the same time, debates over how we define case studies should not be taken to assume that 'anything goes' in case study research. Chapter 1 pointed out two major methodological traditions within which you may situate your own work. If your focus is on empirical questions that lend themselves to hypothesis testing or causality then you will want to design your case study in a way that maximizes **causal inference**, or more simply put, your ability to generalize. But, if your objective is to expand our understanding of a particular concept of phenomena, then your case study should be designed around how closely your object of study relates to the phenomena you wish to understand. See for example the different types of questions that can be addressed through case study research in Table 8.2.

Table 8.2   What do you want to do with your case study? (Definitions and examples are drawn from Bennett and Elman, 2007, with some additions by the author)

1. (Historic) Focused study on a historical event: ***What factors explain the outbreak of the US–Mexican War?***

2. (Interpretive) Deepen our understanding of a particular concept or idea: ***What role does Japan's Yasukuni Shrine play in shaping public memory on the Second World War?***

3. (Empirical) Hypothesis testing: ***Why do states comply with international criminal tribunal orders?***

The first question aims to understand the factors that explain the outbreak of a particular armed conflict, the 1848 US–Mexican War. This type of question is more common for those whose focus is on explaining a particular historic event. Note that here the case is the US–Mexican War, and the study is unlikely to produce claims that are relevant to broader theoretical explanations for the causes of inter-state war. In short, the student could, for example, attempt to understand how the concept of Manifest Destiny, or the belief that the United States of America was entitled to expand across the entire territory between the Atlantic and Pacific Oceans, did or did not play a role in the US decision to go war against Mexico.

The second question aims to further our understanding of memory and armed conflict. Scholars and students of IR have increasingly turned to ideas, concepts, and norms in order to understand how international politics are constituted. Where do identities come from? How are threats constructed? How do we choose to remember the past? How are these historic narratives reproduced within societies? This question takes the case of Japan's Yasukuni Shrine to elucidate how historical narratives of war are created and how they are transmitted. The student could rely on either field research to the Shrine to interview those who visit the Shrine or those who work at its adjacent Yushukan museum or the student could rely on primary source news reports of visits to the Shrine by Japanese politicians and statements they make in relation to their visit and how they remember the past. Nevertheless, while this essay would tell the reader a lot about the role of the Yasukuni Shrine as a place of memory and commemoration in transmitting a specific historic narrative on the past, it would tell us very little about other sites of memory, or the causes of conflict or cooperation in East Asia.[4]

The third question constitutes an attempt to test competing hypotheses as to why states comply with international criminal tribunal orders. The question does not ask whether or not states comply, but aims to understand the conditions under which states will comply. It is thus focused on uncovering causal mechanisms that will bring about the causal effect of compliance. However, given this focus, an essay would have to select cases that are appropriate for analysis. You might ask yourself, what countries have complied with International Criminal Court orders? Given not many countries fall within this category, you can easily design a comparative study that will allow you to process trace compliance decisions. More about questions of case selection and case design will be explored shortly with reference to an example drawn from the International Criminal Tribunal for the former Yugoslavia. In addition to case selection, you will need to identify competing hypotheses in the literature that offer conjectures as to why states comply with international court orders. If you have conducted an effective **literature review**, you will begin to encounter competing compliance hypotheses. Indeed, multiple hypotheses are present in IR scholarship as to why states comply with international law. Here are a few examples of hypotheses you could test:

H1: States comply with international criminal tribunal order only when coerced to comply by more powerful states (Power = Compliance)

H2: States comply with international criminal tribunal orders when it is in their interest to comply (Self-interest = Compliance)

H3: States comply with international criminal tribunal orders out of a normative sense of obligation to do so (Norms = Compliance)

The above three hypotheses offer competing causal pathways or processes that lead to a certain outcome. Through a detailed study of primary and secondary source material you can begin to recreate the decision-making processes that led to a particular outcome in your case study that may either serve to affirm or challenge the aforementioned hypothesis.

Case Study Research Questions and Hypotheses

Now that you have been presented with examples of case study research questions try to formulate your own empirical research question that can be answered through a case study. First come up with your question and second try to think of three competing causal explanations (hypotheses) that could explain a particular outcome.

Research Question:

H1:

H2:

H3:

Now that we have defined case studies as in-depth studies of a single unit or historical episode in order to explain or understand other units or episodes, and we have explored different types of case study research questions, we can now turn to the question of case study design. There are many different strategies available for case study design that includes both single and comparative case studies. After selection of your research question, and your identification of testable hypotheses, your case study design will be crucial to the operationalization of your case study research. In particular, for larger projects such as dissertations, comparison can be a useful tool for strengthening the causal inference that you draw from your research. However, as will be noted in the next section, your case design should reflect both your research question and the properties of the theoretical proposition that you are exploring.

Case Study Design

Case study research design can take on different forms depending upon whether the research question posed is empirical or interpretive. However, in both traditions it is imperative for the researcher to first clearly define why the case or cases have been selected. Case selection marks a crucial first step in case study design. Even for single case studies you must justify how and why your case is relevant to the phenomena you seek to observe. Or more simply, why this case is of interest to you.

Indeed, one common criticism of the case study method is that it lends itself to selection bias on the part of the researcher, which in turn makes any attempt at generalizing findings beyond the limited number of cases that were selected by the researcher almost impossible. In fact, Flyvbjerg noted that some researchers have cast doubt on case studies constituting a 'scientific method', because they contain a bias towards verification and a reinforcement of an author's preconceptions on the case (Flyvbjerg, 2006).[5] Of course, examples abound of case studies where researchers discover that their preconceived notions about their case were challenged by the data they collected.

In order to reduce any appearance of selection bias and ensure that you challenge any preconceived beliefs about a particular case you may have it is important that you think critically about your case selection criteria and case study research design. In particular this is of importance if you place yourself in the empirical research tradition and are attempting to understand causality – justifying your case selection will constitute an important part of your case study research. Bennett and Elman (2007) identified five common strategies for case selection: least-likely, most-similar case comparison, least-similar case comparison, combining cross case and over-time comparison, and deviant cases. For interpretive case studies, where you might not be trying to design your case study with an aim to maximize causal inference, you will still need to justify why you have selected your case and how your case is illustrative of a particular cultural practice or discourse which you would like to explore.

The rationale underlying each of these strategies and examples of IR research that utilized each of these strategies are outlined in Table 8.3. Note that each case selection criteria operates with a different approach to deriving causal inferences from the selected case or cases.

The least-likely case study is argued by Gerring to be implicitly the most commonly used strategy for case selection in case study research (2007: 236). Even though scholars at the time do not explicitly state they are undertaking a least-likely case study, it is useful when you are confronted with a theoretical claim that seems to have some explanatory power; such as, for example, social constructivist literature on norms explaining state behavior, and applied to a

Table 8.3   Common Strategies for Case Selection[6]

Selection Criteria	Rationale	Examples
Least-Likely	'Sinatra Inference' – if a theory can make it here, it can make it anywhere. Start from hard cases to demonstrate confidence in a particular theory.	**Evangelista** (1999) – Arms Control during the Cold War and impact of Transnational Actors, **Klotz** (1995) – US sanctions on South Africa during the Cold War. **Katzenstein** (1996) – role of norms in 'hard case' of security.
Most-Similar Case Comparisons	Find cases as similar as possible in all but one independent variable, but differ in their outcomes. Demonstrate difference in independent variable accounts for difference in outcomes.	**Ishiyama** (1993) – impact of electoral systems on party system development in Estonia and Latvia, **James Lee Ray** (1995) – comparative study of the Fashoda Crisis, a crisis between two democracies, and the Spanish–American War, a democracy and an autocracy.
Least-Similar Case Comparisons	Select cases that are different in all but one independent variable, but share dependent variable. Demonstrate shared independent variable accounts for shared outcomes.	**Ember, Ember, and Russett** (1992) – applied democratic peace theory findings from modern states to pre-modern societies and found similar outcome.
Combining Cross Case and Over-Time Comparisons	Combination of Cross Case and 'before and after' comparisons. Allows for greater comparison across fewer cases.	**Walt** (1996) – studied the foreign policy of three states before and after revolutions, **Lamont** (2010) – examined why states cooperated with an international criminal tribunal under authoritarian regimes and after democratic transitions.
Deviant Cases	Disconformatory cases. Select cases that do not conform to theoretical expectations. Can be powerful tool for generating new hypotheses and uncovering new variables.	**Elman** (1997) – examines Finland's war with the United Kingdom as a deviant case within democratic peace theory.

hard case, such as security, which has traditionally been dominated by realism thought (Katzenstein, 1996).

   The next two comparative case selection criteria are drawn from Mill's Method of Agreement and Method of Difference and were further developed by Przeworski and Teune. The most-similar case comparison involves selecting cases that are almost identical in all but one **independent variable**, but do not share the same **dependent variable** and test for whether or not the one divergent independent variable accounts for divergent outcomes. Przeworski and Teune (1970) refer to this research design as Most Similar Systems Design, in which common factors are controlled and the divergent factor is argued to account for a divergent outcome.[7]

The least-similar case comparison involves selecting cases that share only a single independent variable and test for whether or not that variable accounts for a shared dependent variable. Drawing on Mill's Method of Difference, the least-similar case comparison attempts to bring together cases, or countries, that share little in common except a single variable and a particular outcome the researcher seeks to explain (Faure, 1994). Of course, in practice, it is impossible to either find cases that truly only share one independent variable, or in relation to the most-similar method, share all but a single independent variable, and neither can cope with dependent variables that have multiple causes (Bennett, 2004).

Therefore, the most-similar and least-similar case designs should be taken as general case selection criteria. For example, if most-similar case comparisons can include countries in a single region, such as studies of economic growth in the East Asian 'tigers', or democratization in the post-Soviet Baltic states.[8] Least-similar case comparisons can include countries taken from geographically and culturally distinct regions, such as can be found in cross-regional comparative studies of democratization.

The combined cross case and over-time comparison requires you to select multiple cases and compare them across different points in time. This design allows you to generate more cases out of a few. For example, when exploring state cooperation with the International Criminal Tribunal for the former Yugoslavia it was possible to look at Croatia and Serbia under presidential authoritarian regimes (before 2000) and their democratic successors (after 2000). Table 8.4 illustrates how what had initially been a case study with only two cases was expanded to four once an over-time comparison component was added to the case design.

Table 8.4   Cross Case and Over-Time Comparison

	Croatia	Serbia
Presidential Authoritarian	A1	B1
Parliamentary Democracy	A2	B2

Finally, the deviant cases are those cases that do not conform to theoretical expectations, and your task is to understand why. These are cases that are dis-confirmatory or a specific theoretical conjecture. On all accounts they should conform, on the basis of theoretical expectation, but they do not. Take for example the democratic peace theory, which holds that no two democracies will go to war with each other. Miriam Fendius Elman, however, selected a case of two democracies going to war, Finland and the United Kingdom, to establish new findings that suggest we should look more closely at the types of democracies in explaining why democracies do not go to war with other democracies (Elman, 1997).

Now that we have outlined common strategies for case study selection, we can turn to how you will go about linking your observations within the case study to observed outcomes through process-tracing and the identification of causal mechanisms.

Causal Mechanisms and Process-tracing

An important tool that helps you demonstrate causality in your case studies, no matter what case study selection criteria you have applied, is that of process-tracing. Process-tracing is a widely used qualitative analysis technique that helps illuminate how variables interact with each other. Process-tracing can be used to highlight causal mechanisms or causal pathways. Case studies, by definition, provide contextually rich descriptions of how a certain historical episode took place and through a structured case design you can explore in detail the underlying processes that link your independent variables and dependent variables. In short, your aim is to trace the sequence of events that brought about the outcome you are attempting to explain. You accomplish this through field research, such as searching for archival documentation or interviewing participants in the event under examination. In short, process-tracing allows you to also explore what causal mechanisms brought about a particular outcome in your case study, and thus provide deeper explanatory insight for the reader.

For example, in my cross case over-time comparative study of state compliance with orders issued by the International Criminal Tribunal for the former Yugoslavia I explored why states complied or failed to comply with orders issued by the Tribunal. I wanted to understand the motivations and processes that brought about compliance outcomes and see whether causal mechanisms of power, interests, or norms explained state behavior. In order to do this I selected cases where states were ordered to transfer individuals indicted by the Tribunal and explored how states responded to Tribunal requests in the 1990s and the 2000s.

In the above example, the question was focused on states' compliance with ICTY arrest orders, which meant that case selection was made relatively easy. I was able to include all relevant cases as I only looked at those cases where a state was faced with complying with an arrest order issued against one of its own nationals. This excluded, for example, the former Yugoslav state of Slovenia,

Table 8.5 Creating a Cross Case Comparison and Structuring Your Case
Study

International Criminal Justice and the Politics of Compliance (Lamont, 2010)

Aim: Explain variation in state cooperation with the International Criminal Tribunal for the
former Yugoslavia (ICTY) among former Yugoslav states.

Case selection criteria: Former Yugoslav states that were subject to requests to
cooperate from the ICTY.

Cases: Bosnia-Herzegovina, Croatia, Kosovo, Macedonia, Serbia and Montenegro.

Hypotheses tested: State cooperation can be explained by power, self-interest, or
norms?

Problems of Comparison: Bosnia-Herzegovina and Kosovo were under international
administration and had robust international peacekeeping forces deployed on their
territories, which could execute arrest orders on behalf of the Tribunal independently, so
these cases were studied separately.

Findings: Material or norm-based approaches alone cannot explain outcomes, but
rather legal argumentation to rationalize compliance or non-compliance acts in the
1990s either facilitated or complicated later acts of compliance in the 2000s.

---

which while part of the 'former Yugoslavia' was not confronted with such an
order. Second, the period of time that was under study, was relatively easy to
delineate. The Tribunal was established in 1993 and stopped issuing new indictments in 2005 and as of 2008 had security custody of most of those indicted,
so the temporal scope of these case studies was limited to 1993 until 2008.
Finally, as many of these states underwent significant political changes in the
early 2000s, and for the most part the conflict took place in the 1990s, I divided
each study cross time looking at first the 1990s and then the 2000s and highlighted potential **explanatory variables** and processes through looking at both
the domestic and international politics of compliance decisions.

When thinking of your own case study project, you will note the better you
understand your case the easier it will be to justify your case selection. Table 8.5
illustrates how in order to design the aforementioned case study it was important
to know from what period of time the ICTY was issuing indictments and which
states received the preponderance of these indictments. While 161 individuals
were indicted by the Tribunal, and the Tribunal secured custody of all individuals
at-large, one could argue a quantitative study of compliance would tell us a lot
about state cooperation with the Tribunal. However, as noted earlier, a quantitative 'counting' of outcomes, transfers to Tribunal custody, would only give us the

causal effect, that the Tribunal was able to gain custody of war crimes fugitives. But, the focus on arrests only cannot tell us much as to the processes that underlie decisions to cooperate with the Tribunal on the part of states.

Thus, the lesson drawn from the above example is that the most important consideration you should take into account when designing your own case study is making sure your research question 'fits' your research design. If we take the questions drawn from Table 2.1 (see p. 33), you will note that they are all questions that merit a case study response. If for example, we take the question, 'What factors explain the 2011 Tunisian Revolution?' we have a clearly bounded single country case study that seeks to explain a single event. An essay that responds to this question will produce a historically focused explanation of a single event. But, at the same time, the question is limited in the sense that it does not ask about the causes of revolution in general, but rather attempts to understand the causes of the Tunisian Revolution. This is not to say that your response to the research question will not have implications for a broader category of similar cases, for example other Arab Spring revolutions that broke out in the Middle East and North Africa, but rather that the factors that explain the Tunisian Revolution cannot, on the basis of your case study, be assumed to explain other cases of revolution.

Chapter Summary

Case study research is commonly used in IR, but at the same time case study design is not as simple as the method might appear. Case studies are cases with purposes, or the study of a single unit or a small number of units in order to understand other similar units. How we arrive at that understanding of similar units differs between empirical and interpretive research agendas. Indeed, when we think of case study research, we should take into account that there is a broad universe of case studies that extends beyond causal empirically focused studies. Nonetheless, there are common steps to designing case study research. The first step of case study research design is to ask a research question, which either attempts historical explanation, to deepen our understanding of a particular idea or concept, or to test hypotheses or generate new ones. As such, the goal of a good case study is to both produce knowledge about the case, but also provide some cumulative knowledge about the broader universe of cases. The second step is to select your cases and justify your case selection criteria. Your case study design will then inform the operationalization of your case study. Qualitative tools such as process-tracing can also be used to uncover causal mechanisms or you can focus on discourse to highlight narratives or the impact of discourse within a particular case study.

Suggested Further Reading

Andrew L. George and Andrew Bennett (2005) *Case Studies and Theory Development in the Social Sciences.* Cambridge, MA: MIT Press. This book provides an important overview of case study design in the social sciences and will be of interest to primarily postgraduate students.

John Gerring (2004) 'What Is a Case Study and What Is It Good for?' *American Political Science Review,* 98 (2): 341–54. This article provides a concise overview of case study research. It begins by defining case study research before presenting some strengths associated with case study research designs.

Jack S. Levy (2002) 'Qualitative Methods in International Relations', in Frank P. Harvey and Michael Brecher (eds), *Evaluating Methodology in International Studies.* Ann Arbor, MI: University of Michigan Press, pp. 131–60. This chapter, while making reference to Qualitative Methods in its title, provides examples of different case study designs used in IR.

Charles Lipson (2005) 'Using Case Studies Effectively', in *How to Write a BA Thesis: A Practical Guide from Your First Ideas to Your Finished Paper.* Chicago, IL: University of Chicago Press, pp. 99–109. This chapter provides a basic introduction to case study research design for undergraduate papers.

Notes

1   Levy's chapter on qualitative methods in *Evaluating Methodology in International Studies* (2002) is focused more on the case study method than qualitative methods more broadly. Levy also argues 'nearly all case studies involve comparisons' (p. 133). Jack S. Levy, 'Qualitative Methods in International Relations', in *Evaluating Methodology in International Studies*, edited by Frank P. Harvey and Michael Brecher. Ann Arbor, MI: University of Michigan Press, 2002, pp. 131–60.

2   In response to Colin Elman, who noted neo-realism's inability to predict foreign policy in 'Horses for Courses: Why Not Neorealist Theories of Foreign Policy?' *Security Studies*, vol. 6, no. 1, 1996, pp. 7–53. Waltz makes this distinction in arguing neo-realist theory cannot explain foreign policies of individual states. Waltz notes 'theories are sparse in formulation and beautifully simple. Reality is complex and often ugly.' Kenneth Waltz, 'International Politics is not a Foreign Policy', *Security Studies*, vol. 6, no. 1, 1996, p. 56. Case study, through a focus on context specific knowledge can be seen more as a reflection of 'reality' in scholarship by bringing in numerous variables and generating new hypotheses.

3   Charlotte Epstein, *The Power of Words in International Relations: Birth of Anti-Whaling Discourse.* Cambridge, MA: MIT Press, 2008. Epstein studies the Whaling Commission to highlight the power of discourse in changing perceptions, and state responses to, the practice of whaling. Another example is Kevin C. Dunn, *Imagining the Congo: The International Relations of Identity.* Houndsmills, Basingstoke: Palgrave Macmillan, 2003.

4   Of course this is not to minimize how insights into specific examples of cultural practices of commemoration and narratives assist in understanding how these processes work and therefore could be of potential relevance to other cases.

5 Flyvbjerg also points out that often case study researchers have their preconceived notions and biases challenged during the research process.
6 Definitions and examples that are presented in Table 8.3 are drawn from Bennett and Elman (2007) with some additions provided by the author.
7 Also see Andrew Murray Faure, 'Some Methodological Problems in Comparative Politics', *Journal of Theoretical Politics*, vol. 6, no. 3, 1994, pp. 307–22.
8 For an example of the latter See John T. Ishiyama, 'Founding Elections and the Development of Transitional Parties: The Cases of Estonia and Latvia, 1990–1992', *Communist and Post-Communist Studies*, vol. 26, no. 3, 1993, pp. 277–99. Ishiyama explores the impact of electoral systems on party system development in Estonia and Latvia, two states that shared a common experience of being annexed by the USSR in 1940 and gaining independence following the collapse of the Soviet Union.

9

FIELD RESEARCH IN INTERNATIONAL RELATIONS

Field research has assumed an increasingly important role in IR research agendas over the last two decades. The end of the Cold War and the move away from state-centric approaches to explain and understand international politics necessitated a deeper understanding of a wide range of social actors that include local communities, non-governmental organizations, non-state armed groups, and individuals. Furthermore, the popularization of case study methods in IR has brought about an increased focus on process-tracing, **causal mechanisms,** and historical explanations, which require in-depth field research in order to unearth the contextually rich primary source material needed to shed light on complex social processes.

While field research has long been at the core of ethnographic, anthropological, and even comparative politics research methods, IR theory's high level of abstraction and state-centricity has, in the past, left subaltern discourses, the role of non-state actors or decision-making processes within states and international organizations out of focus for students and scholars within the discipline. As such, despite the proliferation of research agendas that seek to understand international organized crime (Lampe, 2012), trafficking (Kupatadze, 2010), terrorist finance (Wittig, 2011), human rights activism (Kurze and Vukusic, 2013), among other fieldwork intensive agendas, IR methods training has been slow to provide students guidance as to the specific challenges they are likely to face when attempting to operationalize core qualitative or quantitative data collection techniques such as surveys, questionnaires, or **interviews,** in sometimes difficult research environments (Mertus, 2009: 1).

This chapter will explore a broad range of dilemmas and challenges faced by researchers when going out into the field. Any time you interact with people during the course of your research, you will always encounter unexpected challenges and ethical dilemmas. Following the preparatory steps outlined here can help you mitigate the negative consequences of these unexpected challenges; however, you will quickly learn that when planning and carrying out interviews, focus groups, or other forms of research that require you to interact with people in order to collect new data, you will have to be flexible and accommodating toward those who have chosen to participate in your research project.

Despite the fact most research projects require a substantial amount of time spent outside of the university, or the office, to gather primary data, students often embark on field research with very little or no prior training as to what to expect and the challenges they are likely to face during their fieldwork (ibid.). Table 9.1 highlights some of the common practical, ethical and sometimes security dilemmas that you might encounter in relation to both field access and field research operationalization.

Table 9.1 Field Research – Practical, Ethical and Security Considerations

Practical	Ethical	Security
• What questions should I ask? What are the gaps in knowledge? • Who do I need to talk to? • How do I get access to them? • Do I need official permission to conduct research at my field site? (Visa, official permission to conduct research in a particular jurisdiction)	• Have I secured (or do I need) ethical approval from my home institution? • Will my research involve the participation of vulnerable adults or children? • Will I secure the informed consent of all research participants? • What steps will I take to protect the anonymity of research participants? • Does my research have the potential to result in harm to research participants?	• Is my field site in an insecure environment? • What does my home country's Embassy advise in relation to travel to my field research site? • Is my field site in a conflict or post-conflict environment? • How am I, and my research project, likely to be perceived by those on site?

Before continuing with the process of planning your field research you should take a minute to answer all the questions provided in Table 9.1. Not only should you ensure that your field research is well planned in terms of practical matters, and that you have secured ethical permission from your own institution's relevant ethical review board, but you should also be aware of how your research is likely to be perceived within the community where you will carry out your research. Whether that community is a neighborhood close to home or a highly politicized conflict environment, you should be aware that you, as a researcher, are not likely to be perceived as neutral.

The types of research questions posed by students studying international politics, such as those focused on understanding the causes of conflict, accountability for mass atrocity, or contentious politics under authoritarian regimes, means that often our research interests take us to parts of the world that are politically unsettled. For example, Norman notes, in an edited volume dedicated to the topic of 'Surviving Field Research', some of the intense fears and security concerns with which she was confronted when carrying out fieldwork in the Palestinian territories:

> Participatory methods involving focus groups or large gatherings may reflect researchers' aim of establishing trust through inclusive meetings … However such gatherings may present a high-risk situation in active conflict zones in which such assemblies are directly targeted, or in latent conflict zones in which such congregations may be infiltrated by plants or spies. (Norman, 2009: 79)

Norman's experience highlights the difficult nexus between research methods and the complex realities of conducting field research. It also foreshadows how important perceptions are and how easily motives can be questioned. In some cases we must take into account the prospect of violence against participants in our research, and attempts by actors on the ground to manipulate our research findings, or intimidate other participants. In short, more often then not, the realities of the field do not conform to textbook descriptions of how to conduct field research.[1]

In order to remedy this general lack of field research methods training for researchers in IR, the following sections will provide a practical guide to help you plan your own field research and prepare you for field research dilemmas you might encounter in the field. This will be done with examples of how researchers confronted a number of challenges during the course of field research in diverse fieldwork settings. The question of why field research is often a necessary component of the research process will be briefly revisited before a short definition of field research is provided. Then the next section, which focuses on questions of access and methods will turn to the question of how to carry out field research and challenges that you may encounter in trying to reach out to research participants. This will be followed by a discussion of harm, consent and transparency in fieldwork. Finally, throughout the chapter you will find insights from a wide range of geographic and cultural contexts, such as experiences and examples of field research carried out in the former Yugoslavia, Palestine and Georgia, Japan, and Libya.

Why Field Research?

As students of IR, our contribution to existing scholarship requires us to bring to the table new knowledge about the world around us. For a growing number of IR research agendas, this task simply cannot be done through traditional desk-based research from your home institution or organization. A number of questions require us to depart from existing assumptions in the literature and attempt to gather new data about rapidly changing phenomena. How do internal armed conflicts impact civilian populations? What are the causes of political violence? How effective are policies aimed at promoting post-conflict reconciliation? Why are some territories well governed, while others are not? What does the decision-making process look like within a particular state, or international organization? Finding responses to these questions will likely require you to come up with a strategy to gather new primary data and make use of the qualitative or quantitative data collection techniques noted in Chapters 5 and 6.

Secondary scholarly sources are often of limited utility and existing datasets often do not contain the type of detailed contextual information necessary to answer research questions posed within IR. For a PhD researcher, it is not common for the type of topic-specific data we need to explore our research question to have already been collected in the form of surveys or questionnaires, so we must begin the think about designing our own data collection strategies and think about ways to operationalize these strategies during the course of our field research. Often existing data is incomplete or unreliable and, in some cases, it might not even exist all. Even **official documents** or statistics, can be highly problematic as noted by Kukhiandze et al. Indeed, when Kukhiandze et al. embarked on their study of cross-border smuggling in Abkhazia and Tskhinvali, they observed:

> No branch of the Georgian government has enough statistical or analytical data on the socio-economic situation in the breakaway republics. The statistical agencies of the self-proclaimed republics also do not possess exact information on economic activities in their region. (Kukhiandze et al., 2004: 8)

Another researcher, also working in the Caucasus, encountered a similar challenge. While researching terrorist finance along the Georgia–Chechnya border, Wittig pointed out:

> Generally speaking, conducting empirical research of terrorist financing is very difficult, given that primary documentary evidence is acutely rare, and interviewing those involved or suspected to be involved in financing terrorist actors are, unsurprisingly, reluctant to speak to researchers. (Wittig, 2009: 249)

Wittig's quote is illustrative of the dual challenge that often faces researchers: the lack of existing primary data and the reluctance of interlocutors to participate in research. Strategies to address the latter challenge will be dealt with shortly; however, in relation to an absence of existing data, when I conducted research on state cooperation with international criminal tribunal orders, from 2005 until 2008, information on arrests and transfers of war crimes suspects to

International Criminal Tribunal for the former Yugoslavia custody was readily available, but there was almost no information on the underlying motivations and processes that led states to comply or not comply with these arrest and transfer orders (Lamont, 2010). In this case the overall data on numbers of transfers was reliable; however, the data itself provided few clues as to the process that led to transfers actually taking place. Furthermore, I was faced with the challenge of locating research participants who were knowledgeable of these motivations and would be willing to talk to a researcher about them.

Beyond the urgent need to access accurate and reliable data, there is also the fact that field research can perform an important function through the process of bringing new findings and insights into scholarly debates. In some cases this may result in researchers discovering important new insights that may help better understand the impact of particular policy decisions, or it could bring forward previously overlooked subaltern discourses. Many contributions from fieldwork intensive research offer either interpretive or empirical paradigmatic insights that would be impossible to produce without having in-depth knowledge of field sites. Take for example Clifford Geertz's work on Balinese cockfights (Geertz, 1972). In sum, more often than not, the types of research questions that are of interest to us cannot be answered without some attempt to gather new data on the topic at hand. Thus, field research is not just the domain of area studies scholars or ethnographers, but is increasingly a core component of IR research.

Field Research: What is it?

Field research is the process of primary data collection, either through accessing primary sources documents, or through interviews, participant observation, questionnaires, surveys or other methods aimed at eliciting responses from human subjects. In relation to attempts to access new primary data through interactions with human subjects, field research often relies on established qualitative or quantitative data collection techniques. All of these techniques require the researcher to secure the informed consent of participants.[2] Collecting information through deceit or without the consent of participants is unethical and can result in severe reputational and professional damage to the researcher, and may also harm the unknowing participant.[3]

Table 9.2 outlines the many different field research activities that are commonly used by IR researchers. While much of this chapter will deal with challenges that you are likely to face when carrying out these activities in difficult environments outside the borders of your home country, field research does not only refer to research that requires you to travel to another country or region. Depending on your research question, all of the field research activities noted in Table 9.2 can also occur closer to home. Field research is not a reference to a specific geographic location but simply describes the broad range of activities

Table 9.2 Field Research Activities

Field Research Activities	Examples
Archival Research – Primary Source Documents	• Personal documents: diaries, letters, correspondences, autobiographies
	• Official (state) documents: meeting records, legislative debates, legislation, executive orders, official statistics, records, etc.
	• Official (corporate/business) documents
	• Official (other) documents: non-state armed groups, political party archives
Participant Observation	• Overt/Covert observation
Interviews	• Structured, semi-structured, non-structured, one-on-one conversation
Focus Groups	• Group interview
Questionnaires & Surveys	• Structured interviews
	• Telephone surveys
	• Self-completion questionnaires

carried out with the aim of gathering primary data through human subjects or archival documents.

However, whether you have come to the conclusion that you will need to retrieve archival documents or you need to ask your classmates to fill out a questionnaire, you quickly encounter the first major hurdle to carrying out your field research, that of access. The problem of access is common to all techniques aimed at gathering primary data. In some instances you will be confronted with the task of securing the permission of an archivist to access official documents. In other cases, you will need to secure permission to interview, or distribute questionnaires to, employees of an international organization. Or, you might need to convince your classmates that completing your survey is a good use of their time.

None of the examples from the preceding paragraph are necessarily an easy task and access certainly cannot be taken for granted. Often getting access to individuals for interviews, or to official documents, requires the researcher to build some form of trust relationship with those working with, or for, an organization or group that is under study.[4] How to do this, and the challenges you might encounter, will be discussed in the next section.

Field Research: Access and Methods

One of the first dilemmas that confront students who are about to embark on field research is the challenge of access. The denial of access can result in your fieldwork project quickly unraveling, and will require you to quickly adapt and search for new sources of information. In order to effectively negotiate access you will first need to know with whom you want to talk. This requires both a clear idea of the kind of primary data you wish to gather and a detailed knowledge of the group, organization, or institution with which you will be conducting your fieldwork.

In some cases, you might find securing an affiliation with an organization, whether academic, governmental, or non-governmental, in your chosen site of fieldwork as an effective tool to gain access to your field site. This is not uncommon as many students pursue internships, or hold jobs or research fellowships, as part of their fieldwork, or alongside their fieldwork. In some cultural contexts, such as Japan, securing a local academic or think tank affiliation can prove essential to gaining the trust of potential fieldwork participants (Smith, 2003). However, you should be aware of any potential ethical conflicts of interest that may arise if you are professionally affiliated with a non-governmental organization or a government while conducting your field research. First, remember that potential research participants are likely to perceive you as being a representative of your organization and not an individual researcher, so you should consider whether or not your affiliation might give potential research participants the impression that they do not have a choice as to whether or not they can choose not to participate. Often in conflict environments and fragile states, your affiliation could even put you in a privileged power relationship over potential research participants. If this is the case you might want to reconsider conducting your fieldwork while affiliated with your host organization.

Knowing Who to Ask and What to Ask

Often one of the first points of contact when approaching an international organization, large NGO, foreign ministry, or political party is an official spokesperson. While a spokesperson can be helpful in providing you with an overview of a particular organization and its official positions on issues, for process-tracing research you will want to talk to those who are, or were, in decision-making roles within a particular organization. Sometimes interviews with spokespersons can prove disappointing and may leave you feeling like you gained little more knowledge than was already publicly available on an organization's website.

To move beyond spokespersons, you will need both a good knowledge of those working within the organization at hand and its internal structure. The more background research you have done on your fieldwork site before you embark on your attempt to gain access the better. For example, if you are researching the International Criminal Tribunal for the former Yugoslavia, it is essential to understand the Tribunal is divided into distinct sections: the Office of the Prosecutor, the Registry, and the Judicial Chambers.[5] Asking someone from Registry about prosecutorial decisions will either elicit a response that might not be informed or suggest to your interview subject a lack of familiarity with the Tribunal on the part of the researcher.[6]

Once you have established with *whom* you need to talk, you can begin reaching out to potential interview subjects. One thing to always keep in mind when making interview requests is that your interview subjects are likely very busy and may need to be convinced as to why participating in your research project is a good use of their time. While access to some interview subjects can be difficult even for an established scholar, you can start by asking your thesis or dissertation supervisor as to whether or not they can provide assistance in providing introductions to individuals working in relevant international organizations, foreign ministries, NGOs, academic institutions, or living in or near the site of your proposed field research.

Another access strategy is that of **snowball sampling**, or relying on the first individuals you meet in the field to introduce you to other potential interview subjects, who will in turn introduce you to others (Jacobsen and Landau, 2003: 195–6). This effectively allows you to quickly penetrate particular peer groups or professional communities. While snowball sampling is a common field research strategy, there are methodological drawbacks to such an approach that you should be aware of. In particular, snowball sampling can have the effect of locking you into a particular social or professional network. Depending on your research project, this can have the effect of generating sample bias, particularly if the group at the focus of your study is larger than the sub-group which you have accessed through snowball sampling (p. 196).

Snowball sampling, while commonly used as a strategy for gaining access to field research participants, thus includes significant risks for the researcher in terms of data validity. In some cases, an internal risk is generated because snowballing sampling relies on a network of peers or friends. Therefore, you can expect respondents to communicate with each other about your research questions and their responses to your questions. Moreover, sometimes just being aware of the person who passed you on to them can change how you are perceived (ibid.). There is also an additional risk assumed by the researcher and that is attempting to generalize from data gathered by snowball sampling. Indeed, we should always keep in mind that data gathered through this technique only captures a snapshot of the activities and practices of a particular group or social network.[7]

Thus snowball sampling, while a highly effective means of gaining access to a particular network within a short period of time, can very easily result in significant limitations on the data gathered. Take for example a field research project on civil society in a post-conflict country. Let us assume you travel to the site of your research, and your first contact is a member of a large human rights NGO, *NGO A*. This contact introduces you to colleagues both within *NGO A* and colleagues from other NGOs that *NGO A* routinely works with: *NGO B*, *NGO C*, and *NGO D.* You then return from the field with a wealth of information on NGOs A, B, C, and D. However, when you turn to writing about your research findings, you might make conclusions about civil society more broadly in your country of study only to later discover that your conclusions failed to take into account the perspectives of other NGOs, E, F, and G, which held opposing political views to the NGO network that you studied and therefore did not work with that particular community of NGOs.

While the sample bias that arises above is almost unavoidable, you can guard against accusations of misrepresentation by acknowledging how you gained access to your particular NGO community and the limited number of NGO activists interviewed. It is important that you acknowledge the limitations of your data collection technique by not suggesting your findings speak for civil society as a whole within the country where you carried out your fieldwork. Indeed, snowball sampling is a common technique for researchers because it is a powerful means of gaining access to a wider community of potential research participants with relatively little cost in terms of time. Due to the nature of most fieldwork, which imposes limitations on the researcher it terms of cost and time, snowball sampling may prove to be the best way to gain access, even taking to account the drawbacks mentioned above.

In addition, the more background research on your topic that you conduct before setting out on field research, the more you will be aware of the potential limitations of snowball sampling. In conflict and post-conflict settings, being too closely identified with a particular group may not only narrow your findings, but close off access to other groups. Outside of a conflict setting, affiliations can also impact access. Knowledge of how a local think tank is perceived domestically or the reputation of a local non-governmental organization can help you navigate obstacles related to gaining access and trust at your field site. Knowing with whom you are talking and how they are perceived on the ground is of utmost importance.

In sum, at the outset of the field research process it is extremely important that you first have a clear idea of what kind of data you are looking for, and what kinds of field research activities you will be able to carry out. You also need to have acquired a familiarity with either the geographic, cultural and political setting in which your field research will take place, or the organization that you are approaching. While the contents of interviews or archival documents may surprise you once you are in the field, you should have a clear idea of the types of questions you intend to ask of the documents you aim to access before you embark on the field research process.

Field Research: Harm, Consent, and Transparency

The most common field research data collection technique that involves human subjects in International Relations is the interview.[8] Once you know who you are going to interview and what type of interview you will carry out (structured, semi-structured, or non-structured) (Leech, 2002),[9] it is important that you gain the trust of your interview subjects, and later not to betray their trust. In relation to gaining the trust of interviewees, there are two things you should do before beginning your interviews. The first is to write a short description of your research, or **Research Summary**, which is understandable and accessible to your research subjects. In some cases this will be a professional community with a clear knowledge of your research topic, and in others you will need to take into account that readers of your research summary may be a non-specialist audience. If necessary you should translate this document into the native language of those who will be participating in your research.

Your Research Summary should include the following information:

- A brief summary of your research project
- Your institutional or professional affiliation
- Who is funding your research
- How you will use the findings (in published research?)

This research summary can be provided in advance of your interviews via email, particularly if you are contacting potential interview participants through this medium. Otherwise, you should schedule some time at the beginning of your interview to allow the interview participant to read your research summary and ask you questions about the purpose of your research and how the findings are likely to be used.

The second important document you should prepare before departure is your **Interview Consent Form**. An Interview Consent Form carries out two important functions. First, it allows for you to secure, and document, the informed consent of all participants in your field research. Informed consent is necessary because participation in a research project may entail risks for your participants. You should always keep in mind that risks should not always be thought of in physical bodily harm terms. Risks to participants can also be thought of in terms of either harmed prospects for career advancement or the loss of status within a community. You must not attempt to collect primary data from someone for research purposes without informing them that you intend to use their words in your academic or published writing.

Interview Consent Forms generally offer interview participants the option of anonymity; however, the promise of anonymity can also harm our ability to present our research findings to colleagues in a transparent manner. For example, when attempting to process-trace a decision-making process, it makes a difference if you were able to speak with the relevant decision-maker on a given issue. However, if you were able to interview this decision-maker, but you are unable to reference this person by name, the strength and validity of your findings may appear weaker. In order to still provide maximum transparency in the research process, and cope with the weakening of our arguments presented in published research when interview subjects decline to be identified by name, Interview Consent Forms often provide participants with a sliding scale of anonymity. Below is an example of a menu of choices that can be offered to interview participants.

- Consent to the use of name, position, and affiliation in published research (example: John Smith, Chief Prosecutor, International Criminal Tribunal A)
- Consent to the use of only my position and affiliation in published research (example: Chief Prosecutor, International Criminal Tribunal A)
- Consent to the use of only my affiliation in published research (example: an official of International Criminal Tribunal A)
- I do not consent to either the use of my name or affiliation in published research (example: a confidential informant)

From the perspective of the researcher, we would prefer to be able to secure the consent of our interview subjects to use their names, positions, and affiliations in our research; however, due to the nature of our research, and our desire to elicit insights that might cut against, or provide more information that what is provided in the public articulations of an organization, often this is not possible. Once an interview subject has requested a certain degree of anonymity it is your responsibility to ensure their anonymity is not breached.

Field Research in a Foreign Country?

Make sure you have secured the appropriate visa to conduct field research in the country in which you will be carrying out your fieldwork. Host institutions can assist with this. In some cases, you will also need an official letter from a relevant government ministry confirming that your research project has been approved and you have permission to carry out your research.

Consent Forms are not just required for interviews, but they are also required for other forms of participatory research such as the recording of oral histories and focus groups. It is important that you not only secure the consent of all participants but that your participants understand what they are consenting to.[10] Take, for example, the experience of an NGO researcher who was tasked with recording oral histories from elderly residents of a remote area in the former Yugoslavia. The oral histories were being recorded and were to be made available through a web-based digital library. Some elderly respondents were unsure what the Internet was, and this was thus explained to participants as 'like being on a television that you could watch at any time.'[11]

Furthermore, you might find yourself in a situation that during the process of the collection of interviews or oral histories, participants reveal their own participation in a criminal offense. This is particularly a concern when doing research in conflict or post-conflict areas, or researching topics such as human or drug trafficking, or prostitution. Different jurisdictions have different legal requirements as to the obligations of researchers under national law if they come into possession of evidence that a crime has been committed.[12] For example, in Croatia, if an interviewee confesses to participation in a war crime during an interview or oral history, national law requires the researcher to inform the public prosecutor's office.

In some instances, you might find it difficult to secure the written informed consent of participants in a research project. Sometimes, this is for cultural reasons. In many cultural contexts you will find potential research participants responding uncomfortably to a request to sign a written document prior to an interview. For example, Bestor at al. point out in their edited volume *Doing Fieldwork in Japan*, that:

> In a society where the careful cultivation of interpersonal trust is given far more weight than formal contacts and where written contracts often are viewed with distrust, there are many research situations in which American-style legalistic consent requirements would not only be culturally unfamiliar, but would call into question the researcher's cultural understanding and trustworthiness. (Bestor et al., 2003: 14)

In other instances, when researchers are seeking to access individuals involved in illicit activities, the application of traditional methods may be simply impossible. Take, for example, the dilemma described in the paragraph below faced by a team of researchers who where investigating smuggling through Abkhazia and Tskhinvali.

Kukhiandze et al. were faced with a problem that there was almost no reliable official primary documents or statistics available in relation to Abkhazia and South Ossetia and that official representatives from the Georgian Government were either unable or unwilling to provide reliable information through interviews (Kukhiandze et al., 2004: 8). The result was that their research team took the unconventional path of concealing their role as researchers to convince participants in their research that the researchers were actually smugglers. This strategy allowed the researchers to gain an insight into this particular illicit activity that could not have been achieved through conventional fieldwork practices. While you may encounter such examples of risky fieldwork during the course of your research, these unconventional research methods that involve deceit and concealment are unlikely to be approved through your home institution for the purposes of student research because they put the researcher at risk from both participants involved in illicit activities and the state authorities policing them.

Chapter Summary

At this point it should be apparent that field research includes a broad range of activities aimed at accessing new primary data. The most common in International Relations are archival research and interview-based research. Focus groups and participant observation are less common, in particular because of the high cost of carrying out focus groups. Meanwhile, participant observation is a more common ethnographic field research technique. Nevertheless, the common denominator for all forms of research that require you to interact with human subjects is the need to secure the informed consent of your fieldwork participants. In many academic settings, you will also be asked to secure formal institutional approval through an ethics committee for your fieldwork. While research ethics, and the principle of do no harm was discussed in Chapter 3, in the context of field research it is important to recall that ethics review boards or committees will evaluate your project with a particular aim to determine whether you have taken measures to protect your research participants from harm, and whether or not your research involves vulnerable adults and children, and if so, what training or qualifications you might have to work with these groups.

A final observation that was noted in the introduction is that often flexibility on the part of the researcher is the key to fieldwork success. You will often encounter many obstacles to accessing the field. In some cases once you arrive at your field site you will have to rethink your data collection methods. For example, you might find that you are unable to collect survey data and instead will have to rely on interviews to collect data on your research topic. Other obstacles might not relate to methods, but more to challenges in accessing your research subjects on the ground. For example, my fieldwork in Libya, which was conducted during 2013, was complicated even before my arrival by the difficult and time-consuming process of securing a Libyan visa. Once in Libya, my movement was limited due to a dynamic security environment; however, I was still able to conduct interviews. In order to access interview subjects I relied on snowball sampling to talk to a wide range of Libyan and international workers in the field of transitional justice. Often, interview times and locations would change at the last minute, such as a planned meeting with the Free Media Center in Tripoli, or meetings with officials from the Libyan Ministry for Families of Martyrs and Missing Persons which were held in a newly opened Ministry building. Even in difficult security environments, researchers can maintain both personal safety and access to interview participants by simply keeping informed of changing developments and communicating with local interlocutors.

In conclusion, field research is a challenging activity that will confront you with a number of unexpected dilemmas and obstacles. Often your fieldwork is the crucial component of a research process that will determine the success or failure of a thesis or dissertation project. Failure to collect new or relevant data in the field has resulted in many researchers abandoning their theses or dissertations; however, as this chapter has noted, although field research can be challenging, there is no reason why, even in the most difficult circumstances, you should not be able to carry out your fieldwork.

Suggested Further Reading

Chandra Lekha Sriram, John C. King, Julia A. Mertus, Olga Martin-Ortega and Johanna Herman (eds) (2009) *Surviving Field Research: Working in Violent and Difficult Situations*. New York: Routledge. This edited volume provides a rich array of contributions in which authors discuss their own personal experiences conducting fieldwork in authoritarian, conflict, or post-conflict environments. It is required reading for anyone considering field research in fragile or conflict-affected states.

Karen Jacobsen and Lauren B. Landau (2003) 'The Dual Imperative of Refugee Research: Some Methodological and Ethical Considerations in Social Science Research and Forced Migration', *Disasters*, 27 (3): 195–96. This article is a helpful introduction to many of the practical and ethical dilemmas faced by researchers conducing fieldwork with vulnerable population groups.

Theodore C. Bestor, Patricia G. Steinhoff and Victoria Lyon Bestor (eds) (2003) *Doing Fieldwork in Japan*. Honolulu: University of Hawaii Press. While this text may appear focused on challenges faced by researchers conducting fieldwork in Japan, this collection of essays contains valuable insights into common challenges faced by researchers working in cultural and linguistic contexts that vary substantially from home.

Notes

1   There are a wide range of texts that offer guidance on the technical side of how to carry out field research, such as Alan Bryman, *Social Research Methods*, 3rd edition. Oxford: Oxford University Press, 2008. One of the rare books that directly address some of the challenges addressed in this chapter is Chandra Lekha Sriram, John C. King, Julie A. Mertus, Olga Martin-Ortega and Johanna Herman (eds) *Surviving Field Research: Working in Violent and Difficult Situations*. New York: Routledge, 2009.

2   It will be noted shortly that informed consent can be both written or oral.

3   However, this is not to say that the practice does not exist in the field. As will be pointed out later, Kukhianidze et al. argued that posing as smugglers and disguising their role as researchers was necessary in order to gather information from smugglers on their activities. For more on research ethics see Chapter 3.

4   For more on trust and fieldwork see Julie M. Norman, 'Got Trust? The Challenges of Gaining Access in Conflict Zones', in *Surviving Field Research: Working in Violent and Difficult Situations*, edited by Chandra Lekha Sriram, John C. King, Julie A. Mertus, Olga Martin-Ortega and Johanna Herman. New York: Routledge, 2009.

5   'Organizational Chart', International Criminal Tribunal for the former Yugoslavia, available at www.icty.org/sid/326 (last accessed 9 February 2014).

6　Employees of the Tribunal have commonly lamented that they are often approached by researchers who have little or no understanding of how the Tribunal works, and in these situations they are unable to provide the researcher with responses to questions posed during an interview. This sentiment was communicated during discussions with ICTY staff during fieldwork conducted in The Hague in 2007.

7　Also see Norman's discussion of both the utility and limitations of snowball sampling in the context of field research in Palestine. Norman, 'Got Trust?', pp. 79–80.

8　For different types of interviews and strategies for conducting interviews see Chapter 5.

9　Also see Chapter 5.

10　Fieldwork participants should always know that they can stop participating in your fieldwork at any time. Consent Forms do not constitute a contractual obligation to participate in your research. Fieldwork participants should not be made to feel like they are obligated to continue participating in something they may have initially consented to, but decided at a later stage they no longer wished to participate.

11　Interview with Tanja Petrovic, a participant in the Croatian NGO *Documenta*'s Oral History project, June 28, 2013.

12　In the United Kingdom there is no obligation to report evidence of a crime that might be disclosed to a researcher unless it is the subject of an investigation. See Louise Corti, Annette Day and Gill Backhouse, 'Confidentiality and Informed Consent: Issues for Consideration in the Preservation and Provision of Access to Qualitative Data Archives', *Forum: Qualitative Social Research*, vol. 1, no. 2, 2000.

10
WRITING UP YOUR RESEARCH

The final chapter of this textbook will now turn to the writing-up process. Once you have completed your data collection and analysis, you will move on to what are the final stages of your research project, writing up and proofreading. Thus far, the chapters of this book guided you through almost all stages of the research process, from coming up with your research question, to **research design**, to data collection and data analysis. At the end of this process you will be confronted with taking all that knowledge you have acquired through your research and communicating it effectively in the form of an academic essay, thesis or dissertation.

Before you begin writing up, it is important to keep in mind that the research process cannot always be neatly subdivided into constituent parts. While the chapter structure of this textbook provides you with a comprehensive guide to the research process, you should keep in mind that research and writing is not always a step-by-step process in which you progress from one step to another without looking back. It is in fact quite the opposite. Often you will find yourself moving back and forth between data collection, data analysis, and writing as you stumble upon gaps in your work. If you find yourself doing this, there is no need to worry. Indeed, if you find yourself needing to go back and consult your data once again, or double check your analysis, you will discover that you will always find a way to improve your work. Editing and proofreading is just as important to your research as collecting and analyzing your data in the first place. In short, academic writing is a continuous process that requires us to constantly revise our work. Academic writing, like the social phenomena that we study, is not a linear process that guides us to a predetermined end point. Even at the stage of writing up, we should keep an open mind as to potential gaps in our argument that may require us to take a closer look at our data once again.

Academic Writing: The Building Blocks of Your Research Paper

Whether you are writing a short essay, an undergraduate or master's thesis, a PhD, or another piece of academic writing, IR research papers are structured around core components that are common to almost all academic work across the social sciences. This section will provide you with the core components of an IR research paper. You might want to think of them as building blocks that when put together result in a cogently argued research paper.

The core components of an IR research essay, dissertation, or thesis are provided in Table 10.1.[1]

Table 10.1   The Building Blocks of Academic Writing

Abstract
Introduction
Literature Review
Methodology
Data Analysis
Conclusion
Bibliography/References

Internally, each of these parts of your essay, with the exception of the **abstract** and bibliography/references, should also include an introduction, body section, and conclusions. They should also nicely transition into each other. The length of each section, and whether or not each section will constitute a heading or subheading within an essay or its own chapter will depend on the length of your work.

You should always consult your research supervisor for institutional guidelines on the structure that you will be asked to follow. The following sections of this chapter will now present the core features of each of the aforementioned components in greater detail. Here we will also explore an additional section, the abstract, which might not be required of you for most research essays, but is an essential component of scholarly journal articles and longer dissertations.

Abstract

An abstract is a one-paragraph summary of your research provided at the beginning of a scholarly journal article or dissertation. It justifies the relevance of the work, provides the research question, a brief explanation of the **methodology** or methods used, and key findings. For an example of an abstract, you can turn to any scholarly journal in the field of International Relations. While the abstract appears first in academic papers, journal article abstracts are almost always written after the paper has been completed so as to effectively communicate the paper's main argument. Sometimes, students and scholars will need to write their abstract before they write their paper. This is most common when providing abstracts for conference papers, which at the time of a conference call for papers might not yet be complete. If this is the case, once you have completed your paper, you should go back to the abstract to make sure that it accurately represents your research question, methodology, and key findings. It is not uncommon for conference paper abstracts to not accurately capture the contents of papers when they have been written prior to the paper itself because, as noted earlier, we often discover during the course of the research process that our preconceptions that led us to ask a particular question, or adopt a particular research design or method, are often challenged once we begin the research and writing process.

Introduction

Your introduction will serve to both seize the reader's attention and inform the reader of what they are about to read. Although the introduction should strive to get your reader's attention, you should keep in mind that as students and scholars of IR, we are not fiction writers. We should not try to hold our audience in suspense as to what we aim to achieve or demonstrate in our writing. We are not writing mystery novels. In fact, if you do this with a piece of work that you have submitted for assessment, you will likely see your grade suffer for failing to clearly set out your core argument. The introduction should contain a clear statement as to the topic, why it is important, and a roadmap that will provide the reader with the structure of the work.

Literature Review

The **literature review** provides an organizational and analytical summary of existing scholarly engagement with your topic. While the process of reviewing the literature was explored in detail in Chapter 4, here a brief summary of core elements of a good literature review is presented. First, a literature review informs the reader of major points of disagreements in scholarship regarding your topic and lets the reader know how your research question relates to existing work and analytical frameworks that have been used to explore your topic. For lengthier pieces of writing, such as a masters thesis or PhD dissertation, where the literature review often warrants its own chapter, you should introduce the review by letting the reader know about major scholarly debates on your topic. Then you will provide the reader with the organizational structure of your literature review, which will usually reflect the categories, whether theoretical, conceptual, analytical or methodological, in which you have divided competing approaches to your topic. The body of your literature review will reflect these categories, and you will analyze these perspectives and then examine how your research topic or question relates to existing scholarship. For example, do you challenge a dominant perspective in the literature? Have you identified a gap in the literature? For more on the Literature Review, return to Chapter 4.

Methodology

Here you set out for the reader your research design and methodological choices. The methodology section is a crucial component of your academic writing because it will make explicit how you will go about responding to your research question, or explore your research topic. It thus serves an important function in terms of research transparency, as you explicitly state how you will go about answering your research question. And it also allows for replicability, as your methodology section should provide other researchers with the knowledge necessary to replicate your research.

The content of a methodology section will vary significantly depending on which methodological approach you have chosen for your research project, empirical or interpretive. It is in your methodology section that you should clarify for the reader what epistemological assumptions you are making. In many cases this will be done when making reference to your research question and the methods that you have selected to respond to your question. Is your work an empirical explanatory essay focused on providing an explanation for a particular event? Is it an interpretive **discourse analysis** that is attempting to explore the constitution or production of a particular concept or idea in IR?

You should also state the insights you hope to gain from deploying your selected methods, and also any potential limitations to these methods. The methodology section will help allow other researchers to trace what you have done in terms of data collection (whether quantitative, qualitative, or based on **field research**), and analysis (qualitative or quantitative), and thus allows for some degree of replicability on the part of other scholars interested in your research results. For more on research design return to Chapter 2 or for case study design turn to Chapter 8. For method-specific questions see Chapters 1, 5, 6, and 7.

Methodology for Quantitative Research

The methodology section of a quantitative research paper will include a few additional components in order to specify data, **measurement** and provide justification for your methods or models (Bryman, 2008: 670). When specifying data, you should always be explicit about which **datasets** you are making use of for your quantitative analysis. You should respond to the following questions: How are you using these datasets? Where are they found? Who collected the data? How was it collected? If you are generating your own data through quantitative data collection techniques, such as surveys, questionnaires, **content analysis,** or some technique to facilitate the **coding** of documents, you should describe your data collection process to the reader. In the event you have used surveys or questionnaires, you should also specify your sampling procedures (ibid.). For example, did you secure a **random sample** or did you make use of some other form of non-random sampling technique such as opportunistic or **snowball sampling?**

When addressing measurement, you should be explicit about measurement tools that you are using such as **coding** or **scaling.** You should justify your coding or scaling choices that you made, and what you hoped to demonstrate through this process.

Data Analysis

The data analysis section of your essay will constitute the bulk of your writing. Depending on whether you are using quantitative or **qualitative methods,** the contents of this part of your work will likely vary significantly from paper to paper; however, there are a few organizational principles you should keep in mind. The first is structure. You should always make sure that you follow the same basic structure for every section within your data analysis so as to allow the reader to more easily follow the logic of your research process, your findings, and your arguments. Let's say you are examining three **independent variables** across three cases to explain a **dependent variable.** The purpose of your research is to **process-trace** so as to illuminate which **causal mechanism** best explains an outcome. The causal mechanisms, or independent variables, under study are power, self-interest, and norms. The cases are country A, country B, and country C. You could outline your data analysis section along these lines:

I. Country A

   a. Power
   b. Self-interest
   c. Norms

II. Country B

   a. Power
   b. Self-interest
   c. Norms

III. Country C

    a. Power

    b. Self-interest

    c. Norms

The section outline above will allow for you to maintain logical consistency and coherence across sections. In each section within your data analysis, you will examine a particular case, Country A, B, and C. In the sub-sections, you will examine in a consistent manner how each of these causal mechanisms played out in your cases.

The data analysis section of your work is likely to be the lengthiest portion of your work in terms of word count, particularly in qualitative work, because it is here you will be faced with operationalizing your methods of study and analyzing either empirically or interpretively your data. It is also here that you will present your research findings to the reader and describe how you have operationalized your methods. You are in a way telling the reader the story of your research project. For more on data analysis, see Chapters 5, 6, and 7.

Conclusion

Here you will highlight the main findings of your work. The conclusion section is often relatively short compared to other parts of the essay. Remember, that you will have done the bulk of the work demonstrating and justifying your findings in the data analysis section of your essay, so your conclusion should not include the provision of any new data. You should also avoid introducing new arguments in the conclusion. Instead, you should go back to your research question or research hypotheses and provide the reader with your findings in relation to each. When thinking of drafting your responses to your research question or hypotheses, it is helpful to think of these in the form of thesis statements. A thesis statement reflects what is in short the main idea or argument you seek to convey in your work. Sometimes you may not have a clear-cut response to the question you asked. Do not worry if this is the case. This is often the nature of scholarly research, and often the social world does not provide us with the empirical evidence necessary for general statements with natural science law like qualities. It is helpful in your conclusion to keep in mind Rosselle and Spray's advice to students of IR to be humble in your findings and not overstate your claims (Rosselle and Spray, 2012: 48–9).

Bibliography/References

Remember that transparency is one of the essential requirements for a piece of writing to be considered academic writing. The bibliography/references section of your work should always reflect the conventional referencing style requested by your institution or academic journal. The two common styles used in IR include in-text references, for example (Lamont, 2015: 10), or footnote references. Less common are endnotes, which are similar to footnotes, but appear at the end of a research paper. In the event you provide full bibliographic references in your footnotes, unless you are requested to do so, you will not need to reproduce full citations in a separate bibliography or references section.[2] Referencing guidelines are often widely circulated and easily accessible. As mentioned in Chapter 3, the two most common referencing styles used in IR are *Cambridge style* or *Harvard style*. Remember whatever style you have been asked to use, you should always be consistent in your usage. Never mix styles, or provide bibliographic information in an inconsistent manner.

Writing Up Your Research: Step 1 – Write an Outline

Often researchers will provide a broadly similar process when writing up their research. The first step is to write a research outline. You might have already written a research outline at the research proposal stage of your project. In the event you have done so, the research outline that you will write prior to writing up should be much more detailed, as your project may have changed during the data collection and analysis stage of your research, and questions that you had unanswered, or uncertainties about the data, may have now been clarified. Alternatively, you may need to adjust the structure of your outline due to unanticipated discoveries you made during the data collection and analysis stage of your research. You should provide some indication of the internal structure of each of these sections in your outline. Before you begin your writing process try to map out the structure of your work, along the lines of the following example outline:

I. Introduction

    a. What is my topic/question?
    b. Why is it important?

II. Literature Review

    a. Approach #1 to my topic
    b. Approach # 2 to my topic
    c. (*if applicable*) Approach #3 to my topic
    d. (*if applicable*) Additional approaches as warranted

III. Methodology

    a. Research Design – why and how it fits with your research question
    b. Research Method – how have you collected and analyzed your data? How will this method or method(s) provide an answer to your question?

IV. Data Analysis

    a. Examples: Case Studies (Empirical or Interpretive) /**Large-*n* Statistical Analysis/Formal Models** /Discourse Analysis /Content Analysis

V. Conclusions

    a. What are the results of your analysis?

    b. Have you answered the question?

    c. Have you generated new questions?

Once you have your outline try to see if it is internally coherent. Can you follow your argument from the outline? Are there major gaps in logic that are apparent? Do you still have questions about how you are able to respond to your question? Try giving your outline to a classmate or a colleague and see if the outline makes sense to them. If not, try to go back to your data and think about how you can most logically structure your argument on the basis of the outline.

You will need to internally signpost your writing to make the structure easily visible and easy to follow on the part of the reader. This is done through making sure that you have included section headings, and if you have lengthy sections, subheadings. Of course, you should be creative in signposting, and you need not replicate the generic section titles presented here in your own work. Furthermore, sometimes in short pieces of work, such as journal articles, the literature review is integrated into the introduction. Other times you may notice the methodology section has been as well.

Writing Up Your Research: Step 2 – Start Writing

Although you will normally have written some form of outline prior to writing up your research, as mentioned before the rest of the process is often a non-linear process, meaning that you might have already begun writing significant sections of your research prior to finishing your data collection or analysis. For example, you might have already started to work on drafts of your literature review section and methodology sections. Nevertheless, the writing stage of your research should be enjoyable as you will have already made all your difficult research choices, collected your data, analyzed your data, and come up with some responses to your research questions.

One of the greatest obstacles to effectively writing up research is not related to structure or style, but is that of time. Writing up takes time, and you should factor this into your own time management and planning when undertaking any research project. After your data collection and analysis, your writing up process can be time intensive and, if done well, will require you to read multiple drafts of your work before it is complete.

As researchers we are also writers who aim to communicate our findings to a wider audience. As a student our primary audience for our research essay will be our course lecturer, who will be reading essays for the purpose of assessment. However, as mentioned in the Introduction to this book, as students of IR, we are writing so as to hone our research and communication skills with an aim to make a wider contribution to the world around us. Whether it is in the form of writing for international affairs think tanks, the wider public, or academics, in order to conduct good and impactful research, we must also be effective communicators.

Writing: Stylistic Tips

This section will provide some useful tips to improve the readability of your work. First, avoid the passive voice in your academic writing. The passive voice obscures and makes it much more difficult for the reader to understand cause and effect relationships in your writing. This is because the passive voice obscures the subject of your sentence. In other words, the reader does not know who or what is responsible for a particular action. For example take the sentence, 'Bad grades were received in Chemistry'. From this sentence it is not clear who received bad grades. It could be better phrased as 'Students received bad grades in Chemistry'.

Second, avoid unnecessary jargon, or overly technical language. Often, given the depth of analysis provided in our research papers on specific issue areas in IR the use of jargon is unavoidable. In this case, if a word may not be familiar to your audience be sure to provide a definition. Keep this in mind particularly if you are writing on a subject area that includes reference to a subject area-specific vocabulary, such as cyber security.[3] Also, more advanced **quantitative methods** uses specific vocabularies that make reference to the newest statistical data analysis software or programs. Keep in mind that your reader might not be aware of what these are and that short explanatory notes might be necessary.

Third, always write in paragraph form. Make sure that every paragraph has a topic sentence, and communicates a single idea. Concise paragraphs are normally four to five sentences long. If you find yourself writing paragraphs that span for over a page, double check to see if the ideas or concepts discussed in the paragraph can be subdivided into smaller paragraphs. In general, paragraphs should not be made of a single sentence.

Fourth, don't over quote. Your research papers should transmit your own perspective and should be written in your own voice. You should not use the words of others as crutches to help you formulate your own argument. Therefore, you should only use direct quotes when absolutely necessary. In order to make a determination as to whether or not it is necessary to use a quote to communicate an idea, you should ask yourself if there is something in the original wording that is lost when rephrased. If the wording of the quote is particularly compelling and concisely captures an argument that you wish to communicate in your writing, then a quote may be necessary.

As noted in Chapter 3, quotes, along with any reference to another author's ideas or words, must always be referenced. In addition, if you are using a direct quote you should also reference the name of the author in the text preceding the quote. For example if referencing Walt, you could state: As Walt (2014) argued, 'What these critiques lack, of course, is a convincing explanation of how doing more in all these trouble spots would make Americans safer or more prosperous.' Note that, in this instance, the quote appears in the text and with quotation marks; however, for quotes that contain more than three lines of text, you should provide the quote in an indented paragraph. For example, again if referencing Walt, your quote would appear as follows. As Walt argued:

> In fact, because the United States is already so powerful and so secure, there is relatively little the United States could gain in most of these situations, even if they were to turn out well. Furthermore, diving back into the quicksand might easily make them worse. (Walt, 2014)

Every time you use a quote you should state the name of the author in the text preceding the quote. You should also make sure the quote flows nicely with your own writing that precedes and follows the quoted text. Normally, if the quote effectively captures a crucial argument that is related to the text in the paragraph where you have included the quote, this will not require much additional effort. However, it is always helpful to point out to the reader the importance of your quote, and what you are using the quote to illustrate (Lipson, 2005: 153–4).

Finally, use an appropriate tone for your writing. The appropriate tone will generally reflect your audience of academic peers. There is no need for exclamatory marks such as: *Intra-state war is now more common than inter-state wars!* Your audience does not need to be shouted at. With few exceptions in IR, academic writing is always written in a formal tone that is respectful of the audience and other perspectives on a topic. You should always focus on keeping the focus of your writing analytical and not engage in any *ad hominum* criticisms of those making arguments that you are engaging with in your own work. If you have specific questions as to whether or not to use particular pronouns such as I, consult with your lecturer or adviser as to their expectations. In relation to the question of using personal pronouns in academic writing, I often tell my own students that to impose a general rule against speaking in the first person in a research essay can result at times in overly awkward sentence constructions. So, if used parsimoniously, personal pronouns can appear in research essays, although their use should be limited. For example, you might find it makes more sense to simply state:

In this essay I argue that the discourse of counter-terrorism has led to a security-focused approach toward foreign policy-making in relation to North Africa.

However, the same idea can also be conveyed more formally below:

It is argued in this essay that the discourse of counter-terrorism has led to a security-focused approach toward foreign policy-making in relation to North Africa.

In more empirical work, where the author takes a more detached stance from the object under study, you are more likely to find authors avoiding inserting themselves into their research essays through the use of the first person. Meanwhile, the use of the first person can be seen more readily in interpretive scholarship, which sees the researcher as actively interacting with their object of study.[4]

Writing Up Your Research: Step 3 – Write Multiple Drafts, Proofread, and Edit

After you have finished writing each component part of your essay, you will have finished your first draft. However, at this point your work is not yet complete. Remember, it is essential to always write multiple drafts and to always proofread. Your final work that you submit for grading, submit for a thesis or dissertation defense, or to a publisher for publication, should never be a first draft. The first draft should always be completed with enough time to allow you to reflect upon it and improve it. Your ability to do this is often predicated on your ability to effectively plan and manage your time. Make sure that when planning to write that you include at a very minimum a few days to reflect upon your first draft, and perhaps up to a few weeks, depending on the length of your writing.

Your first draft is never the final product. It is your first attempt at writing up. Once you have finished your first draft, it is helpful to put it to the side for a day or two, and then read it again. Often you will be surprised with the amount of editing that remains to be done at this stage. Indeed, when you read your first draft, you should review your work for its overall cogency. Does your essay, thesis or dissertation logically make sense to the reader? Are there significant gaps in your argumentation? Do sections, or chapters, of your work flow nicely from one to another?

At this stage you might find yourself removing entire sentences for being repetitive, or inserting new sentences to provide further explanation because you have not effectively communicated what you had aimed to communicate. Furthermore, you might find significant logical gaps in your argument, or errors in data collection and analysis that require you to go back to an earlier stage of the research process and revisit your research choices. Again, with effective time management, correcting these problems you encounter during the writing-up process should not prove too difficult.

Chapter Summary

Now that you have been taken through all the steps of writing a research essay, dissertation, or thesis, you have at your hands a practical guide to writing in International Relations. IR is a diverse field that encompasses many distinct methodological and disciplinary traditions, as you will find a broad range of writing that falls within the scope of IR. Nevertheless, most writing within the field follows a similar structure that is comprised of core building blocks. These are the introduction, literature review, methodology, data analysis, and conclusion. For some works you will be asked to provide an abstract prior to the introduction, and for more quantitative papers you will need to specify questions of data, measurement, statistical methods or models used within your methodology section.

Of course, the primary aim of all research-based writing in the field is to communicate certain findings of scholarly or policy relevance to a particular audience. We invest significant amounts of time in our research, and often we feel our findings should be widely read. This means that in addition to carrying out methodologically rigorous research, we are required to be effective writers and effective communicators. In this regard, there are a number of additional writing resources that you can draw upon to improve your writing, some of which are noted below as further readings. Finally, it is important to underline that you should always write with your audience in mind, whether that be your course lecturer, your dissertation or thesis supervisor, a specialist community, academic colleagues, or the wider public. The better you understand the expectations of your audience, the easier you will find the writing-up process.

Suggested Further Reading

Alan Bryman (2008) *Social Research Methods*, 3rd edition. Oxford: Oxford University Press. See 'Chapter 27: Writing Up Social Research', pp. 660–89. This chapter provides you with additional tips for writing up research from the perspective of research and writing in the social sciences.

Charles Lipson (2005) *How to Write a BA Thesis: A Practical Guide from Your First Ideas to Your Finished Paper.* Chicago, IL: University of Chicago Press. See Chapters 9 'Writing Your Best' (pp. 143–58), 10 'Effective Openings, Smooth Transitions, and Strong Closings' (pp. 159–76), and 11 'Good Editing Makes Good Writing' (pp. 177–92). Lipson's text provides for some specific guidance on questions of writing style that can help improve your writing.

Laura Roselle and Sharon Spray (2012) *Research and Writing in International Relations*, 2nd edition. New York: Longman. See 'Chapter 4: Analysis and Writing', pp. 46–66. This chapter provides guidance on academic writing and also provides an overview of core component parts of academic essays.

Notes

1   Note that for certain types of writing, dissertations, journal articles, or conference papers, you will normally be asked to include an abstract prior to the introduction.
2   You should always strictly follow the specific referencing guidelines provided by your institution. In some cases, you will be asked to provide a reference or bibliographic list after your footnotes or endnotes.
3   Cyber security jargon that a general audience might not be familiar with could include *bots*, *botnets*, and *zombies*.
4   For more on the empirical–interpretive distinction turn back to Chapter 1.

GLOSSARY

Abstract   A one-paragraph summary of your research provided at the beginning of a scholarly journal article or dissertation. It justifies the relevance of the work, provides the research question, a brief explanation of the methodology or methods used, and key findings.

Agent-Based Modeling   Computer assisted mathematical simulation models that generate data on how agents interact within a given environment that can be analyzed inductively.

Agent–Structure Debate   The agent–structure debate revolves around the question of whether or not events are determined by structural causes, such as institutions or socio-economic factors, or whether or not they are determined by the choices of individual decision-makers.

Behavioralism   An approach to International Relations that posits natural science methods can be imported into the social sciences.

Bivariate Regression Analysis   A statistical test that allows for researchers to see whether or not a relationship exists between two variables.

Causal Effects   The outcomes brought about by a posited causal variable.

Causal Inference   A statement that posits a causal relationship between variables on the basis of observed **causal effects**.

Causal Mechanisms   Independent stable factors that under certain conditions link causes to effects.

Causation   This implies that a change in one variable *causes* a change in another.

Coding   The categorization and quantification of material for analysis. Coding is often used to categorize unstructured data gathered by the researcher for entry into **datasets**.

Correlation   Reference to the co-variance of two variables. Because a change in one variable appears to coincide with the change in another it is often confused with **causation**.

Constructivism   This term has been used to describe both a theoretical approach to International Relations and a broader epistemological tradition referred to in this book as **interpretivism.** In relation to constructivism as a theory of International Relations, constructivists emphasize the causal role of norms in explaining certain outcomes, or they emphasize the need to interrogate social meaning.

Content Analysis A form of data analysis that allows researchers to examine large amounts of data derived from social communication through the categorization and **coding.**

Datasets A collection of related sets of information, usually coded in numeric form.

Decision Tree A means of mapping a player's choices and potential payoffs that does not take into account the choices of others.

Dependent Variable The object that requires explanation or a particular outcome that you wish to explain.

Descriptive Statistics A form of **statistical analysis** that helps provide means to describe our data. It is often used to help present or visualize trends or to collect data.

Discourse Analysis A form of qualitative data analysis that focuses on the interpretation of linguistic forms of communication.

Empiricism One of two broad epistemological traditions in IR, the other being **interpretivism.** It embraces natural science methods to explain the world around us and is based on the assumption that knowledge can be accumulated through experience and observation. This tradition has also been referred to as **naturalism, positivism,** or **behavioralism.**

Epistemology The study of knowledge and how knowledge is produced

Experimentation The experiment is a scientific method imported from the natural sciences that normally tests a **hypothesis** to determine whether a conjectured relationship or process will either verify or falsify it.

Explanatory Variables Variables that explain a certain outcome or **dependent variable.**

External Validity This refers to whether a population sample is representative of a **sample frame.** External validity is most often ensured by attempts to minimize **selection bias.**

Falsifiable This refers to the position that an observation can be found to be false through observation or experimentation.

Field Research The gathering of primary data, either through accessing primary source documents, or through interviews, participant observation, questionnaires, surveys, or other methods aimed at eliciting responses from human subjects.

Focus Groups   A form of group interview in which a group facilitator leads a discussion on a specific topic in groups of six to ten participants. Generally, researchers will carry out multiple focus group discussions on a given topic.

Formalization   The translation of verbal arguments or statements into mathematical form.

Formal Models   The application of mathematical or statistical toots to the study of International Relations.

Game Theory   The application of mathematical models to understand strategic interaction among actors.

Human Subjects   When people participate in research, these people are referred to as human subjects.

Hypothesis   A statement that makes a claim as to a relationship between two or more variables, usually the independent and dependent variables.

Independent Variable   Something that is conjectured to explain or cause the **dependent variable**.

Inductive Reasoning   The generation of theoretical propositions out of empirical observations.

Inferential Statistics   The use of statistical tests to reach conclusions about numerical data that has been collected.

Interpretivism   One of two broad epistemological traditions in IR, the other being **empiricism**. It rejects the notion that natural science methods can help explain the world around us, and instead focuses on social meanings embedded within IR through the interrogation ideas, norms, beliefs, and values. This tradition has also been referred to as **constructivism**, **reflectivism**, or **post-positivism**.

Iterated   This term is used in game theory to refer to repeated interactions among players.

Intersubjective   Intersubjective understandings refer to the observation that agents are constituted through their interactions with other agents. These processes of interaction, illuminated through discourse, are argued to help us understand how the social world is constituted.

Interview   A form of qualitative data collection in which the researcher asks questions of a research participant. Interviews can take on many forms. The most common are **structured**, **semi-structured**, and **unstructured interviews**.

Interview Consent Form   A document prepared for field research that allows you to secure the informed consent of research participants.

Large-*n*   This refers to a large number of cases, or *n*s.

Literature Review   An analytical summary of existing scholarly research on a certain topic that establishes and organizes existing concepts and theoretical frameworks for the reader.

Measurement   The assignment of numeric values to establish the exact properties of a particular object or event.

Methodology   The study of ways through which we acquire knowledge.

Multivariate Regression Analysis   A statistical test that allows researchers to test whether or not a relationship exists between three or more variables.

Narratives   A qualitative research concept that focuses on how memories are constructed in the form of stories about past events such as wars or political struggles.

Naturalism   See **empiricism**.

Observation   The collection of data about some aspect of the world around us.

Official Documents   Published documents released by a state, organization, or business.

Ontological Puzzle   This refers to the type of questions that can be of interest to interpretive researchers. It is contrasted with cause-and-effect puzzles of interest to empirical researchers.

Ontology   The study of being, or the nature of social entities.

Peer-Review   This refers to a blind review process undertaken by scholarly publishers in which a manuscript submitted for publication is reviewed by two or more anonymous reviewers.

Plagiarism   The intentional or unintentional use of someone else's words or ideas in your own work without appropriate attribution, usually done through referencing.

Positive Theory   Refers to theory development in the empirical tradition that focuses on explaining the relationship between variables.

Positivism   See **empiricism**.

Post-Positivism   See **interpretivism**.

Primary Source Documents   Original documents, authored by individuals who had direct access to the information that they are describing, or directly experienced a particular event.

Process-Tracing   The tracing of processes that link possible causes with observed outcomes.

Qualitative Methods Data collection and data analysis strategies that rely upon the collection, and analysis of, non-numeric data. This does not have to be restricted to textual data and can also include speech, film, and other forms of communicative works.

Quantitative Methods Data collection and data analysis strategies that rely upon collecting or coding data in numeric form in an attempt to determine whether or not a relationship exists between two or more variables. This entails the use of either **statistical analysis** or **formal models**.

Question-Based Research A research project in which the researcher poses a question that typically attempts to explain an uncertain relation between two or more variables (**empiricism**) or that problematizes our understanding of an existing variable (**interpretivism**).

Random Sample Every potential research participant within a **sample frame** has an equal chance of being selected for participation. Random samples are sought so as to guard against **selection bias**.

Rational Choice An attempt to explain the behavior of actors in terms of choice, preference, and expected outcomes.

Reflectivism See **interpretivism**.

Research Design This refers to a research plan that sets out how the research will go about responding to a research question. It can also be seen as the basic structure of a research paper.

Research Summary A short description of your research written for the purpose of your **field research** that provides an explanation of your research project and how your findings will be used to research participants.

Sample Frame This refers to the pool of potential survey or questionnaire respondents from which actual research participants are drawn.

Scaling A form of measurement that allows for qualitative data to be converted into metric units.

Secondary Source Documents Documents, which make reference to, and analyze, **primary source documents**.

Selection Bias Can manifest itself in data collection in both quantitative and qualitative research. It refers to situations where some members of a sample frame have a greater chance of being selected for participation than others.

Semi-Structured Interview An interview format that is commonly used because it allows the researcher to pose their questions, but also to ask follow-up questions that reflect the interview participant's responses.

Snowball Sampling   This refers to a strategy to access human subjects during the course of **field research** that has the researcher rely on the first individuals you meet during the course of your research to introduce you to other potential research participants.

Spurious Relationship   This is when there appears to be a relationship between two variables, but the relationship is actually produced by a third variable.

Statistical Analysis   Statistical analysis refers to the analysis of large sets of numeric data in either the form of **descriptive statistics** or **inferential statistics**.

Structured Interview   An interview format in which the individual administering the interview keeps strictly to a script of questions and the respondent is asked to select from a pre-determined menu of response options.

Triangulation   This can refer either to a strategy for data collection, in which the researcher relies on multiple sources of data, such as interviews, media reports, and official documents, or to a strategy for bringing together distinct research methods, such as quantitative and qualitative methods.

Unstructured Interview   An interview format that is more analogous to a conversation. The researcher will at the beginning prompt a conversation on a given topic, but then allows the conversation to evolve naturally.

REFERENCES

Ackerly, Brooke and True, Jacqui (2008) 'Reflexivity in Practice: Power and Ethics in Feminist Research on International Relations', *International Studies Review*, (10) 4: 693–707.

American Anthropological Association's Executive Board Statement on the Human Terrain System Project, October 31, 2007 [released on November 7, 2007]. Available at: www.aaanet.org/pdf/EB_Resolution_110807.pdf

American Anthropological Association (2012) *Statement on Ethics: Principles of Professional Responsibility*. Arlington, VA: American Anthropological Association.

American Historical Association, *Statement on Standards on Professional Conduct*, last revised January 2011. Available at: www.historians.org/about-aha-and-membership/governance/policies-and-documents/statement-on-standards-of-professional-conduct

Andersen, Erika (2012) 'True Fact: The Lack of Pirates is Causing Global Warming', *Forbes*, March 23, 2012, www.forbes.com/sites/erikaandersen/2012/03/23/true-fact-the-lack-of-pirates-is-causing-global-warming/

Art, Robert J. and Waltz, Kenneth N. (eds) (1993) *The Use of Force: Military Power and International Politics*. New York: University Press of America.

Axelrod, Robert (1997) *The Complexity of Cooperation: Agent-Based Models of Competition and Collaboration*. Princeton, NJ: Princeton University, Press.

Balnaves, Mark and Caputi, Peter (2001) *Introduction to Quantitative Research Methods*. London: Sage.

Bartolucci, Valentina (2010) 'Analyzing Elite Discourse in Morocco and Its Implications: The Case of Morocco', *Critical Studies on Terrorism*, 3 (1): 119–35.

Baylis, John, Smith, Steve and Owens, Patricia (eds) (2010) *The Globalization of World Politics: An Introduction to International Relations*. Oxford: Oxford University Press.

BBC News, 'Facebook Emotion Experiment Sparks Criticism, June 30, 2014, available at: www.bbc.com/news/technology-28051930

Bennett, Andrew (2004) 'Case Study Methods, Design, Use and Comparative Advantage', in Detlef F. Sprinz and Yael Wolinsky-Nahmias, (eds), *Models, Numbers, and Cases: Methods for Studying International Relations*. Ann Arbor, MI: University of Michigan Press.

Bennett, Andrew and Elman, Colin (2007) 'Case Study Methods in the International Relations Subfield', *Comparative Political Studies*, 40 (2): 170–95.

Berg, Bruce L. and Lune, Howard (2012) *Qualitative Methods for the Social Sciences*, 8th edition. New York: Pearson.

Berg-Schlosser, Dirk (2012) *Mixed Methods in Comparative Politics: Principles and Applications*. Houndmills, Basingstoke: Palgrave Macmillan.

Bestor, Theodore C., Steinhoff, Patricia G. and Bestor, Victoria Lyon (eds) (2003) *Doing Fieldwork in Japan*. Honolulu: University of Hawaii Press.

Bhattacharjee, Yudhijit (2013) 'The Mind of a Con Man', *The New York Times Magazine*, April 26, 2013.

Boduszynski, Mieczyslaw (2013) 'Comparing Western Democratic Leverage: From Tirana to Tripoli', *Croatian Political Science Review*, 50 (5): 189–203.

Bogod, David (2004) 'Nazi Hypothermia Experiments: Forbidden Data?' *Anaesthesia*, 59 (12): 1155–56.

Brandt, Allan M. (1978) 'Racism and Research: The Case of the Tuskegee Syphilis Study', *The Hastings Center Report*, 8 (6): 21–9.

Braumoeller, Bear F. and Sartori, Anne E. (2004) 'The Promise and Perils of Statistics in International Relations', in Detlef F. Sprinz and Yael Wolinsky-Nahmias (eds), *Models, Numbers, and Cases: Methods for Studying International Relations*. Ann Arbor, MI: University of Michigan Press, pp. 129–51.

Bremer, Stuart A. (1993) 'Democracy and Militarized Interstate Conflict, 1816–1965', *International Interactions*, 18 (3): 231–49.

Brinton, Mary C. (2003) 'Fact-Rich, Data Poor: Japan as Sociologists' Heaven and Hell', in Theodore C. Bestor, Patricia G. Steinhoff and Victoria Lyon Bestor (eds), *Doing Fieldwork in Japan*. Honolulu: University of Hawaii Press.

Brown, Chris (2001) *Understanding International Relations*, 2nd edition. New York: Palgrave.

Brownlee, Jason (2007) *Authoritarianism in an Age of Democratization*. Cambridge: Cambridge University Press.

Bryman, Alan (2008) *Social Research Methods,* 3rd edition. Oxford: Oxford University Press.

Bull, Hedley (1966) 'International Theory: The Case for a Classical Approach', *World Politics*, 18 (3): 361–77.

Burchill, Scott (2001) 'Introduction', in Scott Burchill, Richard Devetak, Andrew Linklater, Matthew Paterson, Christian Reus-Smit and Jacqui True (eds), *Theories of International Relations*. New York: Palgrave, pp. 1–28.

Campbell, David (1998) *National Deconstruction: Violence, Identity, and Justice in Bosnia*. Minneapolis, MN: University of Minnesota Press.

Carr, Edward Hallett (2001) *The Twenty Years Crisis 1919–1939*. New York: Perennial Harper Collins.

Cederman, Lars-Erik (2003) 'The Size of Wars: From Billiard Balls to Sandpiles', *The American Political Science Review*, 97 (1): 135–50.

Collier, Paul and Nicholas Sambanis (eds) *Understanding Civil War: Evidence and Analysis*. Washington DC: The World Bank.

Corti, Louise, Day, Annette and Backhouse, Gill (2000) 'Confidentiality and Informed Consent: Issues for Consideration in the Preservation of Access to Qualitative Data Archives', *Forum: Qualitative Social Research*, 1 (2).

Cox, Robert (1981) 'Social Forces, States and World Orders: Beyond International Relations Theory', *Millennium – Journal of International Studies*, 10 (2): 126–55.

David, Roman (2011) *Lustration and Transitional Justice: Personnel Systems in the Czech Republic, Hungary, and Poland*. Philadelphia, PA: University of Pennsylvania Press.

Douglas, Jack D. (1976) *Investigative Social Research: Individual and Team Field Research*. Beverly Hills, CA: Sage.

Dunn, Kevin C. (2003) *Imagining the Congo: The International Relations of Identity*. Houndsmills, Basingstoke: Palgrave Macmillan.

Elman, Colin (1996) 'Horses for Courses: Why Not Neorealist Theories of Foreign Policy?' *Security Studies*, 6 (1): 7–53.

Elman, Miriam Fendius (1997) *Paths to Peace: Is Democracy the Answer?* Cambridge, MA: MIT Press.

Ember, Carol, Ember, Melvin and Russett, Bruce (1992) 'Peace between Participatory Politics', *World Politics*, 44: 573–99.

Epstein, Charlotte (2008) *The Power of Words in International Relations: Birth of Anti-Whaling Discourse*. Cambridge, MA: MIT Press.

Evangelista, Matthew (1999) *Unarmed Forces: The Transnational Movement to end the Cold War*. Ithaca, NY: Cornell University Press.

Faure, Andrew Murray (1994) 'Some Methodological Problems in Comparative Politics', *Journal of Theoretical Politics*, 6 (3): 307–22.

Fearon, James, D. (2004) 'Why Do Some Civil Wars Last So Much Longer than Others?' *Journal of Peace Research*, 41 (3): 275–301.

Finnemore, Martha and Sikkink, Kathryn (2001) 'Taking Stock: The Constructivist Research Program in International Relations and Comparative Politics', *Annual Review of Political Science,* 4 (1): 391–416.

Flyvbjerg, Bent (2006) 'Five Misunderstandings About Case-Study Research', *Qualitative Inquiry*, 12 (2): 234–7.

Gaaloul, Badra (2011) 'Back to the Barracks: The Tunisian Army Post-Revolution', *Sada – Middle East Analysis*, Carnegie Endowment for International Peace, November 3, 2011. Available at: http://carnegieendowment.org/2011/11/03/back-to-barracks-tunisian-army-post-revolution/fduu

Gabriel, Trip (2010) 'Plagiarism Lines Blur for Students in the Digital Age', *The New York Times*, August 1, 2010.

Geertz, Clifford (1972) 'Deep Play: Notes on the Balinese Cockfight', *Daedalus*, 101 (1): 1–37.

Geertz, Clifford (1973) *The Interpretation of Cultures: Selected Essays*. New York: Basic Books.

Geller, Daniel S. and Singer, J. David (1998) *Nations at War: A Scientific Study of International Conflict*. Cambridge: Cambridge University Press.

George, A. and Bennett, A. (2005) *Case Studies and Theory Development in the Social Sciences*. Cambridge, MA: MIT Press.

Gerring, John (2004) 'What Is a Case Study and What Is It Good for?' *American Political Science Review*, 98 (2): 341–54.

Gerring, John (2007) 'Is There a (Viable) Crucial Case Method?' *Comparative Political Studies*, 40 (3): 231–53.

Gerring, John (2012) *Social Science Methodology: A Unified Framework*, 2nd edition. Cambridge, Cambridge University Press.

Gilpin, Robert (2001) *Global Political Economy: Understanding the International Economic Order*. Princeton, NJ: Princeton University Press.

Grodsky, Brian K. (2010) *The Costs of Justice: How New Leaders Respond to Previous Rights Abuses*. Notre Dame, IN: University of Notre Dame Press, pp. 81–2.

Hardy, Cynthia, Harley, Bill and Phillips, Nelson (2004) 'Discourse Analysis and Content Analysis: Two Solitudes?' *Qualitative Methods*, 2 (1): 19–22.

Harris, Gardiner (2008) 'Cigarette Company Paid for Lung Cancer Study', *The New York Times,* March 26, 2008, available at: www.nytimes.com/2008/03/26/health/research/26lung.html?pagewanted=all&_r=0

Harrison, Lisa and Callan, Theresa (2013) *Key Research Concepts in Politics & International Relations*. London: Sage.

Harvey, Frank P. and Brecher, Michael (eds) (2002) *Evaluating Methodology in International Studies*. Ann Arbor, MI: University of Michigan Press.

Herrera, C.D. (2001) 'Ethics, Deception, and "Those Milgram Experiments"', *Journal of Applied Psychology*, 8 (4): 245–56.

Hoffman, Matthew J. (2008) 'Agent-Based Modeling as Qualitative Method', in Audie Klotz and Deepa Prakash (eds), *Qualitative Methods in International Relations*. New York: Palgrave, pp. 187–210.

Hollis, Martin and Smith, Steve (1990) *Explaining and Understanding International Relations*. Oxford: Clarendon Press.

ISA Policy and Procedures on Plagiarism (2014).

Ishiyama, John T. (1993) 'Founding Elections and the Development of Transitional Parties: The Cases of Estonia and Latvia, 1990–1992', *Communist and Post-Communist Studies*, 26 (3): 277–99.

Jacobsen, Karen and Landau, Lauren B. (2003) 'The Dual Imperative of Refugee Research: Some Methodological and Ethical Considerations in Social Science Research and Forced Migration', *Disasters*, 27 (3): 185–206.

Jackson, Richard (2007) 'Constructing Enemies: "Islamic Terrorism" in Political and Academic Discourse', *Government and Opposition*, 42 (3): 394–426.

Johnson, R. Burke, Onwuegbuzie, Anthony J. and Turner, Lisa A. (2007) 'Toward a Definition of Mixed Methods Research', *Journal of Mixed Methods Research*, 1 (2): 112–33.

Kahler, Miles (1998) 'Rationality in International Relations', *International Organization*, 52 (4): 919–41.

Katzenstein, Peter (ed.) (1996) *The Culture of National Security: Norms and Identity in World Politics*. New York: Columbia University Press.

Katzenstein, Peter J., Keohane, Robert O. and Krasner, Stephen D. (1998) 'International Organization and the Study of World Politics', *International Organization*, 52 (4): 645–85.

Kim, Hunjoon and Sikkink, Kathryn (2010) 'Explaining the Deterrence Effect of Human Rights Prosecutions for Transitional Countries', *International Studies Quarterly*, 54 (4): 939–63.

King, Gary, Keohane, Robert O. and Verba, Sydney (1994) *Designing Social Inquiry: Scientific Inference in Qualitative Research*. Princeton, NJ: Princeton University Press.

King, Gary, Keohane, Robert O. and Verba, Sydney (2010) 'The Importance of Research Design', in Henry E. Brady and David Collier (eds), *Rethinking Social Inquiry: Diverse Tools, Shared Standards*, 2nd edition. Lanham, MD: Rowman & Littlefield, pp. 111–22.

King, Gary and Lowe, Will (2003) 'An Automated Information Extraction Tool for International Conflict Data with Performance as Good as Human Coders: A Rare Events Design Evaluation', *International Organization*, 57: 617–64.

Klotz, Audie (1995) 'Norms Reconstituting Interests: Global Racial Equality and US Sanctions Against South Africa', *International Organization*, 49 (3): 451–78.

Klotz, Audie and Lynch, Cecelia (2007) *Strategies for Research in Constructivist International Relations*. Armonk, NY: M.E. Sharpe, p. 11.

Klotz, Audie and Deepa Prakash (eds) (2008) *Qualitative Methods in International Relations: A Pluralist Guide*. New York: Palgrave.

Kramer, Adam D.I, Guillory, Jamie E. and Hancock, Jeffrey T. (2014) 'Experimental Evidence of Massive Scale Emotional Contagion through Social Networks', *Proceedings of the National Academy of Sciences of the United States of America (PNAS)*, 111 (24): 8788–90.

Kukhianidze, Alexander, Kupatatdze, Alexander and Gotsiridze, Roman (2004) *Smuggling through Abkhazia and Tskhinvali Region of Georgia*. Tblisi: TraCCC Georgia Office.

Kupatadze, Alexander (2010) 'Organized Crime and the Trafficking of Radiological Materials', *The Nonproliferation Review*, 17 (2): 219–34.

Kurze, Arnaud (2013) '#War Crimes #PostConflictJustice #Balkans: Youth, Performance Activism and the Politics of Memory', paper prepared for the ECPR General Conference, September 4–7, 2013, Bordeaux, France. Available at: http://ecpr.eu/Filestore/Paper Proposal/649a00e2-b300-4c06-b0cc-920a72c14bec.pdf

Kurze, Arnaud and Vukusic, Iva (2013) 'Afraid to Cry Wolf: Human Rights Activists' Struggle of Transnational Accountability Efforts in the Balkans', in Olivera Simic and Zala Volcic (eds), *Transitional Justice and Civil Society in the Balkans*. New York: Springer, pp. 201–15.

Lamont, Christopher K. (2010) 'Compliance or Strategic Defiance: The Croatian Democratic Union and the International Criminal Tribunal for the former Yugoslavia', *Europe-Asia Studies*, 62 (10): 1683–705.

Lamont, Christopher K. (2010) *International Criminal Justice and the Politics of Compliance*. Farnham, UK: Ashgate.

Lampe, Klaus von (2012) 'Transnational Organized Crime Challenges for Future Research', *Crime, Law and Social Change*, 58 (2): 179–94.

Lane, Christopher (1994) 'Kant or Cant: The Myth of Democratic Peace', *International Security*, 19 (2): 5–49.

Leech, Beth L. (2002) 'Asking Questions: Techniques for Semi-Structured Interviews', *PS-Washington*, 35 (4): 665–8.

Levy, Jack S. (2002) 'Qualitative Methods in International Relations', in Frank P. Harvey and
   Michael Brecher (eds), *Evaluating Methodology in International Studies*. Ann Arbor, MI:
   University of Michigan Press, pp. 131–60.

Linklater, Andrew (1992) 'The question of the next stage in international relations theory: a
   critical-theoretical point of view', *Millennium*, 21 (1): 77–98.

Lipson, Charles (2005) *How to Write a BA Thesis: A Practical Guide from Your First Ideas to
   Your Finished Paper*. Chicago, IL: University of Chicago Press.

Lowe, Will (2004) 'Content Analysis and Its Place in the (Methodological) Scheme of Things',
   Qualitative Methods, 2 (1): 25–7.

Mansfield, Edward D. and Pevehouse, Jon C. (2000) 'Trade Blocs, Trade Flows, and
   International Conflict', *International Organization*, 54 (4): 775–808.

Maoz, Zeev (2002) 'Case Study Methodology in International Studies: From Story-Telling to
   Hypothesis Testing', in Frank P. Harvey and Michael Brecher (eds), *Evaluating Methodology
   in International Studies*. Ann Arbor, MI: University of Michigan Press, pp. 161–86.

Maoz, Zeev (2011) *Networks of Nations: The Evolution, Structure and Impact of International
   Networks, 1816–2001*. Cambridge: Cambridge University Press.

Maoz, Zeev and San-Akca, Belgin (2012) 'Rivalry and State Support for Non-State Armed
   Groups (NAGs), 1946–2001', *International Studies Quarterly*, 56 (4): 720–34.

Mertus, Julie A. (2009) 'Introduction: Surviving Field Research' in Chandra Lekha Sriram,
   John C. King, Julie A. Mertus, Olga Martin-Ortega and Johanna Herman (eds), *Surviving
   Field Research: Working in Violent and Difficult Situations*. New York: Routledge, pp. 1–7.

Mesquita, Bruce Bueno de (2002) 'Accomplishments and Limitations of a Game-Theoretic
   Approach to International Relations', in Frank P. Harvey and Michael Brecher (eds), *Evaluating
   Methodology in International Studies*. Ann Arbor, MI: University of Michigan Press, pp. 59–80.

Milgram, Stanley (1963) 'Behavioral Study of Obedience', *The Journal of Abnormal and
   Social Psychology*, 67 (4): 371–8.

Milliken, Jennifer (1999) 'The Study of Discourse in International Relations', *European
   Journal of International Relations*, 5 (2): 225–54.

Milner, Helen V. (1998) 'Rationalizing Politics: The Emerging of International, American and
   Comparative Politics', *International Organization*, 52 (4): 759–86.

Mintz, Alex, Redd, Stephen B. and Vedlitz, Arnold (2006) 'Can We Generalize from Student
   Experiments to the Real World in Political Science, Military Affairs, and International
   Relations?' *The Journal of Conflict Resolution*, 50 (5): 757–76.

Moe, Kristine (1984) 'Should the Nazi Research Data Be Cited?' *The Hastings Center Report*,
   14 (6): 5–7.

Morgenthau, Hans (revised by Kenneth W. Thompson and W. David Clinton) (2005) *Politics
   Among Nations: The Struggle for Power and Peace*, 7th edition. New York: McGraw Hill.

Moses, Jonathon, W. and Knutsen, Torbjorn L. (2012) *Ways of Knowing: Competing
   Methodologies in Social and Political Research*, 2nd edition. Basingstoke: Palgrave
   Macmillan.

Neumann, John Von and Morgenstern, Oskar (1944) *The Theory of Games and Economic
   Behavior*. Priceton, NJ: Princeton University Press.

Nicholson, Michael (1992) *Rationality and the Analysis of International Conflict*. Cambridge:
   Cambridge University Press.

Nicholson, Michael (2002) 'Formal Methods in International Relations', in Frank P. Harvey
   and Michael Brecher (eds), *Evaluating Methodology in International Studies*. Ann Arbor,
   MI: University of Michigan Press, pp. 23–42.

Norman, Julie M. (2009) 'Got Trust? The Challenges of Gaining Access in Conflict Zones', in
   Chandra Lekha Sriram, John C. King, Julie A. Mertus, Olga Martin-Ortega and Johanna

Herman (eds), *Surviving Field Research: Working in Violent and Difficult Situations*. New York: Routledge, pp. 71–90.

O'Driscoll, Cian (2008) *Renegotiation of Just War Tradition and the Right to War in the Twenty-First Century*. New York: Palgrave.

Pavlakovic, Vjeran (2008) 'Red Stars, Black Shirts: Symbols, Commemorations, and Contested Histories of World War Two in Croatia', The National Council for Eurasian and East European Research (NCEEER), September 11, 2008. Available at: www.ucis.pitt.edu/nceeer/2008_822-16h_Pavlakovic.pdf

Pavlakovic, Vjeran (2010) 'Croatia, the International Criminal Tribunal for the Former Yugoslavia, and General Gotovina as a Political Symbol', *Europe-Asia Studies*, 62: 1707–40.

Pepinsky, Thomas B. (2005) 'From Agents to Outcomes: Simulation in International Relations', *European Journal of International Relations*, 11 (3): 267–394.

Peskin, Victor and Boduszynski, Mieczyslaw (2011) 'Balancing International Justice in the Balkans: Surrogate Enforcers, Uncertain Transitions and the Road to Europe', *International Journal of Transitional Justice*, 5 (1): 52–74.

Pole, Christopher J. and Lampard, Richard (2002) *Practical Social Investigation: Qualitative and Quantitative Methods in Social Research*. Harlow: Pearson Education.

Pratt, Nicola (2007) *Democracy & Authoritarianism in the Arab World*. Boulder, CO: Lynn Rienner Publishers.

Przeworski, Adam and Teune, Henry (1970) *The Logic of Comparative Social Inquiry*. New York: Wiley-Interscience.

Ray, James Lee (1995) *Democracy and International Conflict: An Evaluation of the Democratic Peace Proposition*. Columbia, SC: University of South Carolina Press.

Research Ethics Framework (REF). London: Economic and Social Research Council.

Richards, David (1996) 'Elite Interviewing: Approaches and Pitfalls', *Politics*, 16 (3): 199–204.

Richardson, Lewis Fry (1960) *The Statistics of Deadly Quarrels*. Pacific Grove, CA: Boxwood.

Risse, Thomas, Ropp, Stephen C. and Sikkink, Kathryn (eds) (1999) *The Power of Human Rights: International Norms and Domestic Change*. Cambridge: Cambridge University Press.

Roselle, Laura and Spray, Sharon (2012) *Research and Writing in International Relations*, 2nd edition. New York: Pearson.

Rousseau, David and van der Veen, A. Maurits (2005) 'The Emergence of a Shared Identity: An Agent Based Computer Simulation of Idea Diffusion', *Journal of Conflict Resolution*, 49 (5): 686–712.

Rozen, Joel (forthcoming 2014) 'Civics Lesson: Ambivalence, Contestation, and Curricular Change in Tunisia', *Ethnos: Journal of Anthropology*.

Sambanis, Nicholas (2005) 'Using Case Studies to Refine and Expand the Theory of Civil War', in Paul Collier and Nicholas Sambanis (eds), *Understanding Civil War: Evidence and Analysis*. Washington DC: The World Bank, pp. 303–34.

Scott, Greg and Garner, Roberta (2013) *Doing Qualitative Research: Design, Methods, and Techniques*. Boston, MA: Pearson.

Shim, David (2014) *Visual Politics & North Korea: Seeing is Believing*. New York: Routledge.

Shively, W. Phillips (2013) *The Craft of Political Science Research*, 9th edition. New York: Pearson.

Shuster, Evelyne (1997) 'Fifty Years Later: The Significance of the Nuremberg Code', *The New England Journal of Medicine*, 337 (20): 1436–40.

Smith, Steve (1995) 'The Self-Image of a Discipline: A Genealogy of International Relations Theory' in Ken Booth and Steve Smith (eds), *International Relations Theory Today*. Cambridge: Cambridge University Press.

Sprinz, Detleft and Wolinsky-Nahmias, Yael (eds) (2004) *Cases, Numbers, Models: International Relations Research Methods*. Ann Arbor, MI: University of Michigan Press.

Sriram, Chandra Lekha, King, John C., Mertus, Julia A., Martin-Ortega, Olga and Herman, Johanna (eds) (2009) *Surviving Field Research: Working in Violent and Difficult Situations*. London: Routledge.

Tickner, J. Ann (2005) 'What is Your Research Program? Some Feminist Answers to International Relations Methodological Questions', *International Studies Quarterly*, 49 (1): 1–22.

Van Evera, Stephen (1997) *Guide to Methods for Students of Political Science*. Ithaca, NY: Cornell University Press.

Walt, Stephen, M. (1996) *Revolution and War*. Ithaca, NY: Cornell University Press.

Walt, Stephen, M. (1999) 'Rigor or Rigor Mortis? Rational Choice and Security Studies', *International Security*, 23 (4): 5–48.

Walt, Stephen (2005) 'The Relationship between Theory and Policy in International Relations', *Annual Review of Political Science*, 8: 28–29.

Walt, Stephen M. (2011) 'How to Do Social Science', *Foreign Policy*, September 29, 2011. Available at: www.foreignpolicy.com/posts/2011/09/28/how_to_do_social_science

Walt, Stephen M. (2011) 'International Affairs and the Public Sphere' *Essay Series: Transformations of the Public Sphere*, Social Science Research Council (SSRC), July 21, 2011. Available at: http://publicsphere.ssrc.org/walt-international-affairs-and-the-public-sphere/

Walt, Stephen M. (2014) 'Is Barak Obama More of a Realist Than I Am?' *Foreign Policy*, 14 August 2014. Available at: www.foreignpolicy.com/articles/2014/08/19/is_barack_obama_more_of_a_realist_than_i_am_stephen_m_walt_iraq_russia_gaza

Walter, Barbara F. (2002) *Committing to Peace: The Successful Settlement of Civil Wars*. Princeton, NJ: Princeton University Press.

Waltz, Kenneth N. (1979) *Theory of International Politics*. New York: McGraw-Hill.

Waltz, Kenneth N. (1996) 'International Politics is Not a Foreign Policy', *Security Studies*, 6 (1): 54–7.

Walzer, Michael (1977) *Just and Unjust Wars: A Moral Argument with Historical Illustrations*. New York: Basic Books.

Weller, Nicholas and Barnes, Jeb (2014) *Finding Pathways: Mixed Methods Research for Studying Causal Mechanisms*. Cambridge: Cambridge University Press.

Wendt, Alexander (1998) 'On Constitution and Causation in International Relations', *Review of International Studies*, 24 (5): 101–18.

White, Stephen, McAllister, Ian, Light, Margo and Lowenhardt, John (2002) 'A European or Slavic Choice? Foreign Policy and Public Attitudes in Post-Soviet Europe', *Europe-Asia Studies* 54 (2): 181–202.

Williams, John H.P. and Zeager, Lester A. (2004) 'Macedonian Border Closings in the Kosovo Refugee Crisis: A Game-Theoretic Perspective', *Conflict Management and Peace Science*, 21 (4): 233–54.

Wittig, Timothy (2009) 'Financing Terrorism along the Chechnya-Georgia Border, 1999–2002', *Global Crime*, 10 (3): 248–60.

Wittig, Timothy (2011) *Understanding Terrorist Finance*. Basingstoke: Palgrave Macmillan.

Zinnes, Dina A. (2002) 'Reflections on Quantitative International Politics', in Frank P. Harvey and Michael Brecher (eds), *Evaluating Methodology in International Studies*. Ann Arbor, MI: University of Michigan Press, pp. 97–102.

INDEX

Added to a page number 'f' denotes figures, 't' denotes tables, 'n' denotes notes and 'g' denotes glossary.